SCENES OF INSTRUCTION ☀

SCENES OF INSTRUCTION

a memoir ☀ Michael Awkward

DUKE UNIVERSITY PRESS   Durham & London   1999

© 1999 Duke University Press

All rights reserved

Printed in the United States of America

on acid-free paper ∞

Designed by C. H. Westmoreland

Typeset in Dante with DIN Neutzeit Grotesk

Bold Condensed display by Keystone Typesetting, Inc.

Library of Congress Cataloging-in-Publication Data

appear on the last printed page of this book.

for Carol ☀

What I have lost is not a Figure (the Mother), but a being;
and not a being, but a *quality* (a soul): not the indispensable,
but the irreplaceable.—**ROLAND BARTHES,** *Camera Lucida*

My father . . . had gone to the city seeking life, but . . . [his]
life had been hopelessly snarled in the city, . . . that same city
which had lifted me in its burning arms and borne me toward
alien and undreamed-of shores of knowing.
—**RICHARD WRIGHT,** *Black Boy*

We're all consequences of something.
Stained with another's past as well as our own.
Their past in my blood.
—**GAYL JONES,** *Corregidora*

Travel folders call you
So do your memories
—**PHOEBE SNOW,** "Isn't It a Shame?"

It was time to put all of the pieces together,
make coherence where before there had been none.
—**TONI MORRISON,** *The Bluest Eye*

CONTENTS ☀

Acknowledgments   xi

Author's Note   xiii

Awkward Silences   xv

Introduction: "Don't Be Like Your Father"   1

Section I: The Mother's Mark   9

Section II: "Are You Man Enough?"   49

Section III: Chocolate City   85

Section IV: "closed in silence"   127

Section V: The Mother's Breast   165

Coda: Tippin' In   198

Works Cited or Consulted   203

ACKNOWLEDGMENTS ☀

A number of people have assisted my efforts to confront the formal, ideological, and ontological challenges I faced during the process of this book's composition. I owe a special debt to my friends and colleagues at the University of Michigan, where this project had its genesis. For discussing, among other things, issues relevant to the academic discourses with which this book is most directly concerned—Afro-Americanist, literary, cultural, and feminist studies— and for encouraging me despite our shared doubts about what I hoped to accomplish, I want especially to thank Julie Ellison, Lincoln Faller, Chris Flint, Anne Herrmann, Michelle Johnson, Robin Kelley, Marjorie Levinson, Earl Lewis, Athena Vrettos, and Patsy Yaeger. I'm especially grateful to Anita Norich, who read a draft of an earlier version of the manuscript and helped me to rediscover its purpose and potential significance. The opportunity during the fall of 1995 to interact with a stellar interdisciplinary group, the Black Gender Studies Faculty Seminar, confirmed the importance of the sort of gendered and racialized self-inquiry I was interested in offering. From that group, I'd like to thank Elsa Barkley Brown and Marlon Ross in particular for what I hope all of us found an inspiriting collaboration. And for making my three years as Director of the Center for Afroamerican and African Studies (when the bulk of this manuscript was drafted) more pleasant and infinitely less stressful than I dreamed possible, I am indebted to Gerri Brewer, Tammy Davis, Camille Spencer, and Evans Young.

I completed this book in Philadelphia during what the great R & B singer Donny Hathaway once called "tryin' times." For helping me to cope, I want to thank Howard Arnold, Houston Baker, Jeff Bedrick, Henry Louis Gates, Tresa Grauer, Farah Griffin, Sharon Holland, Peter Kuriloff, E. Daniel Larkin, Dan Lebowitz, Vicky Mahaffey, Nellie McKay, Elsa Ramsden, and Ira Schwartz. Special thanks to Nicole Brittingham Furlonge and Claire Satlof, whose selfless devotion buoyed my spirits. Also, Henrietta Stephens assisted me with the preparation of the final version of this manuscript, and Tommy Leonardi provided stunning photographic images of scenes from my childhood.

My wife, Lauren, and my daughters, Camara and Leah, love me even when I am not particularly lovable, for which I am more grateful than I can possibly express. The sane and sage advice of my intimate critic, Lauren, helped to make this a more focused and coherent project.

I am very appreciative of the faith in this project exhibited by Ken Wissoker, editor in chief of Duke University Press. Also, I'm grateful to the anonymous readers commissioned by the press and especially to associate editor Katie Courtland, who offered valuable suggestions about how to craft this difficult narrative.

Finally, for granting me permission to share family experiences, I want first to thank my aunt, Peggy McCalla, my mother's lifelong best friend, from whom I have gained a better understanding of my mother and, hence, myself. And I want especially to acknowledge my siblings, Carol, Ricky, and Debby, who've supported me in this endeavor despite their occasional reservations. My siblings continue to sustain me emotionally and spiritually; that "the four seasons," as we used to call ourselves, remain closely connected is proof of the strength of bonds our mother's love helped to forge. I dedicate this book to my sister Carol, who taught me to read, helped to take care of me when she was still a child herself, and continues to offer me lessons in selfless devotion. I don't always heed her advice, often to my spiritual, emotional, and financial detriment, but I always listen.

The photographs on pages 13, 14, 20, 53, 172, and 200 are by Tommy Leonardi. The *for colored girls* cover art on page 137 is by Paul Davis. The Benetton photograph on page 166 is by Oliviero Toscani. The rest of the images are from the author's private collection.

I've attempted to protect the privacy of many of the people about whom I speak by changing their names, some of their characteristics, and aspects of the events recounted here. I've compressed events, created dialogue, and sketched a composite neighborhood character, Stink (the actual nickname of a childhood acquaintance), as a necessary form of narrative shorthand. Also, where possible, I've preserved the anonymity of academics and administrators who may not wish to be named.

In 1988 I wrote to Alice Walker, asking her to participate in a lecture series I was organizing at the University of Michigan to celebrate the fiftieth anniversary of the publication of *Their Eyes Were Watching God*. She wrote me a gentle, encouraging rejection, which I've saved, in part because internationally renowned people write to me infrequently, but also because I was impressed by the envelope's lowercased designation of the author as *a walker*.

Ignoring the injunction against equating fiction writer and fictional character, I connected Walker with her restless, militant character Meridian, who marches tirelessly for justice during the civil rights movement. *a walker*, I concluded, connotes restlessness, a searching self who knows that truth, like love, is what Walker's forebear, Zora Neale Hurston, calls "uh movin' thing" that "takes its shape from de shore it meets, and it's different at every shore" (284). Who knows that in order to comprehend a world structured in dominance, "you got tuh go there," to search literally and figuratively through, among other potentially instructive sites, our mothers' gardens and our fathers' trunks. The quotidian objects that mark these familial spaces—rusty rakes, splashes of color, and the thorny remnants of neglected perennials; well-preserved pictures, unattached, odd-shaped buttons, and the faint odor of a long-wilted carnation—contain memories suffused with encoded meanings that we can begin to unpack only if we are both attentive and creative.

I felt inspired by Walker's example to order my own stationery. I experimented with color and font, and with paper grade. But ultimately my efforts failed to yield enveloping richness. *m awkward* is what Toni Morrison calls in *Sula* "a nigger joke," "the kind white folks tell when the mill closes down and they're looking for a little comfort somewhere. The kind colored folk tell on themselves when the rain doesn't come, or comes for weeks, and they're looking for a little comfort somehow" (4). As I made huge analytical leaps to connect Walker's symbol, Morrison's formulation, and my name, I remembered long, guilt-filled moments when I wished that instead

a walker

Prof. Michael Awkward
Department of English
University of Michigan
7611 Haven Hall
Ann Arbor, MI 48109

"a walker" envelope

of burdening me with her family name, my mother had given me the slightly threatening surname of my absent father, whom I didn't know: "Cutler."

A few months after receiving Walker's letter, I found an inspiriting meaning beneath the surfaces of a word that had made me hesitant to speak my name to strangers: "difficult to manage." Compelled by depictions of post-emancipation acts of black misnaming in such novels as Morrison's *Song of Solomon* and Gloria Naylor's *The Women of Brewster Place,* and by emphases in humanistic and social scientific scholarship on the essential importance of counterhegemonic resistance by oppressed peoples, I decided that being hard to handle wasn't a bad thing for a black man. Subsequently, I've felt less compelled to injure anonymous store clerks and university staff people who asked me the stupidest question a white person could possibly ask a black American: "Where'd you get that name?" And my refusal, on such occasions, to respond with my long-prepared retort, "From your slave-owning great-great-grandpa!" became itself empowering.

I've felt less urgency in these and other situations to repeat family myths about my great-great-grandfather, which insisted, if I remember my mother's narratives accurately, that he fell dramatically off of the low rungs of ladders whenever his white boss wanted him to do

SANDY SPRING, MARYLAND
SEPTEMBER 14, 1991

"AND GOD MADE ALL OF US"

The cover of family reunion program

dangerous work. This employer responded to my forebear's behavior by insisting that he change his name from some unrecoverable designation to "Awkward."

My family's historian, Kenneth W. Awkward, in the compelling essay that appears in the 1991 *Awkward / Awkard / Offord Family Reunion Handbook,* acknowledges that our name's origins cannot be traced definitively. Rather than give more credence to such speculation, he offers a heroic narrative of "three Awkward men [who] left the West Indies (in the 1820's) and went up to Canada" and "came down to the United States with the soldiers (again in the 1820's)." This narrative is deemed "plausible" by the historian because a number of family members told him "the exact same story." Still, it is not especially persuasive to me because in addition to failing to resolve the issue of our pejorative naming, it foregrounds heroic, self-determined action on the part of the "Awkward patriarchs" while evading the historical fact that, even if our family's Western roots are in a now-romanticizable Caribbean, a dehumanizing slavery and subsequent forms of oppression existed there, too, and doubtless accounted for our naming.

I've decided to stick closer to—and play subversively with—the story my mother told me. (Kenneth rejects as implausible a similar tale in which a male forebear, a carpenter who "frequently dropped his tools," was deemed by his farmer employer "so clumsy" that he decreed that "his last name would be changed to 'Awkward.'") Given their respective social power, I suspect that the original Awkward man heeded his frustrated boss's instructions because he felt he had no choice. Of course, his acquiescence could be viewed as cowardly capitulation to whites. But he may also have been someone who, like the invisible man's grandfather, recognized that American life is "a war" that blacks do not have the weapons to win through open combat. Laughing along with his employer's "nigger joke" might have been merely a facet of his strategy to protect himself and future generations from detection as we seek subtly to "overcome" and "overwhelm" the enemy.

Having invested this racialized familial narrative with empowering possibilities that, in my view, effectively undermine aspects of my forebear's boss's pejorative plans, I have begun to come to terms with a surname passed on to me along maternal lines of inheritance, like so much else. Subsequently, I've felt less compulsion to discard it or to attach the same significance to it that this mythical white boss intended. Whichever family myth I embrace, my name—like the chain link that Tarp, another of invisible man's mentors, filed to escape imprisonment and passes on to Ellison's protagonist—has obviously "got a heap of signifying wrapped up in it" (379). Like so much other evidence that, from a certain vantage point, could be seen as mere confirmation of whites' Adamic control over names and, hence, meaning, *m awkward* "signifies a heap more" than my forebear's employer intended.

The following narrative is not the story of my name, but it may explain why I loved my mother enough to keep it.

INTRODUCTION ❋ "Don't Be Like Your Father"

This book explores my coming-of-age as a black American male in the wake of social, political, and cultural changes inaugurated during the turbulent 1960s. At the core of the narrative are the academic commencements in which I participated. Because commencements mark the culmination of specific stages of the educational process and initiate other searches for knowledge and insight, they offer emotionally charged occasions that allow me to examine my intellectual development. Further, they provide rich opportunities for me to measure my own actions and developing sensibilities against socially prescribed norms of, among other things, racial, gendered, and heterosexual behavior. From the general uniformity of caps and gowns and celebrants' ordered marches into and out of auditoriums decorated with glistening American flags to cautionary addresses by prominent figures, the traditional elements of academic commencements allow institutions to dramatize graduates' submission to the dictates of local, state, and federal law.

One result of my participation in such scenes of instruction is that I have become a scholar of twentieth-century Afro-American literary and cultural traditions. As such, I am well acquainted with depictions of commencements in black narratives that investigate the ironies of education in racist environments. The racial dramas surrounding commencement in, for example, Richard Wright's *Black Boy,* Ralph Ellison's *Invisible Man,* and Maya Angelou's *I Know Why the Caged Bird Sings* demonstrate that such celebrations are often sites of struggle between operatives of white society and forces of black resistance, both of whom seek control over the form and content of Afro-American expression.

Following the examples offered by such authors, I emphasize how events surrounding my own commencements, and aspects of the ceremonies themselves, placed me at odds with social constructions of black maleness. My struggles were not as communally resonant as those described in Angelou's narrative, where members

Anna Marie Awkward, summer 1986

of the graduating class respond to a departed white speaker who argues that black aspirations to be more than "maids and farmers, handymen and washerwomen . . . [were] farcical and presumptuous" by offering an inspiriting rendition of the black anthem "Lift Ev'ry Voice and Sing" (152). They were not as economically costly as young Richard's choice to read the valedictory remarks he has composed in defiance of his principal, who promises to help get the boy into college in exchange for his agreeing to read a speech that the school's white benefactors will not deem offensive. And, certainly, they were neither as eloquent nor as lucrative as the invisible man's repetition of a Washingtonian graduation speech for a group of monied whites who reward his accommodationist discourse with a college scholarship and an expensive briefcase. But they were occasions that tested my resolve, the seriousness of my convictions, and my comprehension of the social worlds I inhabited and by which I often felt inhibited.

Even when they are analyzing autobiographical texts and speaking self-reflexively, scholars generally emphasize social issues and patterns over the unexpected, unsystematizable twists and turns that characterize an individual life. As I see it, they do so because they believe that scholarship should examine how texts, attitudes, events, and behaviors are produced by a complicated amalgam of political, cultural, and religious beliefs and disputes that permeate and define a segment of society at a particular moment in time. Certainly, my own training limits my capacity, when I am performing traditional scholarly tasks, to deal cogently with the idiosyncracies of my intellectual journey. But because speaking of that journey remains important to me, I have turned, in the following pages, to autobiographical writing.

The academic memoir has emerged as a popular form of writing in part because of the aforementioned limitations of traditional scholarly discourse. But it is also, I believe, an indication that identity politics have become as inhibiting a critical straitjacket as the struggle to produce objective interpretive truths had been for earlier generations of academicians. The formulations of identity associated with even the most progressive versions of multiculturalism require that we claim to see our own—and others'—lives as conforming unproblematically to one of a series of master narratives that attempt to codify the particulars of various social groups' relationships to white male power.

Certainly, formulations of group identity can be used to predict or help account for individual behaviors and attitudes. But we are also all aware that individuals maintain some degree of power to determine how they respond to external stimuli. None of us is doomed to perform others' elaborate scripts of race, gender, or other social circumstances.

As the following pages demonstrate, I've worked diligently to avoid becoming a predictable product of my circumstances. Still, I've been troubled on occasion by a nagging suspicion that I am just that—a predictable product of my circumstances—though not in the ways that people who believe in a biologically determined division of intellectual labor, interests, and skills would expect. Indeed, my personal and intellectual interests often seem less a matter of choice than part of a "mission" that I "felt duty bound to fulfill," to echo Paule Marshall's evocative line in *Praisesong for the Widow* (42). As I understand it, this mission has been to figure out how most adequately to deal with being acutely aware, for as long as I can remember, of the social, political, psychological, and economic impact of men's domination of women. My often painful, always confusing, and still-ongoing mission, and the foundations for my acceptance of the bedrock feminist claim that men as a class oppress women as a class, were passed on to me by my mother through family narratives that spoke hauntingly of my absent father's physical, verbal, and spiritual abuse.

Having come of age intellectually in the late 1970s and early 1980s during the emergence of feminist criticism and theory and of black literary theory as important academic discourses, it would have been impossible for me to have avoided them. But I was, indeed, attracted to these discourses in part because they provided me a way of thinking about my own life, including the fact that I loved my mother, who was an alcoholic and who, particularly when she was drunk, offered her four children detailed accounts of her victimization. Sympathizing with my father, who broke my mother's right arm and left wrist, terrorized his small children, and withdrew abruptly from our lives, was impossible. For me, loving my mother required that I try to understand why she drank, why she frequently neglected her children's needs, and why she remained so emotionally remote during much of the first two decades of my life. Loving her meant recognizing logical connections between my father's brutality and her drinking. Even before I started elementary school, I knew that to consider only the pain that her alcoholism caused me would have meant that I did not take her pain, her stories, and her cautionary injunction, "Don't be like your father," seriously enough.

Doing anything but pursuing black feminist insights would have meant being like my father. I could no more have rejected feminism than I could have chosen not to love my mother. But prevailing formulations of identity politics insist that to talk openly about my love for her and my interests in, and difficulties with, certain versions of feminism is to risk appearing not to love her. To speak extensively about why I am a black male feminist is to expose myself to charges that I have visited upon my mother a discursive violence similar in intensity to the unimaginable physical pain she suffered at my father's hands. But given my experiences, given her experiences, I'm not sure how else I can explain the personal and professional choices I've made, choices about which I've been asked repeatedly over the last decade and a half. Indeed, how else can I, a self-defined, and flawed, black male feminist, justify my love and myself?

No text has assisted my efforts to think through such matters as much as Wendy Lesser's *His Other Half,* an engaging study of "men's relationship to the feminine—and . . . the way that relationship comes out in works of art" (5). In her investigations of the work of artists such as D. H. Lawrence, Dickens, and Hitchcock, Lesser is uninterested in texts that merely confirm the existence of, and the damage caused by, gender inequity, texts whose interrogation offers easy, comforting support to feminist ideology's already well-documented claims. Instead, she is attracted, as a reader and as a critic, "to the points at which most pressure is brought to bear, to the places where the [male] artist risks (and one often hears) the charge of misogyny" (4).

Lesser insists that such risks are *necessary* if one hopes to encounter provocative artistic representations of women by men, and unavoidable for women who wish to speak frankly about those daring representations that they admire. Also, and quite important for my purposes, she locates males' relationships with their mothers as the source of such risky endeavors. Indeed, in the beginning of her powerful discussion of mothers and their writer-sons, she argues that such mothers and sons must learn to cajole audiences into accepting their assigned roles. Lesser's statement reads as follows:

> Whenever a man sets out to write a story about a mother (or *his* mother, for it comes to the same thing), it is also, inevitably, a story about the extortion of sympathy. Two kinds of sympathy are extorted:

the reader's and the male author's. That is to say, it becomes a story both about the sympathy the author had to feel for his mother and about the sympathy we have to feel for him because that other sympathy was forced from him.

This story about extorted sympathy also becomes a story about how that man came to be a writer. For in feeling another's pain, he begins to learn how to create characters beyond himself; and in extracting sympathy from us without making us resentful, he learns the skills of mediating between himself and an audience of readers. (23)

Mothers and sons can be equally adept at extorting sympathy, a narrative skill that the mother teaches the son and without which discursive power is unthinkable. By imitating the mother, the author-son comes to see storytelling as the art of investing the relationship between speaker and listener, or author and audience, with the psychic drama that characterizes his relationship to his female forebear.

Lesser's formulation recognizes the generative nature of artful female expressivity. Lesser's mothers are not unwilling pawns in male efforts to extort sympathy but teachers who pass on to their sons this essential narrative skill. Indeed, they are self-conscious, self-empowered, and empowering models of textual control.

Seen from such a vantage point, my mother's discussions of her abuse provided her with a means of exerting control over her environment and her audience, including—especially—me. She compelled me to empathize with her plight, and to be attracted to, and want to produce, texts that explored the sorts of issues her narratives addressed. Certainly, hers were cautionary tales, which, like all such tales, must be heard—and repeated—again and again, circulating within the culture among a host of complementary and competing stories, if they are to maintain their capacity to influence the attitudes of sons, mothers, and others concerning sexual and racial politics.

If my mother was indeed trying to extort her children's sympathy (and why else would she have told us, before any of us had memorized the contours of his face, that our father broke her right arm by stomping on it?), she summarized her narrative's major theme in a line she repeated often to her two sons: "Don't be like your father." I've spent much of my life trying to understand precisely what it means not to be "like" him, and searching for acceptable modes and models of behavior.

This book constitutes my risky attempt to circulate the major themes of my mother's narratives, and to demonstrate that I've absorbed their form and content well enough to contribute to feminism's efforts to challenge patriarchy's unabated rule. A record of events that have marked that still-ongoing search, it combines autobiographical recall, textual criticism, and institutional analysis in a form that, following Henry Louis Gates Jr., we might call "autocritography." Gates uses this term in a promotional blurb for a book of critical essays by Houston A. Baker Jr. to signify "an autobiography of a critical concept."

If autobiography is a genre in which contributors shape their self-representations in response to earlier texts, "autocritography" is a self-reflexive, self-consciously academic act that foregrounds aspects of the genre typically dissolved into authors' always strategic self-portraits. Autocritography, in other words, is an account of individual, social, and institutional conditions that help to produce a scholar and, hence, his or her professional concerns. Although the intensity of investigation of any of these conditions may vary widely, their self-consciously interactive presence distinguishes autocritography from other forms of autobiographical recall.

What follows, then, is my effort, in James Olney's words, to "discuss and analyze the autobiographical act as [I] perform . . . it" (25), to account for and offer evidence—from my childhood, scenes of professional instruction, and readings of contemporary events and expressive cultural texts—of my attentiveness to my mother's narratives.

I am not naive enough to claim that my gender has not been an obstacle to my pursuit of feminist truths; indeed, I am quite aware of the incompatibilities between such truths and masculine self-interest. In my effort to produce an insightful black male autobiographical inquiry, I've chosen not to focus primarily on incidents that could be seen, even by the most skeptical of gatekeepers, as nascent signs of feminist consciousness. Rather, I linger primarily on moments that dramatize the tensions between male self-interest and a recognition of women's systemic oppression. I believe that only by exploring such tensions, by remaining both self-interested and cognizant of the myriad costs of misogyny, can the activity that Tom Digby terms "men doing feminism" contribute to this ever-expanding social, intellectual, and philosophical project.

Such exploration requires something other than the timid recapitulation of safe, predictable formulations by a distractingly self-conscious interloper. Indeed, it requires a willingness to take risks. Despite the care I've used to construct this narrative, I am well aware that it is risky to linger on my youthful attempts to negotiate the always politically fraught fault lines of race, gender, class identity, and sexuality. Indeed, for some, this book may confirm masculi-nist perceptions of the dangers for males of failing to accept the benefits and costs of their gendered legacy. For others, it may offer further proof that men are unable to resist using even those females they purport to love in order to increase their store of material, cultural, and psychic comfort. For still others, exposing an ambivalence I share with countless other affirmative action baby boys and girls about the costs and consequences of our apparent inclusion in the crazy quilt of American society may suggest that I am insufficiently grateful for the assistance of important individuals and institutions. And as I know all too well, through some afrocentric eyes, I may seem too grateful for such assistance.

But given the persistence of pejorative meanings attached to black male subjectivities, if a feminist discourse informed by an acute awareness of such perceptions is not a risky venture, its social and intellectual contributions will be, at best, negligible. I hope that the risks I've taken in the following pages—pages that offer what, following Lesser, I've come to think of as a narrative of "extorted sympathy"—seem justified.

I read voraciously in the autumns, winters, springs, and summers before I graduated from sixth grade. I consumed library books, magazines, newspapers, and trashy, sexually explicit novels that I borrowed surreptitiously from the shelf of my mother's closet. Later, during high school, two books— A Farewell to Arms, *by Ernest Hemingway, and* The End of the Road, *by John Barth—emerged from the mountain of texts I'd encountered to become my manuals. Compelled alternately by Papa's brooding cynicism and JB's broad, bawdy satire, I vacillated between the two novels' disparate representations of their protagonists' lack of faith in modes of thought that had been normative for pre–World War I, premodern Western societies. Hemingway's novel seemed to emphasize the importance of limited human connection despite its difficulties, whereas Barth's suggested that even limited connections were, if not impossible, potentially disastrous.*

So by the spring semester of my sophomore year at Brandeis, when I encountered The Bluest Eye *near the end of a class on twentieth-century Afro-American literature, I was already passionate about, and familiar with, the secular art of close, personal narrative scrutiny. After a semester spent reading, discussing, and skimming critical writings on canonical texts including* Native Son *and* Invisible Man, *I knew that Wright's and Ellison's were at the top of a very short list of quintessential moments in black expressivity. Still, my cursory first readings did not lead me to recognize these novels as aesthetic accomplishments or savvy representations of black life as I'd experienced it.*

However, elements of Toni Morrison's novel hooked me immediately: its critical appropriation of the Dick-and-Jane primer; its prefatory emphasis on reconstructing what Claudia, its first-person narrator, terms not the "why" but the "how" of black female degradation; and that narrator's failed efforts to intervene to save the degraded subject—Pecola—from psychic fragmentation and social death. Soon after reading this novel, I became desperate to understand the analytical implications of Morrison's formal experimentation. Precisely what were the motivations for and the impact of her use of two narrators? Her decision to name the four sections of the novel after the seasons beginning, like the calendar of school-age children—and their teachers—with autumn? Her prefacing each of the sections narrated by the omniscient narrator with one of the sentences from the primer? And how, exactly, are the dual narrative voices connected to Pecola's schizophrenic splitting into two voices after she is raped by her father?

Also, I was mesmerized by the self-conscious revisions by a now-mature Claudia of her life. Although I recognized that The Bluest Eye *had much in common thematically with Ellison's and Wright's representations of the difficulties of black male maturation, the male-authored novels lacked for me what I found so vital in Morrison's novel: a quality of urgent, mournful, and revisionary remembrance.*

That compulsion to reconsider the past is most clearly evinced early in the novel in a passage that Claudia offers just after describing a particularly difficult bout with the flu to which her mother responds in typically brusque fashion. Significantly, this reconsideration does not require that Claudia reject her childhood interpretation and, with it, any hope that the reader will seriously consider the plausibility of her youthful perspectives on a range of matters. Rather, it is offered as an expansion and extension of her previous views of the sources and consequences of her childhood pain.

> *But was it really like that? As painful as I remember? Only mildly. Or rather, it was a productive and fructifying pain. Love, thick and dark as Alaga syrup, eased up into that cracked window. I could smell it—taste it—sweet, musty, with an edge of wintergreen at its base—everywhere in that house. It stuck, along with my tongue, to the frosted windowpanes. It coated my chest, along with the salve, and when the flannel came undone in my sleep, the clear, sharp curves of air outlined its presence on my throat. And in the night, when my coughing was dry and tough, feet padded into the room, hands repinned the flannel, readjusted the quilt, and rested a moment on my forehead. So when I think of autumn, I think of somebody with hands who does not want me to die. (14)*

In addition to the sorts of questions it raised about the novel's own designs, this passage suggested for me the potential psychological and emotional benefits of reexamining one's past as a knowledgeable, articulate adult armed with greater insight and a workable, clearly defined agenda. To revisit joyful and painful experiences with remnants of a child's heart and an informed angle of vision, The Bluest Eye *suggested to me as an eighteen-year-old college sophomore, is to open up the possibilities of re-making myself and, perhaps, others.*

Beyond her desire to find *"fructifying"* value in her painful experiences, this bruised, inquisitive child writes to recall her failed efforts to legitimize the life of her friend, Pecola, who goes mad because nearly everyone she encounters uses her as a scapegoat. She is mistreated by her shamelessly self-centered parents, gossiping women who blame her for being the target of her father's perverse desires, a gang of boys who ritualistically surround and hurl racialized insults at her, and Claudia herself, who acknowledges her participation in the community's efforts to confirm its own tenuous sense of self worth by reinforcing Pecola's pronounced feelings of worthlessness. A narrative of strategic recollection, The Bluest Eye suggests that Claudia re-members the past because of her need to atone for her contributions, benign though they may have been, to Pecola's demise.

It hardly mattered to me that Claudia was a fictional girl, and I was not. That she came of age in the pre–civil rights forties, and I in the revolutionary sixties and seventies. That she lived in a small, nondescript city in the Midwest, and I grew up in Philadelphia, the cradle of American liberty, the place where assiduously preserved monuments of the nation's origins can seem to overwhelm the clearest signals of the wide gulf between national rhetoric and self-evident truths like slavery and sexism. What mattered was that Claudia thought, deeply, self-consciously, about the connections between the past and the present, between herself and Pecola. I loved Claudia because I recognized that her struggles were my struggles, including the struggle to figure out how to situate oneself in relation to a community's simultaneously self-protective and injurious values.

Perhaps reading Morrison's first novel placed me irretrievably on the road to becoming a scholar of Afro-American literature. Certainly, after reading Claudia's efforts, I began self-consciously to consider the pliability of the meanings of the past.

While Morrison's The Bluest Eye uses the cyclicality of seasons to structure its narrative, I've organized the sections of my own acts of autobiographical recall around occasions of institutional disengagement. These occasions, called alternately graduation (emphasizing the division of one's academic career—one's life in school—into marked, measurable categories) and commencement (the commemorative recognition of a new scho-

lastic beginning), invite reassessments and recollections of the self one was and the self one has become as a result of experiences in institutions from which one is about to depart. My sense of the interpretive significance of commencements began at the end of sixth grade, when I first arrived at the inescapable conclusion that, like the past, present, and future, my personal and institutional lives were inextricably bound together.

On the mid-June 1970 morning of my graduation from George Washington Elementary School, I looked as good from head to toe as I ever had. My typically unkempt hair, which I'd gotten cut into an attractive short Afro the evening before, was oiled and combed. My brown Easter suit pants had creases so sharp I was sure that I could use them to slice any neighborhood hardrock who crossed my path. My chocolate brown shoes were polished and shining, and my brown clip-on tie topped off what I thought was an impressive ensemble. Looking me over, my mother nodded approvingly, and Carol, who switched effortlessly from older sister to maternal surrogate when our mother was drinking, marveled at the fact that I'd remembered to lotion my typically ashy face and hands. "See you at graduation," my mother said to me as I left the apartment to gather with my classmates before our mile-long walk to historic Mother Bethel Church.

Bethel, the "mother" parish that spawned hundreds of African Methodist churches across the country, was founded in 1816 by Richard Allen and Absalom Jones, black Philadelphia ministers who'd objected to the confinement of black worshipers to the balconies of white churches. I'd heard that Reverend Allen, in particular, was so beloved by his congregation that the church's members saw fit to encase his mummified remains in a crypt in the basement of the church. Apparently because of Bethel's historical significance and Rittenhouse Square location, the local ABC television station had assigned a camera crew and a reporter to cover the proceedings. When we heard this news at our final rehearsal, my classmates and I whispered excitedly to one another, thrilled that our graduation would serve as the concluding, feel-good section of the broadcast.

Mother Bethel is located four blocks from where I'd lived until I

McCall Elementary School, the author's first school, which he attended with Rittenhouse Square's upper-middle-class residents

The author's first remembered residence, near Center City

The revolutionary war hero and future first president, Crossing the Delaware River. Artwork carved into the exterior of George Washington Elementary School.

was nine, and about a block from McCall, the elementary school my siblings and I had previously attended. McCall served, in addition to some poor black kids who lived on the borders of the district, a ritzy Rittenhouse Square population, the children of doctors, lawyers, and various other affluent white professionals. Walking the final four blocks between George Washington and Mother Bethel— institutions with distinct parental claims on me (as an American citizen who hadn't begun to question the nationalistic rhetoric I'd been force-fed at school and elsewhere, and as a black Philadelphian who was at least vaguely aware of the self-righteous ferocity of civil rights and Black Power battles)—I traversed familiar streets, passing familiar stores, bus stops, and the newly refurbished playground whose former state of disrepair had made me hesitant to enter it before we moved.

The familiarity was comforting. Assuming the role of tour guide, I was uncharacteristically talkative, pointing out landmarks to my classmates, for whom these streets were largely unexplored territory, and to Miss Davis. Miss Davis was a thin woman with shoulder-length blond hair that she wore in a ponytail. She came to class decked, as the fashion of the day dictated, in wild-colored miniskirts and dresses and thin black boots that reached the bottom of her bony knees. She was a marvelous teacher blessed with boundless energy, a smoky, southern twang like Liz Taylor on a hot tin roof, and the gumption to use any and all standard teaching paraphernalia—especially thick, unfinished yardsticks and pokers—to keep the most rambunctious boys and, on occasion, girls in line.

I'd come to Miss Davis's class a year ahead of schedule because in the fall of 1968, during my first term in George Washington, my fourth-grade teacher, Mrs. Robinson, recognized that I already knew all of the material she was supposed to teach me that year. I'd been a good student at my previous school, McCall, but I knew that a number of my classmates there were probably more intelligent and certainly more studious than I was. I got skipped not because I'd become appreciably smarter during the summer between third and fourth grade but because I'd moved from the outskirts of a largely white, upper-middle-class school district with an excellent elementary school to an overwhelmingly black housing project and school where the resources, parental involvement, and scholastic expectations were palpably inferior.

My gregariousness during our graduation day walk seemed to surprise and please Miss Davis, whose constant prodding of me to answer questions in class suggested that she thought of me as shy or as someone who preferred anonymity to the pressures of ostentatious display. Certainly, I was typically quiet in class as I pondered with equal seriousness such topics as how to improve my basketball game and why my mother drank so much.

In many ways my activities were "normal"—I played freeze tag and climbed the always chilly, dome-shaped monkey bars; I played basketball until I was bone tired, collected all of the cards the loose change I could find would buy, and paid close attention to radio broadcasts and *Daily News* stories about the 76ers, especially my favorite player, Hal Greer; and I dreamed sweet dreams nearly every night about my classmate Denise. I greeted Denise each school day with a quick wave, a shy smile, and an unexpressed longing that one day she, too, would recognize that we were soul mates.

Despite that surface normalcy, I was always aware of feeling what one of my friends recently called, in describing me, a profound sense of melancholy. I was a pouty, teary-eyed boy, unable to assume a happy-go-lucky attitude or to shake the sadness of remembered and unremembered life experiences. I was aware of constantly trying to prepare myself for the next trauma, the next disappointment, the next conflict, resigned to the inevitability of serious, all-consuming, long-lasting pain, and hoping merely for the wherewithal to survive it.

That is not to say that I was unmoved by subtle and not so subtle pleasures of my life: there was the repressed delight I felt during an exhibition in my neighborhood when Hal Greer observed my jump shot and told me that I had "good form"; the tantalizing chill of waking from unremembered wet dreams; the soothing shelter of the unconditional love of my grandparents, whose laughter—hers a sweet, girlish chuckle, his an infectious, high-pitched, down-home cackle—continues to represent the sounds of joy for me; the salty sting of Wise potato chips, four bags of which my mother purchased for her children during each late-night trip with Mr. Freddy to find "some cold beer"; the sadistic satisfaction of squashing pregnant roaches; and the camaraderie my siblings and I shared as survivors of our ongoing war with my mother's alcoholism.

However, none of these pleasures penetrated my psyche for long or deepened my understanding of what it meant for me to be alive in the world. More often than not, even when I was luxuriating under its influence, I would ponder the appropriateness of my lingering too long over anything that suggested pleasure. Was Hal's comment about my form his stock line for ghetto urchins? Were my grandparents really as happy with each other or with us as they seemed? Should I eat potato chips purchased during my mother's journeys to satisfy her alcoholic urges? Did unborn roaches, huddled uncomfortably together in their tannish rectangular sacks like frightened slaves in the bowels of menacing ships, feel pain when I squashed the life out of their mothers? And would my siblings and I have been as close if our mother didn't have a drinking problem?

But more than any other subject, I pondered the origins, appearance, and consequences of my burn. Other mothers (and fathers) in my neighborhood abused alcohol, other families were on welfare and were as poor as mine, other fathers had deserted their families, other mothers lived with abusive men to whom they were not married. While my poverty and our familial situation were painful, certainly they weren't unique. But my burn was, or at least seemed to be. It was my distinguishing mark, what I learned in high school to think of as my Hemingwayesque wound, a tangible standard of deviation, a symbol and a partial explanation of my deep childhood suffering.

Despite my physical imperfections, I'd been told often enough that I was cute by adult female relatives and friends of my mother to believe that I probably was. Certainly, I never felt traumatized by the prevalence of images of standardized white beauty. (I had sleep-disturbing crushes on white girls in my predominantly white second- and third-grade classes, and I developed equally intense and generally unrequited feelings for black girls when I was a student at predominantly black elementary and junior high schools.) More debilitating than being poor, and certainly more of a problem than being black, was the fact that I was permanently disfigured when I was two years old.

I was always—am always—aware of my burn. For as long as I can remember, I've felt it, like a strained muscle whose dull ache reminds you of its traumatic condition. Perhaps because of nerve damage that occurred when layers of skin and inches of hair on the left side of my face were permanently singed off, my burn throbs, pulsates, and demands recognition of its existence from me. It is as though time had anesthetized my forehead, allowing me to constantly feel the contents of the pan roll naggingly down my face.

As closely as I can reconstruct it—and, fortunately, I have no firsthand recollection of the incident—I got burned because of my curiosity, hunger, and impatience: I wanted so much to see, eat, and be filled by the chicken my mother was frying that I pulled the cast-iron pan in which it was cooking down from the hotplate my mother was using and onto my upturned forehead. The scalding liquid peeled layers of skin from my entire forehead, made its way down the upper left side of my face, left a dime-sized spot amidst the hair just above and in front of my left ear, and stopped at my left cheekbone. The chicken grease then slid onto my left shoulder and forearm, my right hand, and my upper stomach, secondary areas where the marks have faded partially or fully.

Compared to the damage done to burn victims I've seen— their vision and use of limbs significantly impaired, their entire faces covered by hideous scars—my accident caused minimal physical damage. Still, I've never achieved a healthy level of acceptance of my disfiguring mark and have told my wife, only half jokingly, that instead of buying a red sports car at the peak of my upcoming midlife crisis, I'd go to a plastic surgeon and beg him to cover up the scars on my face and make me beautiful.

When I was a child, people made fun of my burn constantly. My siblings extemporized a verse, a nonsense song whose words—"It ain't one thing but the next best thing to a . . . Burnt Duck!"—often made me cry and inspired me to locate their easily insultable imperfections. Several kids in the neighborhood teased me mercilessly. To some, I was Burnside (Raymond Burr's wheelchair-bound detective was popular then); others called me Peanut Roaster, or Bernie Dolan. I heard these names everywhere I went: in elevators, in the school yard, in class, on the basketball court. "I'm hungry, boy. Why don't you give me some of that fried chicken?" "It's burning up over there, huh, boy?" "Guess that grease didn't fry all your brains, huh?" "Bring it on, Burnside, and I'll slap the ball 'gainst your greasy head!"

My burn came to define my community identity. I wasn't the skinny, big-headed, sad-faced boy who got skipped, or even one of the drunk lady's sons. In a sense, I was my burn. Because I was also struggling with other problems that threatened my sense of self-confidence, this teasing made me consider the depth of my "inferiority complex," to use the psychiatric designation my mother learned from talk radio and employed to describe her own lack of self-esteem when she was growing up.

Being deemed intelligent by my teachers helped me to maintain a degree of self-confidence and reinforced my own tendency to find rational rather than violent means of dealing with my problems and my surroundings. However, as I searched for reasoned responses, I knew that even the most pronounced evidence of school smarts could not protect me from the sting of insults from members of my community who did not themselves deem my admittedly ephemeral advantages to be significant at all, or certainly not sufficient to level the social playing field. All that my minimal self-confidence did for me in the face of these insults was to keep me from being crushed by them. I learned the art of silent self-protection, of silence as self-protection.

We'd moved in June 1968, two months after I had an eye operation to improve the apparent focus and vision of my lazy right eye, and a week after I completed third grade at McCall. My mother's boyfriend, Mr. Freddy, a short, wavy-haired, good-looking man who had "Mom" and a faded red heart tattooed on his right upper arm, loaded our belongings onto the truck he used to transport furniture for a variety of Center City antique stores and drove them about a mile and a half from a roach-infested apartment building on Ninth Street near Lombard to the Southwark Housing Projects.

Southwark is a four-square city block complex, completed in 1961, that consists of three twenty-five-story high-rises and roughly four hundred strategically placed two- and three-story houses. Though we arrived in the projects less than a decade after they opened, signs of deterioration, infestation, and decay were everywhere. The first such sign I detected was the graffiti-lined elevator we commandeered to take us up to our nineteenth-floor apartment. On the floor of the elevator was a pool of rancid urine that trembled like jostled, not quite coagulated Jell-O.

Despite the sight and smell of the elevator, we were all well aware that Southwark was a significant step up. It provided us relative spaciousness—a living room, a dining area separate from the kitchen, three bedrooms, and a fenced-in porch with a spectacular view of South Philly—along with a large playground just across the street. As the rusty cables of the elevator slowly pulled us up to our new apartment, I looked at the nervous smiles on the faces of my family members and hoped that the hard times connected with our cramped former space might be ending.

During that walk to Mother Bethel, I thought of those times: of my father's savage beatings of my mother (incidents she told her children about so frequently that I felt I'd been a silent witness to

South Philly's Southwark Project high-rises. The author lived in the second building from the left.

them); of the first boyfriend of hers I remember, Mr. Cisco, slamming a hammer against her skull in a fit of calculated rage; of my mother knocking me unconscious with a thick, curved leg of our broken table in response to some now forgotten transgression.

But mainly I thought of the fun my siblings and I had: of laughing giddily as we used our communal bed as a trampoline until Mr. George's or Miss Fanny's voice rose up menacingly through the floor and commanded us to stop; of listening endlessly to the Temptations' "I Wish It Would Rain" and Marvin and Tammi's "Ain't No Mountain High Enough"—the two 45s we owned—on our cheap record player; of going with Ricky across the street to the apartment of my mother's friend, whom we called Aunt Naomi, to watch *Thor* and *Fantastic Four* cartoons on the color television that dominated her perfumed bedroom; of teasing Debby for carrying our pet bunny around by its ears and, we were convinced, eventually killing it; and of acting out a play about a damsel-in-distress that Carol directed, with Debby as the damsel with no line to remember except "Help," and Ricky and me alternating in the roles of the brave, handsome prince and the mean palace guard the prince must battle to free her. While the guard's role provided an occasion to scowl menacingly and to improvise grunts, groans, insults, and angles of attack, the prince got to save the damsel and to say the wonderful lines "Hark, I hear a cry. It is from the Princess of Nottingham. I must save her at once."

Less than a week earlier, my worthiness to accompany my classmates on this walk to this historic American site had been called into question. Along with two of my buddies, Bobby and Skeeter, I was reprimanded and sent home for the day by my school's genial white principal, Mr. Williams, because we veered off our typical center-stairway path and walked down the hallway of the darkened second-floor wing where the classrooms of the predominantly white population of severely handicapped children were located.

As we neared the unfamiliar stairway on the south side of the building, we were accosted by a loud, deep, menacing voice that ordered us to stop. When we turned around, we saw a tall, thin, wispy-haired white man in his thirties rushing toward us.

"What are you doing here?" he shouted at us.

"Here where?"

"In this hallway."

"Going to Miss Davis's class."

"You have no business being in this section of the school. Our students have done nothing to you, and cannot defend themselves. Why must you continue to pick on them?"

"Huh? We was just going to class. We're in the sixth grade, and our rooms are right upstairs from here."

"Come with me. We're going to see Mr. Williams or Mr. Boyd or someone with the authority to prevent you from harassing these poor children."

As we walked to the principal's office, I thought of my mother's constant admonitions against making fun of the weaknesses of others. She was forced to remind us frequently because disability—physical and psychological—was so rampant in the Southwark projects. There was an elderly Parkinson's sufferer whom kids called Shaky, whose involuntary head, hand, and arm movements seemed exacerbated by his heavy drinking. And Miss Katie, whose vision had been burned away by lye thrown in her eyes by an angry lover with whom she continued to live and on whom she'd become totally dependent. And Tiptop, rumored to have gone insane during a tour in Vietnam, who structured his life around brisk, aimless wanderings through South and Central Philadelphia in wild, clashing, thrift shop polyester outfits and, judging by the gingerness of his steps, painful platform shoes. And the pleasant widower who walked his small dog in the playground near the baseball field, who couldn't speak above a whisper because, unlike Mr. Cisco, he had survived cancer of the throat. And the throngs of old folks whose limbs had given out and who traveled up and down on elevators and across our urban jungle on canes, crutches, walkers, and wheelchairs in various states of repair.

Constant, desensitizing encounters with these imperfect bodies, my acute sense of my own imperfections, and the regular public spectacle of my mother, inebriated, swaying in a whiskey- and wine-soaked breeze, squashed any inclination I might otherwise have had to stare at, make fun of, or harass anyone.

My mother was the first parent to arrive, her face a mask of stern sobriety for which I was grateful. When she sat down next to me, I gave her a cautious half smile, which she didn't return.

"What happened, Michael?"

"Nothing, Mommy. We was just walking through the hall and this dumb teacher thought we were gonna do something to those retards."

"We who?" She looked around and noticed Bobby, whom she recognized as the skinny little boy who lived in the first floor of our building, and Skeeter, whom she'd never seen before.

"Oh. What retards?"

Just then, the principal's office door opened, and Mr. Williams stepped out, greeting my mother with a wide smile, and motioned to us to enter his office.

"Miss Awkward, please come in. You, too, young man." Grabbing her elbow, he guided her to a chair near his desk.

"Mr. Williams, what's my son done?"

He told her of the teacher's suspicions, and of the verbal abuse repeatedly heaped upon the disabled children by the school's able-bodied population. After informing my mother that he'd decided to send us home, he looked directly at me. "Michael, you've been an exceptional student here, but if you get into any more trouble, I'll be forced to hold you back a grade. You're younger than your classmates, which means that you may be too easily influenced. Maybe you need another year with us before you move on to junior high. Do you understand?"

Because he had acknowledged that my friends and I had committed no major infraction, and because I was a good student with a spotless disciplinary record, his threat seemed excessive. But I was well aware of the cards he was holding. I had been skipped, and he had the power to unskip me.

"Yes, Mr. Williams, I understand."

He stood up quickly and showed us to the door. "Thanks for coming, Miss Awkward. If your son doesn't get into any more trouble this week, I'm sure I'll see you at graduation."

I waved to Bobby and Skeeter as my mother and I left the office. "Mommy," I said after we got off of school grounds, "he ain't gonna keep me back just 'cause I was walking down that hall, is he? That's not fair, you know? It's not."

"I guess he's got enough bad boys to deal with without having to start worrying about you, too. Don't you think?"

"I guess so. But I'm not bad."

"I know, Michael Cycle. But you got to be careful. You understand?"

I knew that my mother meant that I needed to monitor my behavior generally, not merely avoid repeating this particular infraction, but I replied, "I know I'm not walking down that hallway again!" She smiled a quick, close-mouthed smile, then tried to repress a giggle that turned into a hearty laugh. "No, I guess you won't, huh?"

I smiled, in spite of myself.

We arrived at Mother Bethel a half hour before the luncheon and graduation ceremonies were scheduled to begin, prompting one of the church's staff members to invite all one hundred or so of us on a tour of the church's basement. Figuring that it was more problematic to compromise my sensitive nasal passages and sharp appearance than my reputation, I joined the enthusiastic boys and girls who gleefully followed the woman. But on confronting the basement's stench, dust, spiderwebs, mildew, and, finally, Reverend Allen's crypt, I quickly retraced my steps and devised my excuse: if anyone asked, I'd say I had to go to the bathroom.

When I got back upstairs, relatives and friends of the graduates had begun to arrive. Soon thereafter, my classmates returned from their foolish encounter with dust and death and were pointed toward their assigned seats in the rows of tables on which we would eat and view the proceedings.

I can remember a few details about the ceremony quite vividly. I recall that our assistant principal, Mr. Boyd, announced that the news crew scheduled to film part of our graduation had been called to cover an important breaking story. I remember marveling at the variety of cameras that mothers, fathers, aunts, and family friends brought with them to record this moment in their children's lives. Also, I recall wondering, as people finished their food and had their paper plates and plastic utensils removed, when, and in what condition, my mother was going to arrive.

After Mr. Williams welcomed the relatives and friends of the graduates and briefly discussed the highlights of the school year, the doors to the church opened, and in stepped my mother and one of her friends, whom my siblings and I called Aunt Minnie.

When they stumbled into the center of the church, holding onto each other for support and loudly whispering to each other to be quiet, I wanted to disappear, even if it meant joining Reverend Allen's remains in the dusty basement. I turned my head momentarily away from the spectacle and stared blankly ahead, unable to focus my vision or my thoughts. When I summoned the courage to look around, they had settled into the only easily accessible empty seats that were to the right of the makeshift stage, and I convinced myself that my mother's entrance had made no impact on anyone but me. The assembled crowd kept on smiling, drinking warm water, picking at bitter fruit cups with plastic forks they'd neglected to give to the waitresses, and listening intently to Mr. Williams.

A few minutes later, we were asked to line up to receive our diplomas, and I was grateful for this sign that the proceedings were almost over. As we waited for our names to be called, a few of my male classmates remarked on my mother's inebriation. "Your moms is flying, huh, Mike?" "She fucked up, man!" "Damn, Michael, she more buzzed than a mothafucka!" "I wish I could get me some of that shit she been drinking!" I stared straight ahead, trying to ignore them and to suppress the tears welling up in my eyes. And as my name was called, I walked up to Mr. Williams, wiped my eyes, shook his hand, and smiled briefly at him. I heard him say, "Good job, young man," as I stepped away from him and walked back to my seat.

After he'd given diplomas to all of the assembled students, Mr. Williams announced a surprise final event: acknowledging the performances of the five students who'd scored above the national average on the California Achievement Test. The student with the highest overall score would receive a gold medal with the raised profile of our school's namesake, the nation's first president, and a check for five dollars. "Let me now call the names of the students, who should come up, face the audience, and receive our heartfelt congratulations."

I heard my name called first, followed by Doris's, DeWayne's, Marty's, and Stanley's. As I walked up, I saw my mother stand up, and I heard her exclaim, "That's my son! My son! My baby boy! Minnie, he got skipped last year, hear? So he's younger than the rest of his class, and look at him!"

I felt the tears well up again. As my classmates joined me, I tried to read their responses to my mother's audible chattering and to being singled out in this unexpected manner. In vain, I searched among the Christian icons prominently displayed around the room for a soothing or analogous image, but my three years of studying Catholic catechism taught me, if nothing else, that comparing my suffering with Christ's represented the height of self-absorption. I couldn't block out my mother's slurred words, which I heard distinctly above the applause. "He just got skipped, hear, and he's still one of the smartest in his class!"

When the applause died down, and my mother had finally stopped talking, Mr. Williams continued. "Ladies and gentlemen, the student with the highest score on the CAT is . . . Michael Awkward."

The applause commenced again, along with my mother's audible sobbing. "That's my boy! My boy, hear! See that, Minnie! See that!" I stood, paralyzed. I stared straight ahead, hesitant to turn my head even slightly either toward my mother or away from her, afraid of what she would do if I looked at her and of not being able to see her at all if I turned away.

Suddenly I started sobbing, deep, long-repressed tears that burned my cheeks and contracted my stomach muscles, forcing me to bend over slightly and cover my face. I could smell the sickeningly sweet Jergens lotion I'd spread on my hands just before I left our apartment. The thumb of my right hand brushed against the corner of my legally blind right eye, which began to burn. I didn't want to cover my eyes, because I needed to be able to see my mother; didn't want to wipe the tears away, because I knew that doing so would make my eyes burn even more; didn't want to be standing in front of these people, who I was sure thought I was an overly emotional fool.

Stanley, who was standing next to me, looked at me, clearly happy for me and embarrassed by my display, and put his hand on my shoulder like he did when we were on the basketball court and he wanted to indicate gently that I'd made an ill-advised move, pass, or defensive play. "Why you crying, boy? Stop acting like a little bitch! Go get your prize."

I couldn't. Stop crying. Stop being a bitch. Go get my award. I didn't want to risk further, potentially embarrassing scrutiny. Instead of being able to focus on and take pride in my accomplishment, instead of planning where I'd put my medal or how I'd spend my loot, I could think only about my mother's shameful behavior.

A few long seconds passed, until Mr. Williams, who seemed to sense that I couldn't move, invited me to come forward to receive my award. My tears came now in a steady, silent stream, and as I turned my back to my mother and walked toward the podium, I violated one of her cardinal rules by wiping them and my snot onto my jacket sleeve. When I reached him, Mr. Williams shook my hand, gave me the medal and an envelope, and said, beaming at me, "Congratulations, son. I guess I'm going to have to promote you now, huh?" I couldn't meet his eyes, couldn't smile, couldn't say anything. I shook my head and walked back to my seat.

When I sat down, classmates slapped me on the back, shook my limp, wet right hand, and asked to see the medal. Several of the mothers sitting nearby asked me if I was okay. Unsatisfied by my teary, tentative nods, one particularly concerned mother, whom I'd seen a few seconds earlier out of the corner of my eye point a flashing camera at me, rested a palm on the back of my neck and handed me a small, thick piece of glossy paper with a dark, rectangular middle bordered by an ivory edge. "Look at yourself," she said, and touched my cheek with one of her soft, chilly fingertips. "Keep this, okay?"

I thanked her, smiled, and stared at the dark middle of the paper she'd given to me. When Mr. Williams dismissed the gathering, I remained seated, watching the dark space magically lighten, brighten, and take shape. As people moved toward the door, I saw two of my classmates materialize—Danny and Tom, the only two white boys in Miss Davis's class—with Danny looking toward a still-dark subject of the photo and Tom looking down, smiling at an object he was holding in his hand, my George Washington medal.

When my mother and Aunt Minnie approached me, sitting alone at the empty table, their talk, laughter, and alcohol-drenched breath portending their arrival, I saw my hair, then my suit, then my face, and, finally, my eyes, appear. In the picture, I stared straight ahead, eyes pinkish and filled with tears, mouth slightly open, no sign of pleasure or pride of accomplishment on my face. I looked as I knew I felt: overwhelmed, bothered, bewildered.

"Oh, Michael, I'm so proud of you!" my mother exclaimed, in a slightly more subdued voice than she'd used previously. She searched my face and obviously didn't like what she saw.

"Yeah, me too, boy," Aunt Minnie said.

"How could you, Mommy?"

"How could I what? Oh, you mean come late? Your Aunt Minnie couldn't find an outfit she was happy with, hear? Her clothes are all

The author, in tears after receiving the George Washington medal,
which classmate Tom *(right)* admires as Danny *(left)* looks on

too big. I told her she wasn't eating enough since Dave—I mean
your Uncle Dave—died. Ain't she getting skinny?"

"Mommy . . ."

"I'm proud of you. Come on, let's get out of here. I need me a
smoke real bad."

Most of my classmates had already started heading back toward
Southwark with their families. I saw Stanley half a block away,
walking with his mother, and wanted to run to him to explain why I
had cried. I needed for him to know that I wasn't a bitch, that my
mom's drunkenness had upset me, that I was moved by the award,
that I'd never cry like that again.

"Come on, Michael, let's stop at Aunt Minnie's for a while."

"Nah, Mommy, I want to go . . ."

"Come on, boy. Just for a little while. Then I'll make you a
special meal."

"But Mommy, I want to go play."

"All right, then. I'll see you later. Come on, Minnie."

I put the medal and envelope into my jacket pocket and watched
my mother and her friend stagger toward Lombard Street. A few
feet away from the steps of the church, Aunt Minnie looked into her

pocketbook and shook her head. My mother searched her pockets and pulled out a small handful of balled-up dollars. Instead of turning west on Lombard in the direction of Aunt Minnie's—and my family's former—apartment building, they stayed on Sixth Street, walking in the direction of South Street, where a state liquor store was conveniently located.

I ran to them before they crossed the street. "All right," I yelled. "Let's go. Where y'all going, anyway? You forgot where Aunt Minnie lives?"

I grabbed their elbows and steered them toward Ninth Street, chattering about anything that came to mind. When we reached the steps of Aunt Minnie's building, it was clear that the hot sun and the time that had elapsed since their last drink had sobered them up quite a bit. "Come on, Mommy, we walked Aunt Minnie home. Now I want my special meal."

"But I wanted to stop in for a second or two."

"Come on, Mommy. What you going to make? See you, Aunt Minnie."

"But Anne, I thought you was going to come in for a second and get a taste."

"See you, Aunt Minnie," I repeated, still holding my mother's elbow and directing her down Ninth Street toward Southwark. "Mommy, you want to see my medal?"

"Sure, Michael. But let's walk down South Street, okay? I need to make a quick stop."

When we arrived home, my mother clutching the thin neck of a bottle of whiskey, I put my medal on the kitchen table and hid the check and the graduation photo of me in my winter coat pocket in which I kept my Hal Greer basketball cards. I hung up my suit, put on my Wrangler shorts, a short-sleeved shirt, sweat socks, and sneakers, and walked back into the kitchen. "Mommy," I yelled, "I'm going out."

"What you want me to make for you?" She'd already opened the bottle and downed most of the contents of a tall glass she had filled with whiskey, so I knew that she wouldn't be cooking anything that was edible.

"I don't know. Surprise me, okay?"

"Okay."

"Mommy, where can I cash my check? I want to buy some more cards. Or play some pinball."

"I'll walk you to the bank tomorrow."

"Okay. See you later."

"Be home by 5:30, hear?"

As I walked into the playground, hypnotically drawn to the variegated thumps and clangs of hard plastic balls striking cement, wood, and steel, I saw Denise, who was wearing cutoff jeans and a peach-colored short-sleeved shirt, sitting on the swings talking to some other girls. I slowed down as I reached the swings, hoping she'd look up, and terrified that she would. When she saw me, she smiled and waved at me. My heart pounded as I waved back, grinned broadly, and walked toward the basketball court. I was sure she might like me. I wished I knew what to say to her, how to approach her, what boys and girls who liked each other talked about.

After I walked past her, I saw that a couple of my male classmates, including Stanley, were already playing with a group of older boys. "Heard you started crying today, Bernie," one of the oldheads said, shaking his head. "Guess you better go swing with them girls, you little faggot."

"Fuck you!" I replied, genuinely angry for a second, though not merely or even primarily at him. I knew he was just playing with me, sounding on me. Eventually I smiled and joined in. "Wait till I get on the court. I'ma bust your ass."

"Bring it on, Bernie Dolan. Bring it on."

I played, talked about, and watched basketball, watched Denise swing, joke with her friends, then leave the playground, watched some of the oldheads pass around and swig from bottles of Colt 45, and stared through the fence at the hole that construction workers were supposed to have transformed into an Olympic-sized pool two months earlier. When I got back to my apartment, it was six o'clock, and my older sister, Carol, told me Mommy had been asleep since she got home at four. Carol pointed toward the empty bottle on the table. "When'd she get this?"

"After my graduation. We got home at about two o'clock."

"Wow! She killed that, didn't she? What's this medal?"

"I won it."

"Yeah? For what?"

"I dunno. For the CATs."

"Huh?"

"I had the best score. You know, she came to my graduation with Aunt Minnie. They were both high as a kite."

"Really? Man."

"Yeah. What's for dinner?"

"There's some lunch meat in the refrigerator. Mommy took out some chicken I guess she was going to fry before she fell out. When I came in, roaches were crawling all over it, and it was starting to smell funny, so I threw it in the incinerator."

"Oh. She was supposed to be making me a special graduation dinner."

I awoke the next morning to the sound of my mother rifling through and slamming her bureau drawers. "Where is it," she kept repeating. "Where is it?"

I stuck my head into her room and asked, "What you looking for?"

"Oh. Good morning, Michael Cycle. I'm looking for my money. You seen it?"

"I ain't seen it. Maybe you left it at Aunt Minnie's?"

"I called her already. She says it's not there."

"Oh."

"Michael, when you want to go cash that check? This morning?"

"Yes."

"Okay. Why don't you let me borrow the money until my check comes? It'll come in a couple days. Okay?"

"What? No!"

"I need the money now to buy some food with."

"No. No. That's mine."

"Come on, boy. Now go wash up."

"So, Michael, you won the big prize, huh," Ricky said after I emerged from the bathroom and joined my siblings at the table. He'd graduated from George Washington the year earlier, and he knew the significance of the medal next to his cereal bowl.

"Yeah. But what do I do with it?"

"Just look at it, I guess. And carry it around to impress the ladies."

Ricky, Debby, and Carol had already eaten bowls of cornflakes. I sat down and poured myself one.

"Y'all, Mommy wants the money I won along with the prize. Five dollars! Says we need food."

"Really!" Debby exclaimed. "Five dollars. What you gonna buy me?"

I smiled and rolled my eyes at her.

"Seriously," Carol said. "You think she's finished drinking yet? 'Cause if not, you can't give her the money; she'll just drink it up."

"Ask her what she wants from the store, and offer to go buy it," Ricky suggested.

"Yeah."

Just then, Mommy appeared, her small purse in her hand. "Come on, Michael Cycle. Let's go."

"Let me finish my cereal first, Mommy."

"Come on, hurry up then."

I wasn't hungry and tried to prolong the meal as much as possible. The cornflakes seemed to have no taste, even when I scooped the bottom of the bowl for the treasure of sugar collected there. After five minutes, I stood up, took my bowl to the sink, and walked toward the door. "I'm ready, Mommy." Carol came over to me and whispered, "You gonna give it to her?"

"Nah."

"Good."

As we made our way to the bank, my mother and I barely talked. I went over again and again what I'd say if she asked for my money. "It's mine, Mommy, and you ain't gonna go buy nothing with it but some pluck anyway. You can't take my money. No way." When we reached the virtually empty bank, my mother asked me for the check.

"No," I shouted.

"But Michael, you have to have ID to cash a check. You got anything?"

"No, but . . ."

"Then give me the check."

Reluctantly, I handed her the check, still in the envelope with the school's name and address embossed on it. My mother found an unoccupied teller and handed her the envelope and the card she used for identification to cash her welfare checks.

The cashier smiled down at me. "So you're Michael, huh?"

"Yes," I said sullenly, realizing that the likelihood of the cashier giving the money to me was slim. Adults rarely even talked to kids when their parents were around, let alone gave them money. "I won the money at my graduation. I'd like two dollars in quarters, one dollar in nickels, and the rest in dimes, please."

The cashier smiled and looked at my mother for confirmation.

"Miss, please give me a five dollar bill, okay? I don't know what's wrong with this boy today."

"Yes, ma'am," the cashier replied, handing the crisp, new bill to my mother.

I stuck out my hand, which my mother ignored as she opened her purse and deposited my money inside it.

After we'd left the bank, I held out my hand again. "Mommy, give me my money."

"I told you I need it. I'll give it back to you when my check comes."

"Mommy," I pleaded, tears streaming down my face. "It's mine."

Her face hardened. "I'll give it back to you, now hear? Let's go, Michael."

"No."

"Come on."

"No."

"Well, I'm going. You stand there like a statue if you want to. I'm going to make a quick stop at the store, then I'm going to your Aunt Minnie's for a little while. See you later."

As my mother turned away and toward South Street, I saw the scars of surgical stitches on her right upper arm just below the white cuff of her blue short-sleeved shirt. Whenever I saw them, I felt that I was violating my mother's privacy or in danger of being pulled backward into the past to witness scenes of her own painful personal history. Cut deeply into her flesh, this symmetrical, Frankensteinian mark evinced that, like Humpty Dumpty, she'd literally had to be put back together again after my father had shattered her thin arm. (On another occasion, he broke her left wrist, but repairing it required less visible medical intervention.) For someone who knew its origins, that mark gave unobstructed access to part of my mother's soul, spoke unambiguously about painful experiences, the effects of which she attempted to dull with alcohol.

No matter how many times I saw it, the mark unsettled me, softened my anger toward my mother, and compelled me to try to understand her, particularly when her behavior affected me negatively. Standing outside the bank, I recalled strings of words she used to describe her ordeal—phrases, half sentences, and simple sentences whose full meanings were clarified by her gestures: "Your father stomped on my arm. . . . Broke it in two places. . . . The pain. . . . The doctors had to operate. . . . Took a bone from my leg—right here—put it in my arm. . . . I was in traction for months. . . . Couldn't move it. . . . Carol took care of me. . . . Wasn't more than six at the time. . . . Don't be like your father. . . ."

Unlike me, she could fairly easily have hidden her mark, but she seemed to feel no compulsion to do so. Although she worried about other aspects of her appearance—her strabismic eye, her graying hair, her huge nose, her thin legs—her mark never seemed to make her feel self-conscious. In fact, in warm weather, she wore short-sleeved and sleeveless shirts that revealed it to everyone who came in contact with her.

Standing outside the bank, I knew that my mother's appropriation of my money was grossly unfair, like taking candy from a baby or stealing coins from the cup of one of those blind men we'd see stationed with their old, fat, slobbering, snoozing guide dogs when we went shopping in Center City. But her mark made me want to believe that what had transpired between us was a loan or a gift rather than theft. I watched her walk away, with no idea how I'd pass the rest of the day, or the long, hot summer before me.

That evening, as I left the basketball court and headed for home, I saw Denise sitting alone on one of the swings. She was looking down at either her sandaled feet or the ground. As I approached her, my pulse quickened, and my thoughts became jumbled. Fortunately, I was no longer sweating—I'd been watching others play for at least half an hour—but I worried that I stunk and that white streaks of dried sweat had formed on my forehead. Wiping my face quickly with my tee shirt, I walked over to her. She didn't look up. Her lack of attention to me was emboldening, and I sat down on a swing next to her.

"Hi," I said softly.

Denise looked up at me. "Oh, hi, Michael." She looked back at her feet.

It was both thrilling and frightening to be near her, the thrill heightened, perhaps, by the fear. But because of my nightly dreams of meetings like this, at sunset with soft breezes tinged with sadness that cooled the air, and marked by a calming quiet, this moment felt strangely familiar. In my dreams, when we talked, Denise and I conversed as smoothly as actors who'd memorized a script, so I had faith that the right words would come to me. Enthralled by her short, straightened hair, the tips of her nose and lips, her bare, glistening, honey-brown shoulders, arms, and legs, I stopped feeling mind-numbingly nervous and pursued a line of conversation for which my life had well prepared me: one devoted to displaying deep, unself-conscious sympathy.

"You okay? You seem sad."

"Yeah. I guess so." She looked at me and tried unsuccessfully to change her expression. I smiled, the big, bright smile I used to charm my mother's female friends, the one I practiced in front of mirrors in anticipation of a moment like this, when Denise needed it and would discover or allow herself to acknowledge her overwhelming affection for me. She looked down again.

"You sure you're okay?"

"Michael, did you hear what happened last night?"

"No. What?"

"To Katey." Katey was one of our classmates, a girl with a sly wit and a small, reserved smile. Throughout my childhood, I developed a number of brief attachments that I could hardly understand, let alone explain to someone else. But I knew that I liked Katey because she seemed serious, mature, and thoughtful. When, for example, one of our classmates was exposed as a bra stuffer—evidence of which squeezed between the buttons of her white blouse one afternoon—Katey said, to no one in particular, and with apparently no thought to her own lack of development, "Why would she do that?" If it had been possible for me to have had female friends at that point in my life, Katey would have been at the top of my list.

"No. What happened?"

"A bunch of boys—Benny, Tyrone, and some others, I think—grabbed her in the field over there. They was drinking on the bleachers graduation night and she walked by, and they got her. Right over there." Denise pointed straight ahead, toward left field in the chronically unlit baseball field. The basketball courts and the baseball field were both equipped with lights, but to reduce electrical costs, the playground managers turned on the baseball lights only during night games in July and August.

"What they beat her up for?" I asked, knowing their typical modus operandi.

"Nah. They raped her. Ripped her clothes off her and raped her. Five or six of them. Right over there."

I didn't know what to say. The questions that came to mind—"Why?" "How?"—weren't worth articulating. I sat on the swing next to Denise and started pushing the balls of my feet against the mulch and concrete under them. But because I was hungry, the motion made me feel light-headed and a bit nauseous. I stopped, got off the swing, and walked over to Denise, who looked up at me.

"Is she okay?" I asked.

"I guess so. I wanted to go visit her since I heard, but I don't know what to say. I hope somebody gets those bastards."

The boys Denise named were twelve and thirteen years old. One—Benny—had been a classmate of ours. He was the younger brother of B. J., a plump, dark-skinned boy who was one of the most treacherous gangsters in 5th Street. Recognizing the pressures of his violent legacy, Benny worked diligently to replicate his brother's tough persona and exploits. He strutted like an oldhead, grabbed his dick at every opportunity, represented about 70 percent of Miss Davis's disciplinary problems, and fought—or, as we used to put it, "rumbled"—frighteningly well at the drop of a hat.

As I stood before Denise, trying to think of what to say, I recalled an afternoon I'd spent with Benny in his family's apartment of the thirteenth floor of my building. He and I didn't hang out together regularly, but for some reason he'd knocked on my door an hour or so after his mother had been rushed to the hospital with some unremembered ailment. As we watched cartoons on his family's color television, he talked about all sorts of things: about his fears that his mother—who'd been hospitalized frequently—was going to die this time; about the trouble his tomboyish sister, one of Debby's classmates, was getting into in school; about how much he'd miss Bobby, whose family was moving to North Philadelphia the following month. And Benny told me that he was worried about going to Bartlett in September, where, as the younger brother of a notorious gangster, he would surely be a marked young man.

"13th Street caught one of B. J.'s homeys on Twelfth and South, and shanked his ass to death. You hear me, Mike? Killed that motherfucker. Last week. Then them bastards carved a '13' on his chest. You listening to me, Mike? Carved '13' on his fucking chest, like he was a tree or a desk or something. Fuck that shit, man. I know they gonna try and get me, but I got something for them. You watch."

Standing in front of Denise, I wondered what, if anything, self-protective machismo or the image of a "13" carved into a gangster's dead chest had to do with what he'd done to his classmate.

I thought of Katey and imagined her eyes blackened, her lip busted, her nose broken like a rape victim I'd seen Linc comfort on *Mod Squad*. I looked up at the porch of our apartment, half expecting to see my mother watching me. I thought of my father, whom I knew only as a brutal force.

I didn't know what to say. I felt overwhelmed with sadness for Katey, for Denise, for myself, for Benny, for my mother, for my father. How did they persevere, knowing how much damage they'd inflicted on others or had inflicted on them? My mother's much-stated caution—"Don't be like your father"—rang in my ears, then seemed to fill the space in my imagination typically occupied by my dreams of running away with Denise. These dreams, which caressed me in my sleeping and waking hours, were marked by a subtext of fear and a hint of desperation.

Some older boys walked past us. One of them patted me on the shoulder and said, "Way to go, Bernie!" Suddenly, I was overcome by an urge to protect Denise. "Let me walk you home, Niecy," I insisted, assuming a familiarity I certainly hadn't earned. Further, I'd assumed, without confirmation from any act or fact either she or I could possibly have been aware of, that a skinny punk like me could protect her from the dangers that lurked throughout our neighborhood. And that she wouldn't see me, too, as potentially a threat, a potential violator, a possible participant in the type of violence Katey suffered in left field.

If cool, smart Katey wasn't safe, even with a pack of boys that included someone she'd been in class with for nine months, how could Denise feel safe—be safe—with me? Could I ever think of her as I had again, plot ways of gaining her trust again, dream again of exploring new horizons with her, of kissing her lips and making her smile, or think of her at all without connecting my desires to Katey and Benny, to my mother and father? Sex and violence had inserted themselves between me and this beautiful, living-and-breathing girl before me whom I adored because she was cute and because I loved her voice, her bright-toothed smile, her meaty brown body.

She smiled at me. "I'll be all right, Michael. These niggers know better than to mess with me, or my big brother will fuck them up big time." Her brother's name was Sammy. He was a few years younger than B. J. and hadn't yet achieved Benny's legendary status, but by all indications, he was well on his way.

"Oh. Okay. I hope Katey's okay."

"Me, too. I'm gonna stop by tomorrow, I think."

"Tell her I asked for her." I suspected that boys wouldn't be welcome. "Good night."

" 'night."

"I can walk you home, you know? You really shouldn't sit here in the dark."

"It ain't dark yet. Go on home, okay? See you."

"See you, Denise."

A few weeks later, I was in the playground watching some kids from the summer day camp play checkers, pocket pool, and dominoes. It was over ninety degrees, too hot and humid to move at more than a snail's pace, let alone play basketball. I had no job—I wouldn't be old enough for CETA government work until the following summer—and no better way to occupy my time that steamy early afternoon. I noticed that the pool builders, who were on their lunch break, had neglected to lock the twenty-foot gate through which they drove their cranes, bulldozers, and various other equipment.

To amuse themselves, a few older boys who'd been sitting under the shade of the extended roof of the playground office building began a dangerous game: they grabbed unsuspecting boys two or three years younger than me, put them in the trash cans equipped with wheels that the construction workers used to haul away small chunks of cement, and rolled them toward the cavernous pool hole.

The supply of eight-, nine-, and ten-year-old boys ran out in about ten minutes. Assuming that the brutal game had ended, I watched a couple of girls who were playing checkers and wondered if Denise, whom I hadn't seen since our encounter on the swings, would come to the playground that day. Suddenly I heard a squeak of sneakers behind me, and I was lifted into the air by two boys, one of whom pinned my arms against my body as the other encircled my knees with his arms. They dropped me into a gray trash can whose bottom was covered with newspapers, cigarette butts, and fine crumbs of cement.

"Get the fuck offa me! Get offa me! You motherfuckers. Get off me!"

Running together as quickly as they could to build up momentum, they propelled the can toward the hole. I didn't know how to react. The younger boys had exhibited a variety of responses: a couple successfully tipped the can over before it reached the hole; three or four screamed with fearful glee, like they were diving into a cool, clear pond or going downhill on a roller coaster; all of them eventually disappeared inside the can to protect themselves from the fall.

After I'd stopped yelling at the boys who'd captured me, I stood still and erect, watching the onlookers, the basketball court, the trees surrounding the playground, and the billboard for Afro Sheen on the corner of Fourth and Federal as they whizzed by me. I hoped the trash can would hit a rock, a crack, or a brick that would stop it before it went over the cliff, or that the boys would recognize the error of their ways and put an end to my adventure. When the quickly decelerating trash can reached the edge, the front wheels hung over it for a few seconds, spinning and rattling noisily. Then the can tipped over, and my left shoulder hit the bottom of the rough, rocky hole before anything else did.

The pain was excruciating. It felt as though someone had kicked me with a steel-toed work boot. I screamed unselfconsciously and tried, as I had on numerous occasions when I'd jammed my shoulders playing basketball, to relieve myself of the pain by stretching my arm above my head, which caused me to yell even louder. Carefully pressing my left arm against my body, I crawled out of the trash can. When I stood up and reached the side of the hole, Greg, who had grabbed my legs and helped to place me into the can, appeared and held out his hand to assist me.

"Get the fuck away from me," I hissed at him. But because I couldn't navigate my own way out of the hole, I reluctantly accepted his help. Once I reached solid ground, Greg placed his arm affectionately around my neck and asked, "How come you didn't get down? Didn't you watch the other boys go in? You could have really hurt yourself, Mike."

"Why'd y'all do this to me?"

"We was just playing, boy. You all right?"

The pain jabbed at me each time I took a step. "No. I think my shoulder must be broke." The faces of the spectators reflected various states of amusement and concern. One of the counselors took a look at my pained expression and went into the office to call 911, then asked for my telephone number. After speaking briefly with my mother, the counselor took me across the street to the Community Center to wait for my mother and an ambulance.

She arrived before the ambulance, walking toward me as quickly as I'd ever seen her walk.

"What happened?"

"They pushed me into that hole, Mommy! Those stupid workmen didn't lock the gate, and them South Side boys pushed me in." My mother's presence liberated the moans and tears I had suppressed in front of the counselor and Greg.

"What hurts?"

"My shoulder, Mommy. My left shoulder. I can't move my arm. It feels like it's gonna fall off."

"You'll be all right. They told me a cop car is going to take us to the hospital."

"A cop car? I don't wanna ride in no cop car! I wasn't doing nothing but watching some girls play checkers."

"Michael, the car's right outside. They just want to get you to the emergency room as quickly as possible. They're going to take you to Einstein right up the street. And I'll ride with you, okay?"

A black mustached, large-nosed white policeman approached us. His black nightstick swung against his left hip, and his holstered gun bobbed up and down menacingly against his right hip. Immediately, I directed my attention away from my mother and my pain and toward him. I'd never had any contact with a policeman before, but I'd heard enough stories from older boys in the neighborhood to feel as though I'd suddenly gotten the chills. During the reign of Police Commissioner Frank Rizzo, police brutality against black boys and men was rampant, and I'd had my fill of being victimized for one day.

"Just take me home, Mommy."

"We got to get your arm checked out, hear? It might be broken."

The policeman reached us, removed a notepad from his shirt pocket, and asked me with a mixture of practiced concern and condescension, "Son, who did this to you?"

"Some boys in the playground. Pushed me into the swimming pool hole."

"Who? You want to press charges against the boys who did this? What's their names? We need to know that immediately if you do want to press charges."

"Press what? What's that mean?"

"Take them to court. Get them to pay for what they did to you."

"Huh? Pay money?"

"The boys who did this should go to jail."

"Oh. They grabbed me from behind. I didn't see who it was."

"You sure, boy?"

"Yeah."

He started walking away, stopped, and said, without turning around, "No ambulances are available, so I'm going to ride you to Einstein Hospital. Let's go."

My mother helped me up. "It'll be all right, Michael. Might just be a sprain. But if it's broken, I'm sure it'll heal. My arm was broken in two places and look how strong I am now." She smiled at me, pointing to the thin, flat, flexed bicep of her right arm. "Wanna feel my muscle?"

"No, Mommy." I smiled back at her. "I don't want to hurt myself any more today."

My left shoulder had sustained a bad fracture that took more than eight weeks to heal. With my arm in a cast and a sling, I stayed at home almost all the time, watching the activities in the playground unfold from my scenic nineteenth-floor perch: basketball and baseball games, football practices, double Dutch, hopscotch, and kids, teenagers, and adults trying to stay cool in Philly's heat and humidity. The construction workers finished their task in early August, but as my brother reported, because the lifeguards whom the city had hired to begin in June had received other assignments, the pool would not in fact open until the following year.

I watched the world go by from a safe distance. I didn't see Denise face-to-face again that summer—I did see her once from my porch lookout, walking south on Fifth Street with some boy I didn't recognize—and gave up hope of reaching the horizon with her. I didn't see Katey or any of her attackers. On occasion, I saw the boys who'd rolled me into the hole playing basketball. And each day at noon, I watched the construction workers lock the protective gate around the hole as they headed off for their long lunch breaks.

When I felt absolutely stir-crazy or starved for some sort of physical activity, I threw an assortment of rubber and tennis balls against the gray cement wall that maintenance workers had installed to increase the privacy of neighbors lucky enough to have porches. When the resultant noise sufficiently annoyed my mother, she reminded me of the doctor's warning that, unless I kept my shoulder absolutely still, it would not heal properly. She told me,

With brother Ricky, older sister Carol, and their grandmother, the
author kneels—and smiles—to hide cast on broken left arm.

over and over, about the long months of immobility she'd endured
after my father broke her arm. "Be patient," she said repeatedly.

I never asked my mother for my five dollars. My George Washington medal lost its golden glow before the summer ended. My left
shoulder is one-twelfth of an inch higher than my right, pops when I
do military presses, and aches sometimes when it rains. And my
dreams turned from running away with Denise to running away
from huge 13th Street thugs brandishing nightsticks and sharp, shiny
knives, and falling down deep, dark, musty holes lined with skeletons wearing clothes from a bygone era, skeletons whose fleshless
hands reached for me as I plummeted past them.

In their efforts to invest their lives with an air of inevitability and a sense of
mission, people often construct conversion narratives of professional sum-
moning out of the recollected fragments of personal history. Whatever these
narratives reveal about their subjects, inevitably, they are also intended to
disguise, wish away, or render absolutely irrelevant events and accidents of

fate that people cannot make conform to their governing statements of self-realization. However, these governing statements may no better account for people's choices than those experiences that they are unable to bring under narrative control.

Certainly, we all possess—and are possessed by—instructive scenes from our personal and professional journeys that we revisit on occasion. In the age of intimate critique, humanists in particular are compelled to consider carefully our audiences and the contexts in which we offer our stories of triumph and failure.

While I believe that there are generalizable postulates and meanings that others can glean from my imposition of narrative structure onto strategically chosen scenes from my preadolescent life, I share my stories because I want to encourage readers to compare some of the points I am making about my own complicated becoming to extant theoretical, commonsensical, and nonsensical formulations of the meanings of race, gender, class, sexuality, and desire for black American males and other subjects. Like Zora Neale Hurston's Janie, I hope I've found an audience on whom I can depend for a good thought. Still, I recognize that the receptivity of readers depends on the skill with which I talk about moments in my life, certainly, but also on how my narrative jibes with the suppositions they bring to their roles as active listeners.

An example might be useful here. In December 1989, just a month after learning that I'd been granted early tenure by the University of Michigan, I gave my first paper at the Modern Language Association Convention. Having published a book on black women novelists less than a year earlier, and having spent three years researching and writing about the connections between racial and gendered identity and the interpretation of Afro-American expressive culture, I felt particularly qualified to speak on the topic of black men and feminist theory. Up to that point, I'd strategically avoided publicly addressing the question of the impact of my black maleness on my work, but on this occasion it seemed appropriate for me to come clean about what I understood to be the motivation for my participation in black feminism.

Playing with what many considered the scandalous title of the 1986 collection, Men in Feminism, *I called the paper "A Black Man's Place(s) in Black Feminist Criticism." While I hoped to shed some light on the issue of the interpretive and institutional consequences of male appropriations of feminist methodologies and insights, I was largely concerned not so much with legitimizing male feminism as with explaining myself. So in addition to discussing the constructedness of gender, the complications that self-conscious attention to blackness add to such considerations, and the spaces left in womanist discourses by Alice Walker and Hortense Spillers for conscientious male interventions, I set out to answer questions I'd encountered and often feigned being stumped by: Why do I identify myself as a male feminist? Why do I do the work I do? How does it feel, being an intruder in a discourse made neither for nor by black males, one whose purpose is, in large part, to critique me and my kind strenuously?*

I suggested that my interest in the issues that compel black feminism began when I considered the implications of the fact that my father kicked my mother in her stomach when the fetus that became me was lodged deeply within her womb. According to my mother, that brutal act was motivated by my father's unfounded suspicions that some other man's seed had fertilized my mother's—and, eventually, my—egg.

For the sake of brevity, I left out a number of other compelling features of that story, including my older sister Carol's insistence that it was Debby's paternity that concerned our father, and the fact that I remained in a hospital incubator for weeks after my mother delivered me because of my severe nervous twitches. (As a child, I assumed that they were the result of the shocks to my mother's and my own systems caused by my father's kicks.) Also, I neglected to discuss the eeriness of speaking of this act of paternal abuse while my wife was, at that very moment, waddling around, sitting, or lying uncomfortably in her parents' house, swelled nearly beyond recognition by the fetal presence of our first child, and weakened, as I'd also been for two days, by a stomach virus that we assumed was a mild form of salmonella poisoning we'd gotten from eating eggs on the morning after Christmas. Still, it seemed that I'd shared enough of my story to support the point the paper sought to make: that black males suffer under patriarchy, too, and that the quality of our lives could be improved significantly if we seriously engaged the liberating possibilities of black womanist/feminist perspectives.

A rush of adrenaline helped me to ignore the queasiness of my stomach and the anxiety I felt about speaking of such matters before a large audience that included most of the major figures in Afro-American literary criticism and theory. After my presentation, however, I was only able to half listen to the other speaker, who, along with the panel organizer, coedited the collection in which an expanded version of my paper subsequently appeared. Feigning attentiveness, I looked from my fingernails and unpolished shoes to members of the audience, feeling too ill to be overly concerned about what I assumed would be a fair but strenuous response to a work-in-progress.

In her reply, the respondent asserted that she remained distrustful of black male incursions into black feminism, then equated my autobiographical moves with the efforts of the protagonist of Toni Morrison's Song of Solomon *to protect his abused mother. In the scene she referenced, Milkman strikes his father as a sign of his victorious participation in an Oedipal drama whose object is his own self-aggrandizement. As the respondent offered this purposefully insulting analogy, I thought of many intriguing questions I might raise in subsequent revisions of the paper, including what precisely to make of this discourse of distrust when, by and large— except for friends from graduate school and acquaintances formed at conventions and other professional meetings, where our primary goal is to showcase ourselves—we are all virtual strangers to one another.*

When the respondent completed her remarks, the moderator asked for questions from the audience. The only question I remember being directed at me came from someone who acknowledged that the respondent had shared my paper with her before they'd traveled to Washington, D.C., for the convention. She asked me what I thought about the respondent's comments and, perhaps frustrated by my noncommittal reply, informed me that the best thing I could do for black women was to stop writing about their literature.

Instead of experiencing the sort of productive engagement I had hoped for, I was caught in a classic no-win situation from which neither bristling self-defense nor insincere appreciation of my attackers' perspectives would have extricated me. Even as I chided myself for not accurately assessing the potential antipathy that my use of my mother's narrative could unleash, I knew that I had no other choice but to tell my mother's story were I ever to speak openly about my ideological investments. It was—and is—virtually impossible for a man to justify his interest in feminism except through the body of a woman.

In the scene with which I'd chosen to legitimize myself, I described violence done to a female body that sheltered and nurtured me, done because it sheltered and nurtured what my father and (because my father was married to another woman at the time he and my mother were involved) the law considered my illegitimate presence. This story's symbolic connections to other black male acts of physical, psychic, and spiritual violence may well have made other black females feel equally wary of, and even hostile toward, me.

To the extent that we are able, what scholars and most human beings do who are not hermetically sealed off from others is attempt to exert significant control over our public performances and, hence, others' perceptions of our selves. Being a social animal entails formulating and applying theories that we use to determine whether to accept or reject parts or the entirety of the stories others bombard us with continuously. Because of the theories they'd developed concerning the distrustfulness of black men who come bearing gifts of purported empathetic insight, the respondent and her colleague in the audience assumed that I was unsuited to the role of black feminist ally.

Stunned, nauseous, and incapable of making my way quickly out of the room, I stood patiently as people milled about, murmuring about the session or the intellectual, social, and nocturnal pleasures that awaited them. A minute or two after the applause signaling the conclusion of the session ended and after I'd exchanged pleasantries with two black female acquaintances, a white woman came up to me to inform me that she was a beginning assistant professor of Afro-American literature and that she'd enjoyed my paper. Suddenly she started crying uncontrollably, having found something cathartic in my comments that, combined perhaps with holiday season angst and memories of her own painful familial dramas, moved her to display unaccustomed vulnerability. As I watched her heart-wrenching display, I wondered both if I should put my hand on her shoulder to comfort her and if our similar positions as outsiders in the discourses in which we'd chosen to participate made her feel enough of a sense of kinship with me to display the typically well-camouflaged emotional stakes we have in our professional work and lives.

Soon after receiving encouragement from two distinguished male scholars in my field—one in a letter I received two weeks after the convention, the other during a conversation some months later in which the scholar noted that he'd been ashamed of the respondent's obnoxious, irresponsible potshots—I completed the final version of the essay. The revised version speaks self-consciously about the politics of autobiographical recall in ways that are also an implicit comment on the reception of the MLA paper itself:

> I have decided that it is ultimately irrelevant whether these autobiographical facts, which, of course, are not, and can never be, the whole story, are deemed by others sufficient to permit me to call myself "feminist." . . . What is most important to me is that my work contribute, in however small a way, to the project whose goal is the dismantling of the phallocentric rule by which black females and, I am sure, countless other Afro-American sons have been injuriously "touched." (54)

However well such assertions reflected my dedication to the ideals of feminism, of course I cared deeply—and continue to care—about the ways in which my contributions are received by people committed to that discourse's production and dissemination. But I recognized, even as I wrote these words, that despite disagreements among its practitioners about such issues as pornography and men's participation in the discourse, I'd remain at best a marginal figure within black feminism and, at worst, a male parasite who would inevitably weaken my host.

But if my narrative isn't compelling, are its limitations the result of what some might purport to be my biologically determined resistance to black feminist suppositions? What story might a black male tell of the origins of his feminist interests that would be better received, or whose transparently emotional reception other feminists would feel compelled to critique publicly? Aren't assumptions of unproblematic continuities and discontinuities manifestations of lingering, retrograde forms of the academic crime of essentialism? And haven't scholars on the cutting edge of literary and cultural studies actually claimed victory in the battle to disentangle biology and being?

SECTION II ✳ "Are You Man Enough?"

In late October 1995, I participated in Chicago State University's Fifth Annual Black Writers Conference, " 'Living by the Word': A Dedication to Alice Walker." This conference occurred at the end of a strange week for me, which began with the Million Man March and concluded with a celebration of the career of the black writer most closely allied with the modern feminist movement.

The Farrakhan march represented another in a series of social dramas of black self-definition and inquisition that help to determine, confirm, and consolidate governing notions of racial authenticity. As black televisibility reaches unprecedented heights, black ontology—being down and black enough or, in hip-hop parlance, keeping it sufficiently real—is measured in part by how one positions oneself vis-à-vis persistently simplistic oppositions between, for example, Clarence Thomas and Anita Hill, Rodney King and the L.A. cops, readings of the mass destruction that followed the Simi Valley verdict as riot or rebellion, Mike Tyson and Desiree Washington, O. J. and the variety of living and deceased principals in his ongoing legal and cultural trials.

In my conference presentation, sections of which I offer hereafter along with an examination of Walker's comments about the march, I tried to confront my own dissociation of sensibility by linking the two events interpretively.

In a prefatory section of In Search of Our Mothers' Gardens, Walker defines "womanist" as "a black feminist or feminist of color," "responsible. In charge. Serious," someone "committed to survival and wholeness of entire people, male and female. Not a separatist, except periodically, for health." Like Walker's notions of black womanist commitment, Louis Farrakhan's call to arms emphasizes acts of individual, gendered, and racial responsibility. For Farrakhan, the Million Man March served to counteract negative behaviors by, popular cultural misrepresentations of, and legislative assaults on, black men.

Still, these discourses seem hopelessly at odds. A masculinist marcher and a womanist walker? Part of what is especially chilling in Farrakhan's mission statement is its assertion of black men's divine familial and community leadership rights. That assertion is offered by Farrakhan in the *same breath that he justifies the gendered exclusivity of the march by insisting on turning the historic capital environs into a safe space for both warrior training and repentance. Farrakhan writes:*

> *I'm calling on Black men in particular to stand in unity to declare to the world that we are ready to shoulder our responsibility as the heads of our families and leaders in our community. . . .*
>
> *We feel that we need to atone, to repent, as men, for what we've done to our women. For the way we positioned our women. For the burden that we have put on our women to carry us, as well as themselves. We do not feel that we should any longer burden our women with ourselves, but we should accept the responsibility that God himself has imposed on us as heads of families and heads of communities. (65–66)*

Farrakhan employs a discourse of warfare that plays directly on the perceived threat and potency of transgressive black male energy as it marginalizes black females and feminizes domestic space in perpetuity. Farrakhan goes on to say, "No nation gets any respect if you go out to war and you put your women in the trenches and the men stay at home cooking. Every nation that goes to war tests the fiber of the manhood of that nation. And literally, going to Washington to seek justice for our people is like going to war" (66). Imploring sisters—masculinized by the perversities of American racism that emasculates their brothers—not to compromise this anticipated show of hard black male force, Farrakhan seeks to replace images of the gangsta thug and the irresponsible parent with the symbol of the male warrior organized to perform the time-honored duties of armed national forces: protection and invasion.

Farrakhan's strategies rely on the successful assignment of marginal roles to women both during the march and afterward, when the inspired male warriors arrive home to assume their God-given roles as the heads of black families. Certainly, mass political action such as the Million Man March is potentially more beneficial than melodious intellectual hollers that conclude with our throwing up our collective hands. But Farrakhan's black masculinist solution—offered, in Walker's womanist words, to promote the "survival and wholeness of [an] entire people"—affirms a traditional gender hierarchy that places black men on top economically and politically and assigns to black women inevitably domestic (home, if not necessarily "prone") positions. Farrakhan's rhetoric is a dressed-up, slicked-back version of the Moynihan Report's solutions to the problems of black matriarchs whose power threatens the stability of the black family and, hence, black men and the black nation more generally.

No one asked Walker about her views of the march during the lengthy, occasionally contentious question-and-answer session that began just after I read my remarks. Some months later, long after the thrill of being in her presence, of speaking about a range of topics with creative writers and other critics who also attended the conference, and of witnessing a Chicago neighborhood rally against drug dealers that seemed directly to result from the march, a man affiliated with the University of Michigan's Center for Afroamerican and African Studies gave me a copy of Walker's published remarks on the March. (These remarks were dedicated to her "new brother," Haki Madhubuti, who'd been a force behind both the march and the Walker conference at the school at which he teaches, Chicago State.)

Instead of emphasizing the dangers of phallocentric exclusion, as I did, Walker focuses on the opportunities provided by the march for black men to "regroup as black men; until they can talk to each other, cry with each other, hug and kiss each other, they will never know how to do those things with me" (43). Rather than condemn Farrakhan's gendered gestures, she emphasizes what she considers to be his admirable personal attributes—his capacity for leadership, his willingness to honor his West Indian mother's patois and "wry humor," his pedagogical skills, and his "apparent humility" (43).

The seeming disingenuousness of some of these comments—to call Farrakhan humble is, truly, to stretch credulity—suggests that Walker was aiming primarily to repair gendered rifts manifested in the facile readings and misreadings of her hugely popular novel The Color Purple *and its Hollywood adaptation, about which she speaks in great detail in* The Same River Twice. *Treating their flaws as gingerly as possible, and ignoring altogether the baleful sexual politics evinced by march leaders Farrakhan and deposed* naacp *head Ben Chavis, this response seems at such moments a tortured effort to avoid reopening and pouring salt on old, slow-healing wounds.*

Still, Walker's conciliatory posture does not keep her from examining what is, from the perspective of black gender politics, a discernible sea change attributable, in some measure at least, to feminist and womanist discursive work: the sight of black men gathered to acknowledge and to atone for their social sins, including sins against black women.

Rejecting Farrakhan's rhetoric of male warriors, Walker, a proud follower of the nonviolent philosophy of Martin Luther King Jr., emphasizes her joy at witnessing televisual manifestations of deep homosocial black male feeling—laughter and tears, kissing and hugging—that men in real life and in her fiction often view as signs of weakness, femininity, and perversity. In fact, she reads the march as confirmation of her womanist philosophy as evinced in a transformative moment from The Color Purple *when Harpo lays loving hands on his father, Albert, arrests his certain physical demise, and inspires in his male forebear greater self-reflection and appreciation of putatively feminine aspects of himself that he had fought diligently to suppress. Like similarly salvific moments shared by women in* for colored girls, The Women of Brewster Place, *and* Praisesong for the Widow, *this scene, and the march, demonstrate for Walker the capacity of fathers, brothers, sons, friends, and lovers to transform themselves through displays of filial love, affection, and concern.*

A redeemed Albert says to his former victim, Celie, about the meaning of life:

> *I think us here to wonder, myself. To wonder. To ast. And that in wondering bout the big things and asting bout the big things, you learn about the little ones, almost by accident. But you never know nothing more about the big things than you start out with. (247)*

Walker's character learns to luxuriate in the wonder of life and is grateful for the recognition that its meanings cannot be fixed. Fixity—the inevitable by-product of categorical thinking—is as much a crime against nature for postmodernists as Albert's expression of black male vulnerability is for many traditionalists. By the time I'd graduated from junior high school, I'd had little access to social narratives that legitimized my own unmistakable vulnerability, encouraged me to confront my confusion, or sanctioned my dreamy romanticism and my resistance to notions of a naturally violent black masculinity.

After kissing my mother good-bye on the early afternoon of my junior high school graduation, I walked down the stairs between my

Barlett Junior High School

nineteenth-floor apartment and the sixteenth floor, where my friend Ernie lived. As I did each school day when I was in ninth grade, on this early afternoon in mid-June 1973, I took a path that increased my chances of making it safely inside Barlett Junior High's marble hallways. I began by walking slowly down the fire escape stairs to pick up Ernie. From there, we'd ride the elevator downstairs, then walk to another of Southwark's three high-rises to get our buddy and classmate Larry. Afterward we'd meet up between Sixth and Seventh and Christian Streets with the agitated pack of neighborhood boys, none of whom spoke above a whisper about his fear of having again to invade enemy territory.

On the way to Ernie's apartment, I noticed the faded remnants of my own scribblings of the designation that my male classmates had conferred on me and that a member of the maintenance crew had tried unsuccessfully to remove that morning: dis-zak. It was not so much a nickname—they continued to call me "Awk"—as an alias, rooted in aspects of my name and personality, that I could use to pursue my goal of becoming a graffiti artist.

According to Andre, our resident expert, "Zak" was a graffiti-friendly variation of "Awk" which would allow me to maintain my

dis-zak, the author's graffiti alias

anonymity in the event that I became so much of a public nuisance that some adult wanted to press charges against me. "Dis," on the other hand, emerged from a combination of allergy-inspired goofiness and a self-deprecating sense of humor that inspired me to demonstrate that my illegitimacy and paternal desertion were not painful subjects for me by laughing loudly when my friends serenaded me with snippets of the Temptations' "Papa Was a Rolling Stone." Also, I joked about hoping to be adopted by Hal Greer, whose magnificent career as a professional basketball player ended ignominiously during my final months in ninth grade as a benchwarming member of the team with the lowest single season winning percentage in NBA history.

I'm not sure that this name was an improvement on "Peanut Roaster" or "Burnside" (in hindsight, being dizzy and awkward simultaneously seems quite a burden to bear), but perhaps because the designation's focus was behavioral rather than physical, and its conferral an obvious sign of affection, I claimed it as a part of myself, or as a reflection of aspects of that self.

I enjoyed the danger of writing my name on metal walls before elevators' slow heavy doors opened to admit riders unable to discern the faint, magical odor of just-capped markers because of the stench of our unventilated vessels on which boys and drunk men urinated daily like dogs marking their territory. I loved the discipline, which required that I perfect my signature by picking and choosing from a variety of available styles and find the marker most complementary to that style. I liked seeing my work displayed and was amused by its observable effects on others. When they got on the elevator, adults would shake their heads, and less skilled practitioners would indecorously scrawl "fuck you" under, over, and on my designative display, reactions that I took as signs of their lack of comprehension of the form and of their jealousy.

Most of all, however, I enjoyed the opportunities graffiti provided for me to project another self than that of a shy, sad-eyed, ashy-faced, snotty-nosed, book-smart, basketball-jonesing, occasionally mischievous black boy. Through graffiti, I assumed, for the time it took to write my name at least, a bold, assertive identity unselfconsciously penning such messages as "dis-zak strikes!"

A couple of weeks before graduation, Stink, a charismatic older boy who seemed wholly unconcerned about his derogative designation and possessed sufficient degrees of dick-grabbing swagger to have emerged as a force within our community, confronted me with his suspicions about my graffiti identity. At the time, we were riding on an elevator decorated with my markings. Receiving no immediate verbal response to his question, he warned me that I'd better stop writing myself into being with my pen, or "somebody's gonna fuck you up." After this encounter, I gave up graffiti.

Graffiti was the last of a series of efforts at self-expression I'd undertaken after we moved to Southwark, replacing sketching and occupying my attention along with songwriting. I had a little talent for visual art—that is to say, I could draw a bit better than people who couldn't draw at all—but lost interest when it became apparent that whereas I could create small-headed, muscle-bound male forms patterned after Marvel Comics' superhero styles, I simply couldn't render female faces. No matter how overtly stereotypical I drew them—buxom, longhaired, long lashed, long nailed, hippy, or big behinded—invariably I gave my female creations masculine facial features.

In the last months of eighth grade, I turned to songwriting, figuring that even a romantically inexperienced thirteen year old could compose song lyrics as compelling as some of those that were played continuously on Philadelphia radio stations. Songwriting offered me a venue where I could comfortably express heart-wrenching vulnerability and aching romanticism. I was particularly drawn to black male ballads, which often rejected the masculine guise of impenetrability, bravado, and stoic self-centeredness I had witnessed in the behavior of my friends, neighbors, and, for that matter, in media representations of males. Although I monitored my manly strut in picture windows of Queen Village establishments, I knew I was utterly incapable of projecting the gruff toughness and self-absorption that members of my community associated with manhood.

However, I believed I could be a man like the ones projected in songs sung by Levi Stubbs of the Four Tops, David Ruffin of the Temptations, Bill Withers, Teddy Pendergrass of Harold Melvin and the Bluenotes, Donny Hathaway, and other popular singers of the time.

> *I kiss the ground she walks on*
> *raindrops will hide my teardrops*
> *please don't push me away*
> *I'm on my hands and knees wishing for your return*
> *if I ever hurt you, you know I hurt myself as well*

These songs—filled with adoring, deserted, and desperate lovers—offered tangible models of masculinity to which I could reasonably and comfortably aspire. They were daily musical accompaniment during the hours I spent immersed in the idea of loving some female deeply, unconditionally, and writing about that experience or, more typically, the pain of its termination.

The song that best embodied my youthful romantic perspectives was the Temptations' lovely ballad "Just My Imagination." This song, about a man's boundless capacity to love the admirable qualities he projects onto his object of desire, validated my grossly one-sided approach to emotional involvement and helped to prepare me for its attendant frustrations. A huge hit in early 1971, "Just My Imagination" is R & B melodic perfection resulting from a lovely mixture of orchestral strings and a poignant electric bass, captivating lyrical twists concerning a "lucky guy" who loves a woman he observes each day passing by his window, and Eddie Kendricks's superb falsetto reflections on a lonely, boyish soul's vulnerability, faith, and obsessive desire.

My preadolescent practice of unacknowledged infatuation continued, though because of my raging hormones, I began to feel its attendant pains more urgently. I fell for Rachelle in seventh grade, a beautiful, copper-toned, pigtailed girl from Thirteenth Street, who I was sure noticed me noticing her until—as a consequence of her involvement in activities I could barely imagine—she got pregnant and quietly left school. I pined for Denise in eighth grade, an attractive, vivacious girl who, perhaps because she was aware of my unarticulated affection, littered each conversation we had with loving references to her boyfriend. And Alannah in ninth grade, who like Denise was a North Phillyite, but who, unlike my eighth-grade love, had no romantic attachments of which I was aware and displayed some signs of being interested in me also. She was short, brown, and round faced, had a warm smile, an infectious laugh, and a high-pitched voice with a hint of the South she may have inherited from parents who'd migrated from Georgia or Alabama or some other unimaginable southern climate.

Ernie, Larry, and I walked to our graduation ceremonies with an unaccustomed leisureliness because of the pact reached earlier in the spring between rival black South Philly gangs to "call it off," to cease their bloody hostilities. In the 1960s and early 1970s, black South Philadelphia consisted of four large crews: 5th and South, 7th and Mifflin, 13th and South, and 20th and Carpenter. With our arrival at Southwark, my family and I moved from a sort of demilitarized zone, a safe space betwixt and between the turfs of the 13th and 5th Street gangs, into the very heart of 5th Street.

Having lived the first nine years of my life on neutral ground, I failed to comprehend the gangs' purpose. (Even the neighborhood gang's name perplexed me. In those days before South Street's much-ballyhooed resurgence, the corners of Fifth and South were occupied by businesses—a drugstore, a bookstore, a clothing store, and a shoe store—in which no one in the gang had more than a customer's financial interest.) While watching some boys play basketball one afternoon during the first or second summer I lived in Southwark, I asked Stink what had prompted 5th and South Street's formation. He told me that though he did not know its history, at present it served a pragmatic purpose. It existed not to protect valuable property or to distribute drugs. Rather, as he explained to me, because of choices made ages earlier by the city's and the school system's planners, 5th Street was a purely transgressive outfit, forced to send its teenage boys into others' territories to sample the fruits of knowledge.

"The junior high niggers from 5th Street gotta go to school in somebody else's turf. Furness's in the middle of 7th Street; Bartlett's in 13th Street. Both them motherfuckers wanna fuck us up, so we got to stick together, man. I know your skinny little ass best to be ready to go down with the boys from down the way, or they gonna shank you.

"Youngblood, it's like this," he continued. "It's mostly the niggers from 'cross the tracks—the South Side—who go to Furness. And the ones from the projects on over—the North Side—go to Bartlett. But it's still 5th Street, you dig? We gots to stick together. See what I'm saying?"

"I think I understand. But which tracks?" I asked, not sure if he was referring to the train tracks running down Washington Avenue or the trolley tracks on Fifth Street.

"Washington Avenue, you stupid motherfucker. Trolley tracks don't mean shit."

"Oh."

"You better wake the fuck up, boy," Stink warned, in a voice that combined bemusement and exasperation.

When Ernie, Larry, and I reached Bartlett's cavernous auditorium, I felt, along with the inevitable excitement and nervousness one experiences in anticipation of such events, a sense of sadness. I knew I'd miss the camaraderie I'd developed, through three years of playing basketball and talking shit—about sports, cars, religion, money, pain, fame, girls, and, increasingly, emerging signs of our physical maturation—with boys in my class. With Don, my best friend and chief romantic counsel, an only child who lived with his mother and a grandmother who made him hotdog-and-mayonnaise sandwiches each morning for lunch. Bird, a sweet, tall, gawky boy who loved talking about sports as much as I did. Anthony, my boy, a chubby, cherubic, streetwise North Philly gangster who I was afraid would be killed before he turned eighteen. Skinny, cocky, black cardigan–wearing Fred. Reggie, the straitlaced, devout Jehovah's Witness who took no shit from nobody. Tyrone, fourteen going on forty, who seemed to have access to knowledge about the world I feared I'd never gain. Larry and Ernie.

Throughout my junior high experience, my classroom—made up primarily of North Philly kids bused to our South Philadelphia school, whose neighborhoods' intense territorial disputes became irrelevant at Bartlett because of their common status as outsiders—proved generally to be a calm center in the maelstrom of violent male self-definition and self-assertion that inspired individual and gang rivalries.

If I was saddened by the impending loss of trusted male comrades, I was distressed that commencement meant the permanent loss of proximity to Alannah, whom I knew I was unlikely to see again. For months, I'd hoped to summon the courage to explain to her what had happened to cause the seemingly irreparable and occasionally bitter rift between us. Perhaps she might even have been flattered by the fact that my thoughts had been so jumbled that Friday afternoon when I made my initial, nervous effort to signal the depth of my feelings for her that I focused only on the sound and not the substance of her honey-voiced whisperings of her telephone number. That I'd never asked a girl for her telephone number before. That, for the first time, I was seeking seriously to abandon the safety of unacknowledged affection.

I'd hoped to tell her that I was unsure what I could do to get her to claim me as her boyfriend, and why if, as our friends insisted, ours was a mutual attraction, it was any more my responsibility to compel her than it was hers to compel me. That I was distracted by the intrusive presence of our matchmaking friends and afraid of being attacked by some brutal, bloodthirsty 13th Streeter who hadn't learned or didn't care about the truce. That I couldn't hear her because of the cold late-winter rain crashing against our umbrellas. That I was worrying about her missing her bus.

Would she believe that I'd called fifteen variations of the numbers I thought I'd heard, until my siblings complained of my fruitless, uncharacteristic, and disruptive hogging of the phone? That I'd called Don to ask him to ask her best friend for the number, but because of their own untimely romantic squabblings, he refused? That I'd prepared my apology and explanation down to the last syllable, which I didn't deliver because she'd confronted me the following Monday morning with a cold, stunning silence born of anger, frustrated anticipation, and the pain of believing she'd had her emotions toyed with?

Because I didn't fully understand the ritual of courting, didn't have the right psychic tools or a sufficient sense of self-confidence to insert myself successfully in the game, I was developmentally behind my siblings, all of whom were involved in relationships. On occasion, I'd listen, with more than a little self-protective amusement, to their contributions to inane conversations with people with whom they were involved or in whom they were interested. They spent hours talking on the telephone, trying to seem alternately cool, interested, or bored, but always fascinated, if not with what their mates were saying, then with the artificial sounds of their own voices. "Yeah, Marvin Gaye is really boss, but Jackie Wilson was the man!" "The Bar Kays were doin' it to death, weren't they?" "Isn't Billy jive? Why do you still hang out with him?" "Sure, I wanna go see the Isley Brothers—you gonna take me?"

If this was the general drift of romantic conversations, how could I talk with Alannah about important matters I'd grown accustomed to discussing with my male classmates: my mother's drinking and disconcerting neglect of her offspring? Being sleepy each day because I'd stayed awake until the wee hours of the morning trying to protect myself from the bedbugs that each night, seconds after I turned off the light, marched like murderous soldiers from their nest on my messy closet shelf to gorge themselves with my blood? About my fear that I'd be maimed or killed in gang violence? Would she understand my fascination with Hal Greer? Would she laugh at the songs I'd written about her? Could I ask her if, and how much, my burn figured into her considerations of whether she liked me? Would she explain to me the origins of the large pink-beige mark on her thigh that she wore hideous white stockings in a vain effort to cover?

One late-winter Saturday morning a week or two before I approached Alannah, I sat at the kitchen table with Carol talking about, among other things, where our mother, who had not come home the night before, might be. In a swift, dramatic gesture that I assumed reflected her worry about, and frustration with, our mother, my older sister grabbed a pencil and a piece of paper, smiled, and wrote something that she hid from me with her left forearm. When she was finished, she stared at me intently, a slightly worried and embarrassed look on her face, and told me she'd written a question for which she wanted an answer. In neat swirls, she'd asked, "Michael, are you a homosexual?"

I was stunned by the question and unsure of its motivation. Did I look, act, sound, walk gay? Did she think I desired boys or was unduly attracted to feminine accoutrements and behaviors? Certainly, I wasn't like my male classmate who talked and walked like a girl, or the tough transvestite from Thirteenth Street who wore tighter pants and more makeup than any of the girls in the school. Or Bobby, the swishy white man whom my mother's friend Aunt Naomi had married, who'd invited Ricky and me upstairs separately on the pretense of having us try on some clothes he could no longer wear and asked us in a drunken, desperate voice if he could touch our dicks while our heads were covered by tentlike, musty sweaters.

"Why do you think that? Because I don't go around holding my dick when I walk down the street?"

"No."

" 'Cause I ain't in 5th Street?"

"No."

" 'Cause my voice ain't quite changed yet? 'Cause of the way I walk?"

"No."

" 'Cause I don't have a girlfriend?"

"Yeah."

"Really?"

"Don't you like girls?"

"Yeah. I told you about Alannah, didn't I? About how much I like her."

"So what? I know boys who tell everybody about liking some girl or another just as a front. You planning to do anything with this girl?"

"Um, I guess so."

"Like what?"

"I don't know."

"You want her for a girlfriend?"

"I think so. I guess so. Yeah."

"When you gonna tell her that?"

"I don't know."

"Michael, you sure you're not a faggot? I'd still love you and all."

Refusing to continue to assert my innocence when it was apparent that none of my words and few of my actions—including sporadic gropings with a girl who also lived on the nineteenth floor—could clear my name, I got up from the table, went to my room, and slammed the door behind me. Lying on my unmade bed and casually fingering the bumps left after my unsuccessful battle with bedbugs the night before, I recognized that I'd been deposited at a crossroads, a point of either potentially beneficial transformation or debilitating stagnation. Clearly, in my sister's mind, my just-my-imagination posture was suspect. In order for my sexuality not to be called into question, my closed-door dreaming had to be replaced or at the very least supplemented by real-life, flesh-and-bones drama.

Searching for answers, for a type of truth about myself and the world I couldn't find anywhere else, I pored over my mother's *True Romance* magazines. There were two kinds of men in these formulaic stories: those who beat, raped, loved and left, and were in other ways downright nasty to women, and those who rode in on the equivalent of white horses after the women had been mistreated, who were extremely good looking and/or possessed some exotic, enigmatic, and wholly unnamable quality that drew the women to them and helped them to heal. Aware that I was no more than kind of cute on my best days, I hoped I had that salvific something that someone—that Alannah—would detect, even if she was not aware of what she might need to be saved from and I was only minimally aware of the requirements of the role of savior.

The boys were instructed to sit on the right side of the auditorium, and the girls in the middle, leaving the back and left side seating for family members and friends of the graduates. I sat with boys in my homeroom, next to Larry, close to Ernie and Bird and Don. We chattered noisily throughout the ceremony, thoroughly enjoying this final opportunity to be together en masse. I turned around to look for my mother, hoping to avoid a repeat of my sixth-grade graduation drama. Finally, I saw her, sitting soberly near the back of the middle section of seats, looking small, frail, and a bit uncomfortable near Ernie's and Larry's mothers, both of whom she'd been acquainted with since our Lombard Street days.

The graduation featured the usual pomp and suspect circumstance—singing, speeches, and overpraise—and a glossing over or ignoring of the difficulties, dangers, and threats we'd encountered during our junior high school careers. Glossed over, among other things, were the outbreaks of violence initiated by 13th Street boys outside school grounds. Ronnie's being stabbed near the steps of a Catholic church and hospitalized for weeks. J. V.'s knifing with a blade rumored to have been hidden in the prop box of that year's annual production, *West Side Story*. Frequent pencil, belt, and fist fights that erupted after lunch despite the presence of generally well liked but ineffectual adult male hall monitors. The frustration that, despite the Black Power rhetoric of racial unity, boys seemed to have no choice but to let the accident of residence determine their allies and enemies. The certainty that had a single police car been stationed daily outside Bartlett for five minutes as the boys from Southwark gathered and made our way home (as one invariably was on the days following each serious violent episode), after-school gang violence would have been eliminated.

After I tuned out the mindless platitudes, recognized how restrictive the auditorium seats were, and abandoned my vain search for Alannah, all that was left of the ceremony was the distribution of awards for academic achievement and the outstanding boy and girl.

For those of us deemed sufficiently smart by our teachers, the last two weeks of school had been spent taking tests in academic and vocational subjects that determined who would receive the graduation awards. I'd taken five tests during that period and learned from my history teacher the day after taking the test in his subject that I'd gotten the highest score. So I came to graduation prepared for a little glory.

Bartlett did not offer a challenging academic environment, even for students in the best sections. Except for the lengthy daily algebra assignments given to us by Mrs. Jones, a short, bespectacled, dark-skinned woman blessed with a wonderful sense of humor and the ability to lovingly embarrass students she believed weren't performing up to their potential, I hardly ever had more than ten minutes of homework to complete each night. I never had English homework in ninth grade, because our young teacher—a big, burly, teddy bear of a man who, like a number of others assigned the task of teaching us, was overwhelmed by our capacity for obstinance—stopped trying to impart knowledge to us after the first month of school. No science homework. A little French conjugation, which I did in homeroom each morning.

Despite, or perhaps because of, the lack of formal educational stimulation, I read a great deal during junior high, devouring everything I could get my hands on: my mother's magazines and titillating series of Mandingo novels; basketball books and magazines; all manner of books I withdrew from the public library nestled in the middle of the Italian neighborhood, four blocks from my apartment building; the sports pages and comics section of the newspaper that my mother purchased religiously when she was sober. (On occasion, she also read the city's black newspaper, the *Tribune,* in which my picture and words appeared when I was interviewed in seventh grade along with some other students for a feature on corporal punishment in schools.) I read when I couldn't sleep and when I awoke, when I was lonely and when I was feeling especially connected to my family, friends, or the world in general.

The winners and two runners-up in each category were summoned to stand onstage, and the winners were given certificates acknowledging their achievements. I was called up to receive the math award and took my place on a stage I hadn't previously graced during my years at Bartlett except to get my graduation photo taken. Our auditorium stage was typically used not to celebrate academic achievement but for displays of performative skills: talent shows; plays; our dance troupe, Freekoba, renowned throughout the city; and other special events. From this unaccustomed vantage point, with my eyes cast downward in a self-conscious display of modesty, and in the glare of bright floodlights and stage lights trained on me, I was unable to distinguish anyone in the audience.

In all, I won four of the six academic awards bestowed on my graduating class. Mr. G. even had to call me back to the stage after all the winners and runners-up had retaken their seats because of a mix-up in which initially the history prize was awarded not to me but to the first runner-up. Sitting down again, my certificates in hand, I felt a vague sense of accomplishment. Primarily, however, I felt overwhelmed, stunned, and, for reasons I couldn't quite put my finger on, bitter. If I was indeed, as the surprising results of the tests suggested, an intellectual big fish, albeit in a relatively small and polluted pond, why hadn't it seemed that any of my teachers had taken a special interest in me or gone out of their way to nurture my talents? Why was I not a teacher's pet, not singled out, as other members of my class had been? Why wasn't my intelligence as much grounds for popularity with girls in my class as light skin or a good build or good hair or big money or nice rags?

Had she been fully aware of my intellectual prowess, would Alannah have been so impressed by me that she could have forgiven me, in the ways that I'd imagined males possessing some or all of these traits were forgiven despite their frequently transgressive behavior? In true romantic terms, could my brains move me from bad to good boy, from the cause of her pain to the answer to her prayers?

In my school, my neighborhood, and my household, where my mother expected us to do well in school and rarely praised us for doing so, my intelligence brought me few, if any, perks. There was no debate team, no math or French or science club, no organized programs for relatively gifted or academically motivated boys who could profit from special attention, and no means of satisfying particular interests except entertainment, sports, and gang warring.

Although some teachers tried to fill this void for selected individuals, my male friends in the class, who generally were the offspring of absent fathers and overwhelmed mothers, recognized that we had to figure out for ourselves how to make the transition from a peach-fuzzy boyhood to a hairy black manhood. The authorities charged with overseeing our school seemed neither to have considered our deprivation seriously nor to have sought to analyze, for example, how impressionable boys could develop into productive citizens in an environment where the gang culture, and its adversarial models of maleness, went virtually unchallenged.

In such an environment, our development depended on us neither wholeheartedly embracing nor rejecting the normative feminine values that our mothers sought to instill in us—cooperativeness, goodness, attentiveness, sweetness, passivity. Rather, our challenge was to use and comfortably incorporate aspects of these values into our ways of being black and male.

Besides sports, dance, and drama, the yearbook was the only extracurricular activity I can remember. Certainly, some of the boys in my class were eminently qualified to contribute: Bird won the contest to coin a motto for the year with a phrase that riffed on a popular Sly and the Family Stone song, "It's a family affair . . . at Bartlett"; Andre was the best artist in the school; Barry was musically inclined; and Don and I were, if nothing else, enthusiastic. We kept pestering the yearbook faculty adviser, who'd served as one of a procession of English teachers we'd had during our teacher strike–interrupted eighth-grade year, to add us to the all-female editorial staff, which included our classmates Alannah, Denise, and Marsha.

Our wish to join the yearbook staff resulted, in part, from our desire to work and play with girls we liked and who, because of their duties, seemed hardly ever to be in class. Primarily, however, I think we recognized that we were suffering from intellectual understimulation and general neglect and saw the yearbook's compensatory possibilities. Also, we were hurt by the fact that we'd been excluded, stigmatized, deemed biologically and socially unqualified. While the good, smart girls got singled out for special treatment, we were ignored.

Driven by a combination of hurt and mysterious testosterone

surges, we began to rebel. Don and I cut class for the first time. We became so uncharacteristically unruly in French class that Mrs. Edge, our teacher who punctuated her constant pleas for our attention and cooperation with the phrase "all right now," and spoke the language of love with a distinctive southern twang, felt compelled to telephone my mother to inform her that I'd developed an attitude. We stopped trying to keep the more rambunctious kids in line in English, leaving our overmatched teacher to fend for himself. Befuddled by the apparent institutional indifference to the plight of the sort of smart, well-behaved boys we considered ourselves to be, we tried on the mask of black male boisterousness and uncontrollability, acting out as brashly as our constitutionally cooperative natures would allow.

When the yearbook appeared in late spring, we marveled at the occasionally stylish, amusing, and poignant work the girls had done. Leafing through the yearbook, we realized quickly that it was, in part, a vanity production graced with countless pictures of the attractive editors—nattily dressed, professionally coiffed, and neatly made up for the individual and group photos they'd arranged—who appeared older, more mature, and somehow even more aloof than they did during their brief appearances in class. We laughed loudly at their pathetic efforts at true-to-your-school verse, smiled patronizingly at the lame jokes, but, quiet as we kept it, we were impressed.

After participating in an obligatory display of masculine derision of female work, I sat down at my desk to look more carefully through the yearbook, particularly at the pictures of Alannah. With no danger of discovery and no need to avert my gaze as I did when their flesh-and-bones source became aware of the intensity of my gaze, I lingered, admiringly and almost mournfully, over her bright eyes, her smooth, rich brown skin, her not quite camera-ready, fat-cheeked smile, her stumpy voluptuousness.

Although the chilly silence between us had not ended, we'd somehow survived a host of painful or embarrassing episodes: passing each other wordlessly in the long, empty, hauntingly quiet third-floor hallway (she was doing yearbook business, and I was headed to the counselor's office for news about my prep school application), and summoning the strength to avoid each other's restless hands, tense smiles, and sad, averted eyes; exasperating our friends so thoroughly that they stopped trying to push us together; my so completely miscalculating the feel and physics of an unfamiliar sport during a rare coed gym class that I spiked a volleyball forcefully not merely in her direction, as I'd primarily intended, but into her chest; her letting out a brief, fascinating squeal, and searching behind my shocked expression for signs of malicious intent; my being overwhelmed with regret that we'd never laugh together about this incident, and that I could never ask whether the ball had left a bruise on flesh my thin fingers would never tremble over.

Near the end of the school year, her face finally lost its alternately blank and betrayed expression when she was in my presence, and I sensed that a thaw had at least begun. And though no words had been exchanged between us for months, I took a proprietary pleasure in her photographic images, for if she was not my girl in fact, she remained so in my head and heart.

I appeared in the yearbook twice: in my individual portrait, listed alphabetically at the bottom right of one of the early pages, and, much further back, in the unfocused class photo on the page reserved for our section, which recognized me as class president. (I was elected to this ceremonial post only because the boys outnumbered the girls on the day the vote was taken.) In my last will and testament, a corny yearbook device if ever there was one, I displayed what I believed was my courageous, biting wit by leaving my "alleged attitude" to Mrs. Edge.

When I saw the photo the girl editors had chosen of me to include, I was certain that rather than suffer my silence quietly, Alannah had, with the help of her friends, exacted a measure of sweet, public revenge. In the photo, I looked retarded, drunk, insane, or some startling combination of the three; my big eyes were three-quarters closed, my thick lips formed uncomfortably into the shape they'd assume if bitter lemon juice or some of my mother's foul whiskey had just passed between them, and my Afro, which I'd plaited too tightly the night before, appeared to have been electroshocked in a science project gone awry. It was the picture at which my family, friends, and I had laughed riotously, the mutant, unpurchasable shot in every batch of professional photos I've ever seen. Despite my appreciation of their masterful prank, a joke that represented me in a manner proving that I was not worthy of Alannah's affection, I was unhappy that I'd be forever associated with this monstrous expression.

The selection of this unflattering photo, I was convinced, was further evidence that the faculty adviser was part of an institutionally sanctioned conspiracy to marginalize and devalue even those males who weren't bad. I envisioned these girls and their mentor—who we assumed was divorced and bitter about her husband's mistreatment of her—sitting around, plotting how to use their dictatorial power over official words and images to settle scores. In my most self-involved and stoically suffering moments, the whole yearbook, and my representation therein, seemed a flare-up in the battle between the Avon-enhanced girls and the sweaty, unruly boys.

Generally speaking, particularly after seventh grade, when both sides had managed to throw off their gender-repelling cooties, the girls and boys in my class got along relatively well. Still, the yearbook was not the only manifestation of the often-unacknowledged tensions between us. Indeed, during the bitter winter months of my ninth-grade year, several of the girls from 13th Street decided to organize themselves as an auxiliary militia whose purpose was to beat up individual boys whom they caught walking the hallways alone between classes.

When I first heard of this plan—hatched, ironically, during a lull in male gang violence—it seemed utterly foolish. Who, besides the boys in my class whose sensibilities and cultural styles were much more greatly indebted to female than to male conventions, wouldn't be able to defend themselves against a bunch of girls? My boy Don, for example, quickly dispersed the pack of would-be assailants with two or three hard punches on their arms. Compared to the dangers of organized male assault, which had behind it the force of culture, tradition, and physical power, this girl group activity did not seem a threat at all.

Soon after its encounter with Don, the female mob descended on me one false-spring day as I prepared to mount the stairs that would take me from French to English. A commotion, whose sound was equal parts stifled giggles, jiggling jewelry, and the rustle of stiff-clothed pants, caused me to turn around defensively, and I saw the self-appointed gang approach and quickly surround me. Their countenances, softened by incompletely repressed smiles, signaled to me that what was about to transpire was, in fact, a game, an elaborately designed hoax, behavior unlikely to become ritual because none of its participants believed wholeheartedly in its logic and power.

The gang's de facto leader, a tough project girl on whom the conventional trappings of masculinity seemed more comfortable than those of the so-called softer sex, got up in my face, touched my chest lightly with the tips of each of the fingers of her right hand, and said to me and to her gang, in her best imitation of threatening male tones, "We got you now, motherfucker! We gonna kick your ass!" Encircled by this odd, unthreatening gang, my back against the cold tiled wall, I knew that I could escape easily either by punching my way out or, I surmised, by simply saying "boo" loudly and running over Hope, a sweet, shy, thin, brown-skinned girl with a perfectly shaped Afro and beautiful, sad-eyed features who'd been in my class each of my three years at Bartlett.

My gentle ass whipping was more amusing than anything else. These girls struck the required pugilistic poses but couldn't muster up the malevolence of their male counterparts. Rather than feel humiliated, I felt alternately saddened and tickled by their efforts to act like their male homeys.

I'd faced significantly more physically and psychically threatening situations during that year, with a wide variety of results. I endured Edgar's barrage of insults, aware that confronting him physically meant a certain pummeling because he was bigger than I and, I assumed, better with his hands. I spent much of the year running purposefully away from fast-approaching male members of 13th Street for whom I'd become a marked man in my last year at Bartlett, one of the ones on whom several thugs and would-be thugs wanted to inflict pain.

My primary battles that year, however, were with my mother. My brother, Ricky, who'd spent long years being my mother's domestic adversary, had moved in with his girlfriend's family. He left home largely because he'd tired of Mommy's beating him with shoes and belts, slapping, punching, and digging her fingernails into the flesh in his forearms and hands, and accusing him of being "just like your father!"

When Ricky left, the role of filial scapegoat fell to me, the last in the line of masculine succession. The patterns of the ritual in which I was involved against my will were fairly predictable. After a few drinks of cheap wine or whiskey, Mom would start talking to me (lacking the romantic entanglements of my siblings, I was typically home alone with my mother on cold days) about my father's brutal beatings of her. A look of sadness mixed with horror would descend on her face, the fragile symmetry of whose features alcohol distorted ever so slightly. She'd start to cry uncontrollably, either as a result of remembering that horror or because of the sadness she felt because of her mother's, father's, and oldest brother's deaths. Then she'd transfer her anger from my father to me.

When she first began to turn her wrath on me, I was concerned primarily with easing my mother's burdens and seeking to calm her. So I stoically accepted the insults, the derision, the ungrounded accusations, even the scratches that were much deeper and wider than those I'd periodically get when playing with our cat, Toni. Because I played basketball, scratches, scrapes, and bruises regularly appeared on my flesh, so I never felt I needed to explain to anyone the marks that began to appear with some regularity on my arms.

Aggravated by the pains of unrequited love and simply tired of being a whipping boy, I yelled at my mother to leave me alone when she began her verbal assault one day in the winter of my ninth-grade year. In response, she moved stiffly toward me, hands extended, cursing me, my brother, and my father. Desiring to end the immediate threat and, I hoped, to put a stop permanently to this painful ritual, I moved slowly toward her, yelling, "Leave me alone, Mommy," and grabbed her wrists to keep her from scratching me. Because of a growth spurt that had expanded my body to five feet six inches and 120 pounds, I was taller than and outweighed my mother, whose strength was partly sapped by her inebriation. Unable to free her hands, she kicked at my shins and hotly exclaimed, "Get your hands off me! Uh-huh, backin' me up in a corner. Whatyougonnado? Hit me? Go 'head! Go 'head, hear, you little bastard! Just like your father, aren't you? The apple sure don't fall too far from the tree."

The verbal and physical outburst seemed to calm or exhaust her, and she leaned against the wall, her head bobbing up and down, her arms hanging loosely at her side, mouthing in a barely audible voice, "Ain't this a blip? Ain't this a blip?"

Although I never mentioned this physical altercation to my classmates, I joked with them about the girls' attack. When they asked me why I hadn't hit back, I couldn't bring myself to explain that I hadn't really felt physically endangered, that compared to the male and maternal threats I faced regularly, the psychic and physical damage the girl gang inflicted was minimal at best. Most important, though, I couldn't articulate these sentiments to my classmates because I'd been schooled on tales of male brutality literally from the cradle; and knowing that my mother's history was the source of her abuse of me, I surmised that there must be discernible correlations between the girls' and my mother's behavior. If the boys from 13th Street seemed to live to injure us, what did they do to the girls with whom they coexisted?

"They didn't hurt me," I kept repeating to my buddies. "Plus, I don't hit girls."

"You're a dumb ass, Awk. If they hit you, you damn sure better defend yourself."

"But I don't . . ."

"Them bitches fucking you up and you just stood there and took it? Fuck wrong with you, boy? Let 'em try some shit like that with me, I'll beat the shit outa all of 'em. I'll grab me one or two titties, too, for sure."

The graduation exercises culminated with the announcement of the winners of the outstanding female and male awards. When Mr. G. mentioned these prizes at the beginning of the proceedings, before the academic and vocational subject awards had been given out, the idea of them seemed utterly ridiculous to me. Most of the teachers didn't know most of the students, had had no contact with the great majority of them, and hence couldn't reliably assess our relative outstandingness. Also, "outstanding" in this context was so vague a term that it was virtually meaningless. What criteria did they use to determine outstandingness? Grades? Standardized test scores? Potential for future success? The one criterion I remember Mr. G. mentioning was "contributions to the school," but given Bartlett's manifest lack of organized opportunities for service, extracurricular and otherwise, it was unclear to me what we could have contributed, and to whom.

Because of my ceremonial bounty to that point, my relative success at standardized test taking, and my having been awarded a scholarship to a prestigious prep school, I sat nervously through the last minutes of the ceremony, convinced I'd be chosen. I knew I didn't deserve such recognition—in truth, I hadn't contributed much of anything to the school that I was aware of—but I wanted it, and I suspected that few in the auditorium would have been surprised if my name was called. I sat, shaking like a leaf on a tree, as Nadine, one of the North Philly yearbook girls, the head editor, in fact, tall and pretty and charismatic, walked up to receive the prize for outstanding female. As she strutted back to her seat, grinning from ear to ear, some of my friends—none of whom had known anything at all about the award before the graduation began—patted me on the back and punched me lightly on the arm, sure that I'd be called next.

Mr. G. called Steve instead. Steve was a chubby, jovial, brownnosing North Philly boy who, like Nadine, was from a section other than the star academic group. His behavior often seemed an affront to the norms of masculinity against which all of the males in my class were measured. Although we didn't tease our two budding gay classmates about their soft, high voices, loose-hipped walks, and obvious lack of interest in being anything more than friends with the girls in our class, boys had spent their entire junior high school careers referring to Steve as a "faggot." That obviously derisive characterization had very little to do with his projecting any stereotypically gay traits but was motivated by his atypicality. He eschewed sports, tough talk, girl ogling, fistfights—rituals through which we periodically tested and measured our masculinity—and instead settled on the role of good boy to teachers, for whom he ran all sorts of errands and proved exceedingly trustworthy.

For a number of teachers and a few of his female classmates, who enjoyed having their needs attended to so energetically and efficiently, his cloying, kiss-ass, choirboy, eraser-cleaning routine did not, in fact, represent the personification of all that black boys could not and should not be—as it did for the rest of us. He did not lack personal toughness and integrity, and when he was insulted by some of the boys who had known him before he came to Bartlett, he could defend himself verbally quite well. But even those defensive moments, during which he would set his jaw, gaze sincerely at his would-be assailant, and assert his right to act in any way he felt comfortable, demonstrated his difference, as he never gave any indication that he wanted to smack the shit out of someone for fucking with him too much. At such moments—in fact, at nearly every moment I witnessed his behavior—he acted on the belief that sincerity, honesty, and integrity would work for and change others' minds about him.

That he hadn't excelled academically in any appreciable way—he hadn't been even a runner-up for any of the academic awards—didn't matter to the teachers. That he hadn't won the respect of the majority of his classmates didn't matter, either. What mattered, to the teachers and perhaps to others of the assembled masses who beheld his triumph, was that he represented a safe, pliable version of black boyhood in an institutional and social context dominated by masculine unruliness.

As I watched Steve receive the congratulations of the principal, I felt a level of resentment well out of proportion with my desire for, or belief that I was indeed deserving of, that award. My academic awards began to seem merely a tease, a concession, a begrudging recognition that even in a context where it was supposed to be prized, supported, and encouraged, the only personal quality I possessed significant quantities of that the society insisted it valued—school smarts—was ultimately of no real significance.

This moment represented the culmination of a yearlong process of learning that to be deemed truly outstanding, to win the respect of my teachers, the patience, understanding, and affection of girls, and the favor—or at least the noncontempt—of my mother, I had to be different than I was. Mine was solely a quantitative accomplishment, a victory by the numbers. Qualitatively speaking, the skills and personal characteristics I'd displayed or possessed were only marginally important. Overwhelming evidence of my academic abilities didn't persuade a sufficient number of teachers to vote in my favor. My deep, sincere, tongue-tied affection for Alannah wasn't enough to compensate for my fear and romantic inexperience. And the fact that I obviously wasn't my father didn't convince my mother during her drunken episodes that females could expect to be treated in any less abusive a manner by me than he'd treated her.

After the ceremony, I ended my futile search for Alannah when I saw my mother approaching me with a big, closemouthed grin on her face. When she reached me, she touched my arm lightly and said, "My, my, aren't you something?" I smiled weakly back at her, not sure what to say, and knowing full well how much she frowned on displays of excessive self-satisfaction, vanity, or ingratitude. I wanted to avoid at all costs complaining about not being chosen as the outstanding boy.

"I guess so, huh?" I replied, as I offered her the awards, which I'd rolled neatly together and secured with the thick rubber band, and patted her hand. "Mommy, could you take these home for me? I wanna go to the movies with one of my friends."

"Sure, Michael Cycle, but be home at a reasonable hour, okay? Don't make me worry about you."

"All right, Mommy. I promise."

"I'm proud of you, you know. Four awards! Aren't you something? I thought you might even win that final award. But you can't be too greedy, right?"

"Yeah, you're right. Thanks. See you."

I'd wanted my mother to hug me, kiss me on the cheek, and tell me that she understood how overwhelmed I was by the success of which she was so proud. To tell me that she thought that my resentment—at being passed over for the chubby little brownnoser, being ignored by Alannah, and having been forced to be my mother's own whipping boy—was perfectly justified.

Instead, she turned to leave the auditorium. After she'd moved ten steps away from me, she turned back in my direction, held up the certificates, and smiled at me. I had no idea how to read her gesture.

Bird and I went to see *Shaft in Africa,* one of the sequels to the original black private dick flick starring Richard Roundtree. In this ridiculous installment (which I was viewing with the advantage of not having seen the original), Shaft traveled to some unspecified or unremembered location on the dark continent to rescue the natives who were being sold into slavery by a slimy European who rode around in a stretch limousine during most of the movie with his nymphomaniacal blonde concubine. A horribly inconsistent American condemnation of the African practice of clitorectomy, the film also featured Yvette McGee as the beguiling daughter of an urbanized tribal chief who, unbeknownst to her father, was no longer a virgin. Having firsthand knowledge of what she'd be missing if she submitted to this mutilation, McGee's character schemed to avoid coming under the knife. Like the blonde nympho, this princess quickly became an object of desire for the suave love man and former Afro Sheen model, who—despite the fact that nearly every bad guy in the movie had studied glossy photographs of him and could therefore distinguish his well-groomed do from the home cuts of the black actors with whom he shared screen time—made an effort to learn to appear culturally African so that he could liberate his brothers from slavery's late-twentieth-century manifestation.

I could barely focus on the silly, illogical story and spent much of my energy trying to elicit Bird's hushed, high-pitched laughter by asking him repeatedly, in my best ghetto nigger voice, "Ain't they got they own private dicks in Africa?" But I loved the familiar strangeness in the movie theater, the popcorn-soda-Raisinets-jujubes-musty-humanity-and-reefer smell, the rustling sounds, the hearty laughs and surprised sighs, the clear, large-screen picture, even the sticky, uncomfortable chair on which I sat and was sure would stain my silk-and-wool pants. I was excited by the love scene between the leads, set in a raised crop storage hut that appeared to be a cross between Tarzan's living quarters and a Manhattan loft. And I liked seeing how the movie's music, highlighted by the hit song "Are You Man Enough," fit and didn't fit into the flow of the narrative.

The lyrics of the song were rendered in raspy sweetness by The Four Tops' Levi Stubbs and asked questions with which all the boys I knew—myself included—were actively wrestling.

Are you man enough
Big and bad enough
Are you gonna let 'em shoot you down

How big and bad did one have to be to get the girl? To walk the street unmolested? To limit or eliminate altogether the constant sense of fear that haunted my waking hours and my dreams? Were there spaces and places I could occupy where hardness, badness, and toughness didn't define manhood, where they were only possibilities among a host of equally attractive ways of being male? I wished I could ask Bird, or Ricky, or someone who wouldn't laugh or ridicule me, wouldn't call me a little faggot, wouldn't question my manhood, and would understand, even if he or she didn't know the answers.

As we walked out of the theater and into the humid night air, I shook Bird's hand, embraced him in a back-slapping hug, and told him I'd speak with him soon. "And if you see Alannah," I joked, "tell her I love her, okay?" He smiled, shook his head in feigned exasperation, and headed toward Broad Street to catch the El to North Philly.

One evening that summer, exhausted from having played basketball for several hours in terribly uncomfortable heat and humidity, I decided that rather than walk the extra distance to the relative safety of the well-lit elevators in the back of the building, I'd use the more convenient front-lobby elevators that faced the playground. These elevators' primary function had become to provide maintenance workers with the means of transporting refrigerators, stoves, and other bulky appliances and materials. When I pushed the cold button, one of the elevators' doors opened immediately, and as I stepped toward it, I saw David and Joe, boys who were two years older than I. David, who was known throughout the neighborhood as a crazy motherfucker, and Joe, who was too fundamentally nice to appear so, greeted me. I figured that their appearance at the precise moment I pushed the elevator button was sheer coincidence, that they were leaving one of their apartments to go outside. Their sinister smiles worried me a bit, as did the darkened cabin and the fact that, rather than exit the elevator, they casually leaned against its metal walls, beckoning me to enter.

Tired and thirsty, I stepped from the streetlight-lit lobby into the nearly pitch-black elevator, offering the conventional neighborhood greeting, "What's up," as the door closed and sight of any sort became impossible. "One of y'all got a match or something?" I asked, as their silence gave way to childish snickering, and my wariness turned into real fear. I remembered an earlier elevator incident when David had pulled a knife on Joe and me and ordered us to touch his dick or he'd "fuck you up real bad." In the face of that threat, I had been consumed by a variety of cop-show images: of screaming as the knife pierced my flesh; of my blood mixing with the urine on the floor of the elevator; of David standing over me, smiling menacingly as he kicked my lifeless corpse. I'd reached my shaking right hand into his pants, touched the coarse border of his pubic hair, and removed my hand quickly, as though I'd touched a flame, which seemed to satisfy him. I remembered the look of hurt and deep betrayal on Joe's face. Suddenly I became terrified of what they'd do to me, in the dark, deserted elevator that wouldn't stop before it reached the nineteenth floor.

Hands grabbed my arms, which I struggled to free. A hand covered my mouth, stifling momentarily my efforts to reason with them or to scream or to speak menacingly. Hands and arms and pelvises pushed me to the floor, which I hit with a soft splash, coating my sweat-drenched T-shirt with what I imagined was days-old urine. Fists and knees and elbows and feet slammed against my arms, my stomach, my legs, and my back as I covered my face and tried to collect my thoughts. Why were they doing this? What had I done to them? How much would it hurt? Did it hurt? When would it end?

"What the fuck you doing?"

"Shut the fuck up, nigger!"

"Why y'all doing this? Stop it!"

"What I say? Shut the fuck up!"

When I didn't experience the intense pain I expected to feel from long, uninterrupted seconds of beating, I realized that they were pulling their punches. They weren't really trying to hurt me at all but had merely involved me in a prank, a joke, a game of victim and victimizer. That realization didn't help me to endure any better the seconds before the elevator door opened. But in that moment of clarity, all of the fighting, the posturing, the wolfing and dangerous signifying, the gang warring, seemed similarly staged efforts to manifest a sense of power that the participants were aware all along was, at most, transitory, if not wholly illusory.

Giggling like six year olds or actors playing the roles of insane asylum patients, they kicked me gently in the ass as I rolled off the elevator when it opened on the brightly lit nineteenth floor. I fumbled for my key, opened the door of the deserted apartment, and ran to the bathroom, desperately throwing off my sweat-and-urine-soaked clothing. Sitting in the cold bathtub, I ran the water as hot as I could stand, and as the tub filled and covered my sore body, aching more from hours of basketball than from the mock attack, I started to cry uncontrollably. For what felt like a half hour, I sobbed, my torso rocking involuntarily from a combination of pain, anger, and deep frustration; and I repeated over and over again, "I got to get the fuck outta here. I got to get the fuck outta here."

The day before I was scheduled to leave for Governor Dummer Academy in some place called Byfield, Massachusetts, I went to a drugstore in the Italian Market to purchase discount toiletries. I walked quickly past the pungent smells of the fruit and vegetable stands that covered much of the sidewalk of the Market, leaving shoppers very little room to manueuver their carts, wagons, and screaming children. I watched for sneaky 13th Streeters who liked catching unsuspecting boys from my neighborhood in this neutral commercial turf and robbing them or beating them up. And I avoided being seen by the proprietors of Al's Clothing Store, where I'd worked two consecutive summers with my brother and, later, after school.

As I moved past the fruit stands that dominated the Ninth and Washington Avenue corner and toward the area of the Market where meats, fish, eggs, clothes, shoes, and other items were sold, I felt that someone was following me. Suspecting I was being stalked by someone from 13th Street, I quickened my pace, but when I glanced around, I saw no one looking in my direction except a middle-aged black man dressed in khaki work clothes, who smiled broadly at me. Walking toward me as I slowed my pace a half block from the drugstore, he spoke of the weather or the crowd or some other inane subject. I barely responded. But because I was relieved that he didn't want to stab me, I started to converse with him until, after thirty seconds or so, he asked me to meet him somewhere in 7th Street territory later that evening when he got off of work. Initially, I wanted to ask why, but I quickly realized his unstated intention and sped up again until I turned toward the door of the drugstore. He blocked my path and asked if I was going to meet him. I told him I was going to be busy, that I was leaving town to go off to school, but I knew he wouldn't let me go unless I gave him something to hope for.

"You understand what I'm talking about, don't you?"

Trembling, I shook my head and ran into the store.

To make sure he wasn't waiting for me when I left the drugstore, I spent a full hour choosing deodorant, toothpaste, lotion, and a toothbrush. I walked slowly around the store under the watchful eye of the white female cashier, who seemed convinced that I was prepared to hide a large bottle of mouthwash in my underwear.

I wondered whether I looked gay, or at least potentially interested in altering my clearly conceived sense of my sexuality because of a few words from an old, smelly construction worker. Wasn't I walking tough enough? Hadn't all the work I'd done to remove that feminine switch from my walk been successful? I thought of Carol's question about my sexual orientation and wondered whether others besides my older sister and this man suspected that I wasn't who I believed myself to be.

I spent my last night in Philly before I headed to prep school at home, afraid that the man I'd met would be roaming the streets, looking for me. As I packed my trunks, watched from the porch as my friends and acquaintances played basketball, and leafed through my junior high school yearbook, I wondered whether the sort of aggressiveness that the man displayed was a significant part of what it meant to be a man. This sort of manly assertiveness would have allowed me to inform Alannah confidently that I thought she was really cute, and that I wanted to be her man. Was that the sort of behavior she'd expected of me as we played out our gendered roles of male initiator and female receptor of male interest?

Masculinity, it seemed, in addition to resulting in or helping to produce calculated violence, meant projecting a self-confidence, a fearlessness, that compelled you to go out and get what you wanted. My tentativeness, my dreamy passivity, were unmanly and unlikely to get me anything except hurt, physically and / or emotionally. Perhaps the construction worker sensed that I hadn't sufficiently embraced manhood, that I was overcome with fear of the sort that inhibits bold self-presentation and strenuous resistance to others' acts of assertiveness. If manly behavior included propositioning young boys or strange girls of one's peer group, threatening your friends and acquaintances with knives, beating boys up on pissy elevators, gang warring, and whistling and moaning at attractive women like the construction workers I'd pass as I silently and lustfully watched the objects of our desire walk in Center City, what kind of man was I? What type of man would I become?

I was stuck inside on the porch on a beautiful summer night when the stars made a rare appearance in the typically sooty air. On my last day as a permanent resident of the Southwark Projects, I listened to the thumping of basketballs and the loud squeals of children's playing in the pool, hummed along with the love songs that Debby was sharing with her boyfriend in the living room, and wondered if Alannah was thinking of me, too.

Instead of attending the Million Man March, I taught my graduate course on tradition and twentieth-century Afro-American novels, where we discussed Randall Kenan's A Visitation of Spirits. *Kenan's is a lyrical, richly textured postmodern exploration of the burdens of Christianity, tradition, family, and racial history. These burdens combine to create a particularly toxic form of homophobia that leaves the book's adolescent black male protagonist, Horace Cross, hopeless when he considers the possibilities of being incorporated successfully into his society as a gay male. Hence, he becomes desperate to transform himself magically into a predatory black bird who can roam free in the lush North Carolina environs he loves so fiercely.*

What Horace finds particularly abhorrent is his family members' insistence that a single, restrictive notion of masculinity is appropriate for him, a rigid code of racially exclusive heterosexuality symbolized (as in the case of Ned, the similarly positioned smart boy in The Autobiography of Miss Jane Pittman*) by the label "the Chosen One." Horace feels powerless both to actualize and to escape his family's perceptions of exemplary black maleness. But unlike Ernest Gaines's novel, where that daunting leadership role is conferred by members of a community desperate to achieve fundamental American civil rights, in Kenan's exploration of the post–civil rights South, Horace's "chosen" status is merely a means of confirming the self-important Cross family's enduring significance for a black community from which it seeks to distance itself. The entire novel, in fact, manifests this sort of tension between, on the one hand, the modes of knowledge transmission and social control necessitated in part by virulent racism and, on the other, the difficulties of settling on behavioral strategies of black gendered being in the postmodern present.*

Perhaps because of the Cross family's forgetfulness, the narrator implores the reader to remember the social rituals that continue to be practiced, though Horace's family associates them exclusively with the past. In fact, A Visitation of Spirits *opens with a hog killing that members of the Cross family refuse to attend, a refusal that inspires the narrator's digressive discussions of the generally abandoned practice's social rules and ritualistic benefits. Beyond the narrator's urgent pleas for remembrance, what is most striking about the hog killing is its formalizing of a gendered division of labor and, hence, its distribution of social power.*

As Kenan describes the scene,

> [The women] stand about the hole the men dug the day before, a hole as deep
> and as wide as a grave. The women stand there at its edge: one holds a huge

intestine that looks more like a monstrous, hairless caterpillar. She squeezes the thing from top to bottom, time after time, forcing all the foul matter down and out, into the hole. . . . All the while they talk, their faces placid, their fingers deft, their aprons splattered with fecal matter, the hole sending steam up into the air like a huge cooking pot, reeking, stinking. (7)

Unlike the women, whose role consists of squeezing out the waste that accumulates in the hog intestines into grave-sized holes, the men function in largely honorific ways:

Some older man will give a young boy a gun, perhaps, and instruct him not to be afraid, to take his time, to aim straight. The men will all look at one another and the boy with a sense of mutual pride, as the man goes over to the gate and with some effort moves the three slats that close off the hogpen. . . .

The boy will, carefully, take his aim slowly, slowly, taking his time. He squeezes. The gun fires. The hog jumps, snorts: you will see a red dot appear on the broad plain between the eyes, hear the bang of the gun. . . .

But you've seen this, haven't you? When you were younger? Perhaps . . . (8–9)

The chosen boy squeezes the trigger, other boys dream dreams of being selected for that essential task, and the men exult in their power to confer on the chosen boy the symbolic responsibility of nurturing and sustaining the beloved community's members and social order. The social order whose demise the narrator bemoans marginalizes black women and passes phallic power from one male generation to the next.

Generally, I'm compelled both by the novel's postmodernist formal experiments in storytelling and by the fact that the "chosen" but ritual-less Horace directs the phallic rifle not at a hog but at what he knows his community would deem the abomination of his homosexual self. That he becomes both the chosen one and the hog signals the breakdown in, and perversity of, modes of masculine maturation, an outcome that not only is interpretively fascinating but seems as tragic as any textual response to dictatorial social norms of which I am aware.

In that classroom, on the day of the march, I was concerned primarily that like the narrator, the march rhetoric bemoaned the passing of putatively better days. But unlike Kenan's narrator, the Million Man March's organizers sought to reestablish traditions of gendered behavior that would *elevate men socially and leave women rolling literally and figuratively in men's, hogs', and children's shit.*

There are times when even for a committed intellectual, thoughts of the seeming inevitability of social misery overwhelm the joys of subtle textual representation and analysis.

SECTION III ✸ Chocolate City

In the elite academic settings I've inhabited since 1973 when I became a prep school student through the A Better Chance scholarship program, blackness seems to have had a significantly more subtle impact than it is typically said to have in a number of other institutions and in the world at large. I am acutely aware that race matters profoundly in these settings, but when its manifestations appear in nuanced forms, my capacity to render definitive judgments has been severely tried. Often I've found myself wondering: How do you know? How do you identify with certainty the racialist impulses behind a teacher's, administrator's, coach's, or fellow student's behavior? And to what degree did my own occasional trepidation about being in such settings cause me to read that behavior as potentially racially motivated?

To the extent that I've found these situations challenging, those challenges have generally been a function of the sometimes dauntingly conflictual demands of individuality and race-consciousness. However I felt or feel about my presumed or assumed racial responsibilities, I could not and cannot avoid devising strategies of self-presentation with which that amorphous, all-consuming responsibility was and is on occasion in conflict.

It is precisely because of its curious enactment of such complex interracial dilemmas that the phenomenon of the black public intellectual interests me. This designation came into prominence in 1995 when it was used in a variety of national publications to describe Afro-American professors' mass media discussions of black people. Although arising largely from elite institutions such as Harvard, Oberlin, Princeton, and North Carolina, black public intellectuality of the sort with which "white" publications such as the Village Voice, Atlantic, *and* New Republic *became enamored is generally uncluttered with the jargon and thinly veiled egotism that characterizes much academic prose. In fact, if scholarship is intellectual work that acknowledges and builds on the views of earlier thinkers in related fields, black public intellectual activities are unabashedly unscholarly. Although some have stellar scholarly portfolios—including Henry Louis Gates Jr., the influential Afro-American literary critic and theorist, and Cornel West, the philosopher, preacher, and cultural theorist—others, including Michael*

Dyson, Gerald Early, and bell hooks, have not produced work with more than limited scholarly utility.

It would appear that what matters most in black public intellectuality, particularly in its mainstream media manifestations, is the biological and ideological blackness of the speaker, his or her capacity to speak as a credentialed black person well informed of mass black interests. Whatever other significant social services the black public intellectual renders, the most crucial task he or she undertakes is to crack the impenetrable codes of blackness for the edification of elite and common white folks alike.

In his important 1987 collection of scholarly essays Figures in Black, Gates explained that " 'blackness' is not a material object, an absolute, or an event, but a trope; it does not have an 'essence' as such but is defined by a network of relations that form a particular aesthetic unity" (40). Having achieved a necessary psychic and intellectual distance from this constitutive "network of relations," black public intellectuals are able to see and to speak of blackness as "a complex structure of meanings" (41).

Such de-essentializing gestures require a rethinking of the resonance of terms such as blackness, responsibility, nationhood, and integrity that, for Black Power advocates, constituted measurements of afrocentric righteousness. In fact, before its problematizing in the late 1970s, Afro-American literary scholars believed that " 'blackness' existed as some mythical and mystical absolute, an entity so subtle, sublime, and unspeakable that only the 'very black' racial initiate could ever begin to trace its contours, let alone force it to utter its darkest secrets" (45). If the indisputable measure of black intellectual integrity had been one's desire to articulate to other worshipful converts the truths of a mythical, unknowable blackness, it has evolved in elite academic circles into the capacity to decode its systems of cultural signification without exhibiting more than a trace of romanticized or strategic essentialism.

According to Gates, integrity connotes the absence of violation and corruption, the preservation of an initial wholeness. However, when critical integrity shifts from a desire of "very black" initiates to represent a rich, unsullied blackness to playing by the rules of a semiotic game with a combination of will, skill, and resources, the race of the inquiring intellectual becomes an at least theoretically inessential component. Along with increased opportunities within elite institutions and hard-won prestige for a variety of black discourses often came self-doubt and suspicions that black

individuals had profited from white liberal guilt. Accompanying essential-
ism's delegitimation was the often mindless search for, and reification of,
(credentialed) black bodies. Out of such a confusing time emerged the
contemporary black public intellectual, desperate to find spaces where well-
educated, race-conscious, and media-friendly folks could go to be black,
blue, and relatively free to produce writings in which race centrally, un-
problematically mattered.

In his analysis of black scholarly responsibilities and audiences, Gates
argues:

> We write, it seems to me, primarily for other critics of literature. Through
> shared theoretical presuppositions, the arduous process of "cultural transla-
> tion," if not resolved, is most certainly not hindered. To maintain yet go
> beyond this split text milieu is our curse and, of course, our challenge. (56)

Black scholars with intellectual integrity reflect self-consciously on the
"challenge" of reading and creating double-voiced texts that are fundamentally "split" by their concerns with (among other competing interests)
white and black readers and racial and (inter)national impulses.

In a more recent revisitation of the subject of interracial integrity, Gates
invites us again to consider both the continuing significance of race and the
obstacles to discursive sincerity in racial relations typically marked by
suspicion and strategic misrepresentation. Gates revisits this keyword in
an April 7, 1997, Newsweek article, "Unchained Melody," whose title
references, among other things, the Righteous Brothers' blue-eyed soul
classic as a prelude to discussing Steven Spielberg's Amistad, a filmic
exploration of a slave ship uprising and the legal trials that ensued after the
mutinous Africans reach American shores. According to the article, in
addition to Hollywood players Maya Angelou, Spike Lee, and Quincy
Jones, Cornel West and Gates served as consultants for the film. The
scholar who brought Afro-American literary criticism kicking and screaming into the poststructuralist age, forcing his colleagues to recognize "blackness" and "race" as highly contested social constructs, responds to a question about Spielberg's racial qualifications by saying of "the 'Amistad'
script: 'There is no doubt that it reeks of integrity'" (72).

What, precisely, is Gates up to here? Is he acting as the master('s)
mouthpiece, as more than a few of his critics have claimed? (In that regard,
it is difficult not to read Gates's comments about radical black activists'

rejection of James Baldwin in Early's *collection* Lure and Loathing—*"if someone has anointed a black intellectual, rest assured that others are busily constructing his tumbril" (160)—as partly self-referential.) Is he operating as a verbally adept black trickster who is fully cognizant of the controversy caused by white appropriation of Afro-Americanist forms and cultural materials, including* The Color Purple, Spielberg's *earlier foray into black subjects? Or does Gates's choice of words reflect the burdens of addressing a "split" audience whose white members he expects can take comfort in his confirmation of the possibility that they can deal respectfully with black texts, and whose black members may take solace in his ironic use of the word "reeks"? It is difficult to imagine that someone whose scholarly work is so concerned with black language games and the textual consequences of interracial audience expectations could connect "reeks" and "integrity" accidentally.*

Of course, I could be overreading here, taking far too seriously a throwaway line hastily articulated by an incredibly accomplished—and busy—man for whom Newsweek *inquiries are pleasant though minor distractions rather than potentially career-making opportunities. Indeed, it may even be foolish to compare scholarly and black public intellectual uses even of the same keyword, because they seem generally to represent divergent discursive universes.*

What is clear is that—Gates's wide-ranging knowledge notwithstanding—Spielberg didn't use his services because the Harvard professor and the other black celebrity consultants mentioned in Newsweek *possess singular scholarly insight into the complexities of the Amistad affair. Rather, the endorsements of the project by Gates and the others serve as* certificates of authenticity *reminiscent of the prefatory testimonies by famous white abolitionists that verified and legitimized the formerly enslaved (black) hand and mind that produced the attached slave narratives. Gates cogently explored such structural and ideological issues as early as* 1979 *in* The Reconstruction of Instruction, *the paradigm-shifting Yale black lit-crit manifesto.*

Its revisitation, through the terms of the emerging commentary on the Spielberg film, could possibly occasion an investigation of the nation's lingering sense of the incompatibility between blackness and intellectual expressivity. What relationship obtains, if any, between antebellum doubts about the authenticity and integrity of black slave narratives, on the one hand, and, on the other, the post–Great Society endorsement of Spielberg by the point guard and general manager of Harvard's so-called Dream Team? The black public intellectual phenomenon poses a host of provocative questions whose answers may be of little interest to its mainstream readership, but whose pursuit could prove compelling for those engaged in traditional scholarly activities.

Integrity, for the Afro-American in interracial settings, is virtually impossible to define, defend, or achieve, a fact that I began to understand only toward the end of my prep school years.

On the eve of my graduation from Governor Dummer Academy in June 1976, I got inebriated, to use the word my mother employed in jest to dignify her destructive habit. I got inebriated often during my junior and senior years: in my friend Mark's room, listening to the classical music that he said calmed him, but whose grating violins and jerky wind instruments disturbed my untrained ears and fragile nerves; on darkened, well-manicured playing fields whose plush grass muffled the white noises of Saturday-night school mixers; outside unfamiliar, dimly lit stone and brick buildings before confronting the bass and treble, the joy and pain, of black prep school parties; in the Black Brotherhood meeting room, with puffs of reefer smoke rising slowly above hushed giggles, incense, and unsteady hands trying to wave them out of existence; and when I felt overwhelmed by my fascination with Joan's joyous laugh, her bouncy walk, her sweet smile, her sea green eyes, her short, stylish blonde hair.

I attended GDA from September 1973 to June 1976, a period of still-expanding national commitment to promoting racial, gendered, and socioeconomic diversity in, among other places, elite institutions of learning. During my sophomore and junior years, I held my own in classrooms with white sons and daughters of stable middle-class families and of gaudy opulence who'd had far superior elementary and middle school training and whose presence at schools such as GDA was more a birthright than, as in my case, a virtual miracle. I learned how to eat with a knife and fork, what shepherd's pie and London broil were, and why white people flipped their heads abruptly to one side when trying to reposition hair tickling their cheeks or blocking their vision. And I learned to comb my hair in

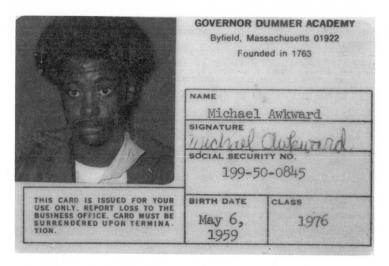

GOVERNOR DUMMER ACADEMY
Byfield, Massachusetts 01922
Founded in 1763

NAME
Michael Awkward

SIGNATURE

SOCIAL SECURITY NO.
199-50-0845

THIS CARD IS ISSUED FOR YOUR USE ONLY. REPORT LOSS TO THE BUSINESS OFFICE. CARD MUST BE SURRENDERED UPON TERMINA-TION.

BIRTH DATE
May 6, 1959

CLASS
1976

The author's prep school student identification card, issued September 1973

front of bathroom mirrors using an Afro pick graced with resonant 1960s symbols—a peace sign and a tightly clenched black fist—without its curved, broken strands falling carelessly into toothpaste-cluttered sinks and inspiring the whiteboy wisecrack "Who's been combing their pubic hair again?"

Among other things, Governor Dummer was a laboratory in which I was forced to learn some of the meanings of race. In part because nothing I'd experienced during the previous six years of my largely segregated existence had prepared me for such a task, I didn't obsess over individual whites' baleful attitudes—the doctor's son who requested in a jive whiteboy's imitation of black vernacular that his black dorm mates call him Reverend Leroy, or the famous athlete's grandson who insisted that his family was footing the bill for my tuition. Instead, I spent a good deal of time contemplating a more familiar subject: the pain blacks caused each other. The unnecessary hurt, the pointless squabbling, the nasty debates about the aesthetic superiority of specific eye, skin, and hair colors and textures, the bloody battles over the supremacy of equally impoverished, equally crime-, drug-, and roach-infested neighborhoods.

Men's blinding, bludgeoning, and battering of black females they claimed in their bodacious discourse as their women.

Because I came of age in the sixties, I was well aware of some of what were, for me, the incontestably appealing aspects of blackness. Our spectrum of pigmentational differences, despite its primarily violent origins and many black folks' persistent aesthetic preference for near whiteness. The surging expressiveness of our forms of religion, music, and dance. The twists and turns the English language took in our heads and our mouths. Our stylish, practiced, stoic cool. But I needed to develop an understanding of blackness that encompassed both the strengths and the flaws, the beauty and the ugliness, of our traditions, our behavior, our modes of living and interacting among ourselves and with others.

Having been a firsthand witness to so much black self-destructiveness, the self-aggrandizing myths that accompanied 1960s black nationalism did not sit well with me. Before I entered prep school, I lived through three junior high school years in which I escaped the certain sting of contact with my putative brothers. To avoid their injurious touch, I sped past immaculate churches, stores, schools, and houses adorned with representations of Jesus in various stages of His sacrificial life. These structures were peopled with Italian Americans who, because of or despite their own history of bloody internecine battle, appeared to shake their heads in disbelief in response to our suicidal squabbles as they fingered their worn rosaries and wondered whether descendants of savages and slaves could indeed be incorporated into the cottony fabric of the country they themselves loved so dearly.

I couldn't accept the notion that white racism was the sole or primary cause of black maladjustment in the 1960s and 1970s, because doing so would have meant that I also had to see it as the source of my mother's alcoholism. Accepting that view would have left me with virtually no hope that my mother would one day overcome her addiction. If racism caused her drinking, and racism was both mutable and the quintessential immovable force, then she would never be free. I didn't expect to influence American race relations in any significant way. However, I did hope one day to understand her problems well enough to offer her the gift of an eye-opening interpretation of her life that would, like magic words, liberate our family.

My cohort—Curtis, Darryl, and I—was introduced to the Brother-hood on our first evening at Governor Dummer soon after I'd vomited the contents of my nervous stomach on the lawn of the faculty member who'd picked us up from the airport when he'd stopped at home to retrieve some papers before depositing us on campus. After we got settled in our rooms in Perkins, a freshman and sophomore boys' dormitory that faced the gymnasium, we walked outside, turning the campus maps we'd found on the desks of our rooms in a variety of directions in a vain effort to figure out the location of the cafeteria. As we talked excitedly about what we had done since we'd seen each other a month earlier at the ABC orientation, three black males slowly approached us.

When they'd completed their wary scrutiny of us, indistinguish-able in its form from the slow, hard, contemptuous urban scoping of potential rivals I'd thought I'd escaped, the husky, slightly bow-legged man positioned in the middle of the trio spoke first.

"So y'all the new Negroes, huh? Well, I'm Kenny. This here's Bill," he said, pointing to his dark-skinned companion, "and the big fella is Sid." With his teeth clenched, posture exaggeratedly rigid, and an air of feigned stuffy formality, he said, "We're pleased to make your acquaintance."

He stuck out his large right hand at a surprised Curtis, who, sensing that this was an important, perhaps even defining, moment, cautiously raised his own while his downcast head signaled his hesi-tance and distrust.

"Don't be giving me that lame, limp, whiteboy shit. What's your name, boy?"

"Curtis."

"Well, Rookie, let me show you how the brothers do it." He grabbed Curtis's right wrist and slowly, patiently, led him through a series of hand and finger movements that concluded with a snap. "Either that, or you give me a pound, you hear me?"

"A pound of what?"

"A pound, boy. Let's show 'em, Sid."

Holding his right hand high above his head, Sid smiled and waited for Kenny to place his right upper arm firmly against his body. At that point Sid—his own right hand extended, its fingers barely touching each other—brought his hand down quickly while Kenny raised his a few inches, their meeting producing a deep, rich smack that seemed to reverberate back from the gymnasium walls facing us.

"C'mon. Y'all ready to go eat?"

I lagged slightly behind, a bit startled at the elaborate hand grasping, palm slapping, and finger snapping I'd just witnessed. Neither the North Philly boys in my junior high school class nor brothers in my neighborhood were much given to handshaking or greetings of any kind beyond a blasé, perfunctory "Hey" or "What's up." During junior high, where my most challenging task was literally to survive black male rage, I envied the girls' uninhibited display of their emotions in general and of their affection for one another in particular and tried to understand why such displays—the kissing, touching, caressing, hugging, and hand-holding that often took place between them—were unacceptable for men.

Consequently, I was intrigued by the Brotherhood's complex sequence of synchronized digital movements, an at once playful and extremely serious manifestation of black male bonding that, like all rituals, had rigid rules. With a fervor I typically reserved for working on my hoop moves, I practiced the shake every chance I got.

I had to perfect a variety of soulful salutations: the seemingly simple pound, which requires the correct combination of angle, finger placement, and velocity to produce the proper, loud, claplike sound; the five-step Brotherhood shake, which concluded with a snap and the extension of our right hands above our heads; and five on the black hand side, which, because it entailed smacking bone against delicate bone, necessitated my finding a partner without a sadistic streak. Learning these greetings was like learning a new language, or at the very least to communicate more expansively in my native tongue.

With these greetings came other racialized demands. During that first walk, our new acquaintances informed us of the names and functions of the buildings we were passing—the gymnasium, the bowl field where the varsity football team played its home games, the library (which also contained a number of classrooms), the little red schoolhouse, the girl's dormitory. Also, they told us of the Brotherhood table, which was located in the back of the cafeteria, where all of the fellows broke bread together. All, that is, except "that honkey-lovin' oreo James," as Sid referred to him.

As the six of us entered the cafeteria, I was overcome with fear of this expansive sea of ghostly pale, ruddy red, and tanned faces. There were no available seats at any of the tables on the right side of the cafeteria except for the table in the back, at which a lone dark-skinned young man sat picking at the food on the plate before him. When he heard Kenny's loud "Yo, Nat," he looked up, waved, and smiled in our direction.

After we got our food and drinks, we headed toward Nat's table. As we were introduced to him, Curtis, Darryl, and I stood motion-less, each trying to remember all of the stages of the Brotherhood shake we'd just learned in case we were called on to demonstrate it. Fortunately, Nat remained seated and merely nodded at us, which allowed us to sit down and start eating. Before I'd swallowed the third tentative nibble of food I was able to direct toward my still-queasy stomach, Kenny said, "This is where we sit. All the time. It's the Brotherhood table. You hear? It's about the only thing we got here, you hear me?"

Periodically, teachers, students, and even the plump, red-faced cafeteria manager came over to the table to greet the veteran and the new members of the Brotherhood. The veterans were polite but looked embarrassed, offering monosyllabic answers to simple ques-tions about vacations, the first football practice, and class schedules with so little enthusiasm that all of these interlopers left quickly.

"White boys don't leave you alone even when you tryin' to eat!"

During several meals in September of my first year at Governor Dummer, the veterans informed my cohort of the Brotherhood's initiatory ritual wherein the veterans stole out of their dormitories under cover of night to douse the sleeping rookies with water. I didn't take the threats seriously, in part because the older boys' participation would require their violation of curfew, for which they could be punished with a month of study hall, the rescission of off-campus weekend privileges, or disciplinary probation.

On that late September night of my watery initiation, I didn't hear the squeaking hinges of my door and the whispered laughter or feel the vibrations of three large males tiptoeing on my uncarpeted floor with two heavy trash cans. In fact, I didn't fully awaken even after they yelled with mischievous glee as the second cold, clear wave of water slapped my face, my neck, my hair, my groin, my torso, and my legs. Apparently, the yell aroused my dorm's two senior proctors, who chased the interlopers and threatened to pursue disciplinary action against them.

After their futile chase, the proctors came to my room, saw my soaked face, hair, sheets, pillow, and pajamas, as well as the can the veterans forgot in their haste to make a quick exit, and asked me how I was doing. While they huddled together in front of my window trying to devise a course of action, I stripped off the wet clothes, dried myself quickly, and put on a fresh T-shirt and pair of underwear. As they escorted me down the hall to the room of a boy who'd gone home a few days earlier after breaking a leg during football practice, I could see parts of the stark white faces of several of my hall mates, standing silently behind half-opened doors, shaking in disbelief.

In response to this attack, my cohort boycotted the Brotherhood table for three days. On the morning after the incident, as we sat by ourselves at the other end of the cafeteria, watching them watching us, Curtis sought to cheer me by demonstrating the sounds, kicks, and chops he would employ from his repertoire of purported black belt karate moves to "fuck 'em up," and Darryl, the most level-headed member of my group, advised me to put my bureau against my door to keep them out as he'd done.

That evening, as I struggled to block Brotherhood access to my room, I recalled a frightening winter night before I was old enough to go to school. While my siblings and I sat huddled together on our bed, my mother and her lover, Mr. Cisco, pushed a huge, cherry-finished bureau against the double doors of our two-room apartment to keep out my father. Overcome by what was apparently an alcohol-induced sense of parental obligation, he banged repeatedly on the door, shaking the dresser's attached mirror so violently I was sure it would drop from its moorings and break into a million invisible pieces that would pierce our eyeballs, nostrils, ears, and hearts.

For the first time, I understood the anguish in my mother's voice when she spoke of his brutality, like when she had to cover the small bodies of her four children with her own as he methodically flicked a hatful of sharp-edged steel bottle tops at us. Drunkenly, almost desperately, he banged on the door and screamed, "I want to see my kids, Anne! Let me see my kids! Come on! Just let me see my kids! Please. Please."

After thirty minutes, I heard his slow footsteps descend the stairs and his loud, anguished sobbing.

Each time I moved my dresser, I recalled my terror and my father's unseen tears. After a week, I stopped barricading my door. Two weeks later, the Brotherhood struck again, dousing me with filthy water from a single trash can when they couldn't get into Darryl's room. The proctors didn't bother to chase them this time, nor did they inquire about my condition. Making no effort to suppress their yawns and sleep-deprived stretching, they told me that I should turn my mattress over and try to get back to sleep.

The Brotherhood never fully recovered in my estimation after this second soaking. Even after I eventually returned to the table and began to hang out with the veterans again, go to parties with them again, and even grow to like them somewhat, I never forgave them. More important, I never again trusted them, never was more than highly ambivalent about the perceptions of black unity that empowered them to treat me in such a manner, left me with seemingly no means of retaliation, and silenced an administration that, had there been white students involved, would certainly have responded with serious disciplinary action.

During my first two years at Governor Dummer, except for the annual Ping-Pong tournament and Saturday evening movies, members of the Brotherhood rarely attended school social functions and were never invited to any of the off-campus weekend parties about whose wild antics others would whisper on Mondays when the faculty was out of earshot. At times, being confined within a protective black male circle minimized any need I might otherwise have felt for a larger social orbit. Eventually, however, spending the great bulk of my moments of leisure with the same small set of people, talking about the same things, and hearing the same jokes from people who constantly derided me began to wear on my nerves.

Part of my difficulty stemmed from my youth and relative inexperience, which meant that I had virtually no power to determine the direction of Brotherhood conversations and activities. One such activity was a Saturday afternoon excursion to Boston during the spring of my sophomore year. After the hour-long bus ride on Route 1, the veterans set out immediately for the red-light district and insisted that we stop at a seedy-looking place called the Top Cat. The Top Cat was a small establishment with a large stage illuminated by a single flashing spotlight, a darkened area with a number of chairs set around small, square tables, and a nondescript bar behind which stood a huge black man with a slicked-back hairdo that made him look like Sammy Davis on steroids.

As soon as we stepped inside, a thin, raven-haired white woman approached us with an exaggerated switch, a face masked in makeup, and directions to two tables in front of the stage. A few minutes after we'd been served drinks, we heard a drumroll followed by a few recorded bars of the sort of campy forties music I heard only on television variety shows like Red Skelton's or Ed Sullivan's or Dean Martin's. A plump, attractive, middle-aged black woman who'd been talking to the bartender when we arrived slithered between the maroon curtains and onto the stage. Her hair was unkempt, her makeup hastily applied, and her limbs and torso were encased in stereotypical stripper paraphernalia: long black gloves, garter belts, a red-and-black feather boa, black fishnet stockings, red high-heeled shoes, and a red teddy.

For a fourteen-year-old virgin boy who went to bed praying for sexless wet dreams, the show was utterly unappealing. Seeing someone old enough to be my mother shake her huge hips, clumsily pull off her gloves and garter belts in conjunction with the crash of cymbals, and exaggerate the wrinkles on her ass bored and, finally, disgusted me. So did the emaciated white waitress—her face heavily powdered and rouged, her eyes underneath a flapping pair of false lashes as bloodshot and sad as any I'd ever seen—who offered three times to show me a good time for twenty dollars. So, too, did the veterans' lurid smiles, their feigned consideration of the waitress's offer, and the delighted, double and triple fives they shared when the stripper bent down to pick up the silver coin one of them had thrown onstage to reveal the crack of her ass.

As we finally left the Top Cat, and just when I believed that the brisk wind had begun to cleanse me of the smoke and smut, one of the veterans proposed that rather than go see Linda Blair's head spin in *The Exorcist* as we'd planned, we go instead to witness Linda Lovelace's reportedly incredible feats of fellatio in *Deep Throat*.

"Nonononono," I shouted, "we said we was going to see *The Exorcist*. And nobody gonna let me into an X-rated movie, anyway."

"They let you into the Top Cat, didn't they?"

"I ain't gonna go. I'm not."

"You just scared, you little faggot. Scared to look at some white pussy."

"I ain't going."

"Alright, already, Rookie. Let's go see that crazy, possessed little white bitch."

This was my first—probably my only—resounding victory in the war of wills I waged against the veterans. I fought not because of a precocious objection to pornography or sage cognition of Lovelace's subsequently much-discussed victimization during the filming of the movie that briefly made her as famous as Marilyn Chambers and Long Dong Silver. Rather, I fought because after my first exposure to the sex trade—to the waitress's melancholy and the matronly stripper's wrinkles—I was afraid that more lurid sights would leave indelible images in my mind that would rival, and eventually come to replace, the comforting vision I conjured up each night of gently bracing my ninth-grade love Alannah's chin with my right thumb as I kissed her.

I longed for an at least temporary respite from the rigid rules of the Brotherhood, which encased me in a dark, sticky cocoon to which I

sometimes clung with equal parts devotion, nostalgia, and desperation. I lived a dual existence: like all of the other students, I toiled in
the library and classrooms, the courts and the fields, the greens and
diamonds of and for GDA. But I was never able to catch the full spirit
of the school—its vaunted traditions, the intangible sentiments it
represented for others that helped to foster group cohesion and
unity—or develop any sense of institutional faith and devotion.

Despite my academic and athletic successes, during my sophomore and junior years I remained on the school's periphery. I
developed no close friendships with anyone outside the Brotherhood, spent hardly any time contemplating my future, and learned
nothing but what my teachers taught me in my classes. Frequently, I
felt overwhelmed with resentment: of the veterans, who demanded
that I live a racially monastic existence; of the school, which seemed
not to care about the intraracial pressures my cohort faced; and of
the ABC program, which had not prepared me for this socially stagnant, fettered, segregated half-life. My fear of inner-city black male
violence was replaced by a fear of ostracism in response to any effort
to establish wider social contacts; my junior high school social discomfort with black girls was replaced by black prep party dance
floor dread and by stultifying and reciprocal white-girl indifference;
and my dysfunctional family was replaced by a dictatorial male clan
that allowed me no room to deviate from its racial script.

Though I was used to the verbal banter and battles of black boyhood, the capping, sounding, and signifying, the Brotherhood's text
consisted of a string of unanswerable insults that, despite the surface
of levity with which they were issued, had an air of disconcerting
seriousness. Instead of capping on each other's skin color, stank
breath, cradle-robbing, tough-fucking, butt-ugly mamas, rolling-
stone, poor-as-dirt papas, and athletic and intellectual deficiencies—
subjects I was used to and could occasionally work to my advantage—the veterans condemned my cohort members for what they
perceived to be our insufficient ideological and cultural blackness.

Whereas black inner-city gangs tested their members' loyalty by
demanding violent displays of hard masculinity, the Black Brotherhood measured affiliation primarily in terms of individual ascrip-
tions to rigid codes of black behavior. The veterans stitched together

for our use on rich New England soil an isolationist philosophy that protected us from soul-snatching assimilation while it projected a view of blackness that was incredibly limited and limiting.

To fully internalize Brotherhood necessitated that we embrace the philosophies and extant practices of Black Power from which it derived. However, as I was growing up, I'd barely heard Black Power rhetoric over the thump of balls against wood, steel, and cement; over the bloodcurdling screams of love gone wrong and of black males' brutalizing of one another; over old folks' unconvincing nostalgia for the pre–civil rights South; over the sudden snap of sealed liquor bottle tops twisted open just before the rhythmic rush of whiskey, wine, and rum.

Though I embraced little of the nationalist rhetoric of the time, I was a ghetto child who recognized the binding ties of race, of culture, of sameness. When Darryl closed his eyes and rocked his head and torso and tapped his feet as he hummed along with the one 45 he'd brought with him from the Bronx, the Persuaders' "Thin Line between Love and Hate"; when Kenny waxed poetic about the wonders of Larry Graham's bass playing as a member of Sly and the Family Stone; when Curtis asked me to teach him to plait his hair; when Bill sported pimp hats, Kangol caps, wide-lapelled jackets, and outdated fly shirts at parties; when Sid placed his face menacingly close to mine, angled his head from side to side, and said in a singsong voice, "Know what I mean, motherfucker"—we were speaking from a common, if not always comforting, cultural understanding. At such moments, our interactions manifested a rhythm and rhyme, a dis and dat, a tit for tat that was familiar, absolving me of the responsibility of explaining or justifying my black looks, music, or other aesthetic preferences, or of asking others to produce their justifications.

What I resisted was the Brotherhood's insistence that familiar sounds and sights were the *only* acceptable ones for blacks in this intimidating interracial setting. Though on several occasions I heard the veterans marvel at the speed and grace with which the varsity women's team played lacrosse, when they saw Curtis and me on the front lawn of our dorm trying to learn how properly to turn the Y-shaped stick so that the net trapped the hard rubber ball instead of bouncing it off our heads, shoulders, and knees, they chided us for playing "that whiteboy sport." When my introductory Columbia Record Club shipment included the greatest hits of Bread and the Carpenters along with Barry White, Bloodstone, Harold Melvin and the Blue Notes, and the Ebonys, the older boys were deeply disturbed that I'd purchased "whiteboy music." When Curtis or Darryl or I chose to sit with white dorm mates or classmates at lunch, the Brotherhood insisted that we wanted to be white.

At times, the pressure they exerted on us to carry on the tradition of principled black segregation was nearly unbearable. Every transgression against their laws they saw as a rejection of Brotherhood, of them, of black people's legitimate rage against the machine of whiteness. With each edict, each criticism, each condemnation, I felt more and more inclined to fight, and less and less willing to navigate our common white institutional structure in the manner they proposed.

My fighting instincts were stirred when I witnessed the truly disconcerting hypocrisy of the veterans. For example, on the very day that he castigated me for having breakfast with one of my white dorm mates, Sid spent nearly a half hour during assembly lovingly caressing the ends of the long, lustrous brown hair of the school's most attractive girl, who'd draped her tresses carelessly behind her seat. And when the new day student whom they nicknamed "Chesty Morgan" sat with a friend of hers at our table, the veterans nearly bumped heads trying to sneak peeks at her cleavage. Thus we learned that Brotherhood sanctions against fraternization didn't include transracial lust. But if lust was acceptable—if it was permissible, in the discourse of that bygone day, to find the white man's woman desirable enough to make proud, princely black selves look as foolish as the Three Stooges—why not friendship? Why not affection? Camaraderie? Why not love, even?

My cohort asked these questions, over and over, rephrasing them continually so as to slip the oreo yoke. We got no intelligible answers. "That's the way of the world, Rookie." " 'Cause of what they did to us, what they still doing to us." " 'Cause getting in the white woman's pants ain't the same as letting her get into your head, fool."

Unsatisfied with these pat, predictable responses, the rookies rebelled. After breaking his leg in a bicycle accident, Darryl stopped attending black prep school parties, ate at the Brotherhood table only sporadically, and spent a good deal of time with James, the exiled ex-brother. And when we could, Curtis and I got to the cafeteria a half hour before the veterans arrived, and ate our meals at as leisurely a pace as we pleased with whomever we pleased.

I didn't reject Brotherhood wholeheartedly. I didn't give up the sounds, the parties, the intense, joyous shit talking during pickup basketball games, the communal lusting over Thelma, J. J.'s so-fine sister on *Good Times,* my nigger bop, the sense of belonging to something larger than myself in an environment in which I was never sure I belonged. But I did try to carve out some space in which I could improvise a bit, to look at the world I was inhabiting in a broader manner than Brotherhood condoned, and to find appropriate avenues for individual expression.

Some time before I arrived, Governor Dummer demonstrated its sensitivity to the social, political, and cultural needs of its black students by recognizing the Black Brotherhood as a legitimate student organization. The most significant measure of the administration's sensitivity was its assignment of faculty drivers to chauffeur us seven Saturdays a year to the various, invariably hard-to-find stops on the black prep school party circuit. In addition to enduring our clashing cacophony of colognes and carefully rationed hair care products on the way to the dances and ignoring the scent of sweat, wine, and weed when they drove us home, these faculty members were faced with the task of finding some cheap, uncrowded diner in which they could pass the time reading a good book or grading a set of papers while we partied.

During my sophomore year especially, these parties were thrilling. I got to see Ernie and Marty, friends from my ninth- and sixth-grade classes, respectively, who lived in private houses with other ABC students and their adult supervisors and attended public high schools in Hamilton and Andover, respectively. Also, these parties provided occasions for me to experience an egotist's joy of dressing up, a small child's anticipation of a big event, and a furloughed prisoner's thrill of temporary escape from near constant lockup and intense institutional scrutiny.

I didn't need to be cool or tough, have money, or be accused of thinking I was cute to party hearty at these events; all I had to do was be black and blue, diligent enough not to lose my scholarship, and uninhibited enough to shake my booty rhythmically for three or four minutes at a time, five or six times a night. We boogied in huge, darkened, acoustically spectacular rooms illuminated by strobe lights and glistening disco balls that exaggerated our knee-bending, torso-wiggling, arm-bopping, shoulder-popping revelry. The flickering lights bounced rhythmically off of our tan and brown bodies, emphasized the angularity of our dancing, and disguised the embarrassing moments when our efforts to do steps we had not quite mastered made us stumble or threw us off beat.

We were black boys and black girls from urban centers across the United States, the vast majority of whom were dealing for the first time with the shocks of homesickness and radical racial difference. Temporarily liberated, we strutted and pimped, switched and pro-filed, bumped and grinded in time with funky bass lines and boss rhythms and rhymes that the white people who dominated our daily lives didn't know anything about, didn't care anything about, didn't feel at home with.

We didn't all come to those parties just to boogie down, blow our whistles, and, if we were both smooth enough and lucky enough, make out with some sweet honey or fly guy; certainly, I know I didn't. Before I went to prep school, I hadn't danced any-where, in fact, except in the privacy of my apartment, when I tried to learn the latest moves from my more socially adept brother and sisters. Like an uninhibited shower singer away from translucent soap bubbles and the soft splash of strings of water against porcelain tiles and naked, goose-bumpy flesh, I felt a shy self-consciousness overtake me outside my apartment.

But prep school partying wasn't just about jamming to the Ohio Players' "Skin Tight" or B. T. Express's "Do It 'Til You're Satisfied" or James Brown's "The Payback," or slow dragging to New Birth's "It's Been a Long Time" or Latimore's "Let's Straighten It Out" or

Smokey's "Baby Come Close." Beyond the hip shaking and grinding was a desire—a need—to inhabit a familiar, if not wholly comfortable, milieu where we could reacquaint ourselves with what it felt like to be something other than a spectacle, something other than an embodiment of phenotypical and cultural difference.

For three hours, once a month, we knew what it felt like to be beneficiaries of privilege we strove mightily to believe was free from the burdens of a bloody racial history. At those times, we sought to be comfortable inhabitors of an ivy-lined, polished-hardwood-floored space where our music, our varied but not wholly dissimilar ways of speaking, our stylish strolls, our head-turned, eyes-rolling, hands-on-hips attitude, our fly guy and girl threads, our anxieties about whether the heat would shrink or unstraighten our dos, were de rigueur.

In those lily-white places temporarily overtaken by the sight and sounds of jungle boogie, we formed a small, migratory nation under a common groove, a chocolate city whose citizens were desperate for the chance to dance, drink, smoke, flirt, and otherwise deny our way out of the constrictions in which the social experiment of integration had placed us. The beat, the funk, the smooth and rhythmic grooves were the sounds of home for us, and we proudly claimed them. In fact, we luxuriated in them, bumping, stomping, and sliding in settings far more luscious than those many of us were used to—the steamy, smelly, blue-light basements and the cramped, carpeted living rooms whose plastic-covered furniture had to be pushed aside to give brothers and sisters the space to get up and get down.

But the hypnotic effects of flashing lights and anonymous misses in skintight britches began to wear off toward the middle of my junior year, when attending these parties began primarily to signal—and, in fact, to increase—my growing sense of alienation. Although I continued to visit, the chocolate city had come to seem more dreamlike than real, insubstantial rather than comfortably familiar, a remnant, like Atlantis or unearthed dinosaur bones, of a long-buried life. Having made the rounds of prep school parties, recognized that they did not yield a sufficient emotional payoff, and acknowledged that without significant drug and / or alcohol inducement, I'd never be able to view public dancing as a form of psychic or physical release, I knew I needed more to sustain me than the funk and flash of blackness.

I longed for something more fulfilling than dances and, on rare occasions, desperate gropings with similarly sad and lonely girls whose names I could barely remember and whose faces I wouldn't have recognized in the light of day. I wanted the opportunity to fight through my shyness, to strive for something more emotionally satisfying than monastic, lovestruck romanticism. The combination of inebriation, black noise, movement, and studied adolescent inscrutability became greatly distressing.

I understand now that these parties weren't designed to foster intimacy. White administrators permitted them because like black slaves' New Year's celebrations with free-flowing alcohol, our parties served as an effective means of social control. They kept us woozy if not happy, mentally and / or physically exhausted from the effort to squeeze all the pleasure we could out of these brief moments, and inspired by a freedom of institutionally sanctioned cultural expression denied us except on such occasions. We filled pervasively white spaces with black noise in the hope that its thumping presence alone could ward off evil spirits and prop up our fatigued, undernourished souls.

The Brotherhood's members dealt with our pronounced isolation by being as drunk, high, and unruly as we could at every party we attended. During my junior year, we developed a reputation: the crazy, get-high niggers from Governor Dummer. Thus stigmatized, we played our parts effectively, stumbling into parties with our bops, chin rubbing, and stylish scoping working overtime, exuding as much badass male attitude as we could.

I never was comfortable with our reputation—I'd spent years in Philly conscientiously avoiding nearly everything that could associate me with such nonsense—but I fell into these behaviors because given the force of Brotherhood strictures against interracial intimacy of any sort, I had no other means of achieving the sort of emotional life I craved. I had no girl sending me perfumed letters and waiting anxiously for me to return home, no family close enough to bring me bundles of food or to come get me on weekends, no friend with a car or knowledge of the world who'd take me to the movies once a month.

By the time the veterans graduated, I no longer felt that my racial identity was tied to my willingness to subject myself to these unpleasant experiences. In September of my senior year, in the middle of a party we'd driven for more than an hour to get to, I recognized that the strain of approaching girls to whom I knew I wouldn't say more than five words, of feigning pleasure as I danced stiffly and wondered what my partners' refusal to look at me signified, was not relieved by anything approaching compensatory pleasure. And as the Isley Brothers' "Fight the Power" testified above the rhythmic claps, coordinated stomping, and exaggerated mirth in the room, I vowed never again to attend one of these parties.

Subsequently I either stayed on campus on Saturday nights or, on occasion, went into Newburyport with Mark. When there was an on-campus mixer, we'd round up Steve or Chip or Ike. Though these mixers—with their overwhelmingly white music and crowd—proved distressing to me in ways black parties never did, they had the benefit of affording me easy escape whenever I tired of them.

Invitational Weekend was GDA's big annual social bash and was open to all students of the school who managed to find dates. Because I was on the Social Committee that planned the event during my senior year, and because I wanted to know what it felt like to take part in at least one major school event before I graduated, I invited a black girl I'd met at a mixer between our two schools and with whom I danced to a local white band's butchered version of B. B. King's blues classic "The Thrill Is Gone."

I approached the Invitational with an acute sense of dread because I'd have to spend almost forty-eight hours with a girl I barely knew. For a shy, romantically inexperienced sixteen-year-old boy, that was problematic enough. However, my situation was further complicated by the fact that I'd finally acknowledged to myself that I was hopelessly infatuated with Joan, a day student whom I'd initially gotten to know while she waited for her rides home and I frittered away my football-less fall afternoons after a routine physical revealed to the school's administration that I was legally blind in my right eye. For at least a month before I'd met Karen, evidence of my feelings for Joan multiplied—I wrote songs about her, doodled her name in my French textbook, talked about her with my friends, hoped to see her face at lunch or as we rushed through the center of the campus between classes, and experienced pangs of jealousy when I learned that she was going to be someone else's date at the Invitational.

When I wasn't reveling in the joy and frustration of my all-consuming desire, I tried to understand my attraction. Was it merely a function of a human need that I had to find some other in whom I could invest myself emotionally? If so, why hadn't I felt similarly for some other GDA girl, or anyone, really, since ninth grade? Did I like Joan because she was white, or despite that obvious fact? Did my attraction to her mean that I'd come to prefer whiteness aesthetically? In taking someone white seriously enough to develop intense feelings for her, was I committing a sin against Brotherhood, against sisters who bemoaned the fact that, as their unscientific surveys proved, successful black men preferred white women? Against my people? Was it unblack to confess vulnerability to someone who resembled a Shirley Temple doll and not Bojangles Robinson's apparently neglected black daughter, or a fifteen-year-old Doris Day with fatter cheeks and a much more wicked sense of humor? And given that one of my mother's greatest fears was that prep school would cause me to lose my connection to my family's and my people's bloody history, would I be betraying her if, like Jermaine Jackson, I told her I'd found that girl, and she looked like Joan?

Whatever else motivated me, I invited Karen to the Invitational in large part because I was afraid of the intensity of my feelings for Joan. Like my trio of bikini-clad *Jet* magazine pinups, which I hid in the back of my closet before she arrived, Karen was to be my ebony shield against the temptations of white flesh. When she arrived for a second time at Governor Dummer, this time escorted by her parents, she had anxieties and an agenda that I willed myself not to consider because I knew, whatever it was, it clashed dramatically with my own. For her, I may have been a means of spending a couple days out of the watchful eyes of overprotective parents, a meaningless tryst, a source of mere flattery, or a possibly smart and industrious black boy with Po-tential. Whatever her expectations, they seemed to magnify what may have been her general shyness and understandable discomfort in the situation, making my perpetuation of emotional fraud even more difficult.

I knew that by inviting Karen, I was acting out Brotherhood's racialist script. But adopting any other course of action—confessing my feelings to Joan or letting this opportunity for black coupling slip away—felt beyond my control. Under different conditions, Karen and I might have gotten to know and maybe even like each other. But because our meeting and uncomfortable time together were so tryingly colored by our race and, for me at least, ambivalence about ideologies of compulsory black unity, we were doomed from the start. Being with her felt like an extended, transposed version of black prep school partying.

Our passionless petting in my room at the conclusion of Invitational Weekend was interrupted by the sounds of two small children, perched on the fire escape outside my window, responding to the sight of teenage naughtiness with what I heard as mocking laughter. I lowered the blind and shouted for them to go away—they flew down the steep steps on thin, scraped, untanned legs, joy and fear etched on the profiles of their faces—and Karen looked at me grimly, reattached her bra, and began reading her school library's copy of Du Bois's *The Philadelphia Negro*.

Relieved to have reached the end of a three-day-long charade of intimacy and desire, I quipped, "I'm from Philly, you know. I used to live in the area he studied." "Yes, I know," she responded blandly, never looking up from her reading, never acknowledging or trying to deflect the embarrassment of the moment, and aware enough of the chill of my saliva at the base of her neck to wipe it off casually as she turned the page.

She contacted me twice afterward—to invite me to a recital she was giving at a famous music school, and later to inform me that she was having a difficult time choosing between the two Ivy League schools that had accepted her, and to invite me to come hang out with her in Boston some weekend. I wanted to want to respond affirmatively, to seize this opportunity for intimacy with an obviously talented, intelligent, and attractive black girl. But I didn't know her well enough to like her, didn't like her well enough to ponder her or my own Invitational Weekend discomfort very seriously, and wasn't attracted enough to her to blot out my deep attraction to Joan.

I got drunk during a mixer in April and told Joan how I felt about her. We had a two-week relationship that wasn't much different from the friendship we'd developed before my drunken confession. Our relationship ended after she caught the flu, missed a week of school, and had time to contemplate the folly of getting involved with me.

During and after those two weeks, I brooded over the possibility that my attraction to Joan signaled that I'd become a charter member of a black male cult of white womanhood. However, I took comfort in the fact that I'd spent nearly three years puzzling over the strange dissonance between myths of white physical superiority and the reality of white girls' typically thin lips, blue veins, stringy hair, blotchy skin, and sun worship.

Still, I wondered. Had Joan been teased by her friends for liking a liver-lipped, bushy-haired jungle bunny? Counseled sternly by her parents? Did racial stereotypes pervade my prep school to such an extent that acknowledging anything other than strictly platonic feelings for a member of a primitive, oversexed tribe was taboo? And why was it so important to me to convince myself that what I felt for her was unsullied by race and by sexual desire?

On the night before graduation, as Mark and I strolled past faculty who were well aware of our inebriation and toward the sounds of dance music, I began to rummage through mental snapshots of scenes from the previous nine months. The pointless eye doctor visit. The headmaster calling my mother to inform her that I wouldn't be allowed to play football. Nervously forgetting, during my first public speaking class performance, how I spent my summer vacation. Autumn boredom. Telephoning hopelessly inaccurate football statistics to the *Boston Globe*. My last black prep school party. The blinding ivy-colored protective ski goggles I was forced to wear during basketball games. Quitting the team that I cocaptained in a fit of rage about lack of playing time. Karen. The alliterative headline "Lax Routs Lawrence" atop a school newspaper sports page

MICHAEL AWKWARD

407 Washington Avenue, Philadelphia, PA 19147

BRANDEIS UNIVERSITY   1973

Black Brotherhood 2,3,4; Social Committee 3,4; THE GOVERNOR Sports Editor
4; Richard Hawes Francis Scholarship 4; Society of Outstanding American High
School Students 4; Honor Roll 2,3.
        "I made a bad start and I've broken ten hearts
        While searching for it everywhere
        I got to find my place in this human race
        I've got to find peace of mind somewhere else."
                        - Ahdul Fakir

Governor Dummer yearbook entry graduation photo

that I edited, reporting of a lacrosse team victory over Rivers. The athletic director's justifiably irate response. A year of honor roll lists without my name. The photo that Mark took of Joan smiling bemusedly during one of the Social Committee's outdoor functions and gave to me despite his inability to understand my attraction. Her laughter when we realized that she'd misspelled "birthday" on the cake she made for me. The lyrics of the Four Tops song I used to accompany my yearbook photograph: "I've got to find my place in this human race / I've gotta find peace of mind somewhere else."

I saw my own reflection in a long mirror in the foyer and was startled by its joylessness. I tried to smile, but couldn't. To laugh at my overwrought pathos, but couldn't. To release some of the pressure strangling me with a long, loud sigh, but my heart and head were pounding, and I became afraid that any sudden movement, any act of self-exertion, would cause one or both to explode.

Feeling overwhelmed by my year of failure, I remembered a wonderful line from the introductory rap to an Isaac Hayes song my mother used to play over and over again when she was drunk and sad. To the friend's fiancée whom he loved, Ike says of his inability to extricate himself from the sticky emotional situation: "It's just like being in quicksand, too—the more you wiggle, the deeper you sink." I was tired of trying to wiggle free, tired of the stress of responding amicably when others' decisions about, or views of, my life pissed me off. Tired of being one of a few dark faces. Tired of being in a place where Led Zeppelin's "Stairway to Heaven" was everyone's favorite song and hardly anybody knew The O'Jays' much different song with the same title.

I wished I could have dealt with the stresses more maturely, that I'd considered the athletic consequences of my visual impairment during the fall as an opportunity to apply myself more diligently to my classwork rather than to barely think about it at all. That I'd used my afternoons to figure out how to write paragraphs as intellectually rich as my unexpressed thoughts about the works by John Barth and Ernest Hemingway and Robert Penn Warren that we studied in Mr. Adams's wonderful class, where I first learned to appreciate textual interpretation. That I'd taken the college application process seriously enough to have applied to more than four schools, none of whose brochures I'd read more than a paragraph of. That I hadn't undermined my reputation as a diligent honor roll student, others' high regard for my levelheadedness, maturity, and commitment, and my own formerly good opinion of my prep school performance.

In trying to immerse myself more fully in the life of the school than Brotherhood had permitted, I nearly drowned. I tried to strategize on the fly, to improvise a way to salvage something from the year. Rum hadn't helped. Nor had attempting to recall the enjoyable times I'd had that year, or the satisfaction of learning that my life as a black man could be lived differently, if not necessarily better, than Brotherhood demanded.

I felt I needed to speak with Joan to reclaim myself, to make the pain I'd endured seem somehow worth it, and, if possible, to experience once more some semblance of the unself-conscious joy I'd felt in her presence before and just after my drunken confession. Mark warned me not to further humiliate myself by begging her to talk to me when she'd made it clear that she wouldn't or couldn't without feeling extremely uncomfortable. But I couldn't imagine it wasn't okay to share a joke with her, to say good-bye.

I walked slowly toward the music blaring from the darkened cafeteria, stripped of its gorgeous wooden tables to make room for dancing. I saw her standing against the locked entrance to the food lines, engaged in banter with some of her friends.

"Can I talk with you for a few minutes, Joan?"

Her countenance sombered immediately. "Um, yeah."

As we walked to a quieter part of the building, I tried to think of something lighthearted to say to her that would disguise my angst, my feelings of failure, my neediness, my anger. I thought of the wasted time, our uncomfortable glances, our strained efforts at small talk when she couldn't avoid being in my presence. I was torn between bitterness and a bizarre sense of gratitude, between anger and affection, between rage and desire. Mainly, however, I just wanted to be with her. I reminded myself not to ask her the question I'd been dying to know the answer to: if she cared for me, why did she abandon me?

"I've missed you."

"I know. I'm sorry."

"How've you been?"

"Okay. A little sad, sometimes. I don't want school to end. I don't want everything to change."

"It already has."

"Michael, I'm going back, okay?"

"Why don't you want to talk to me? What did I do wrong? Why don't you want to be around me anymore?"

"It's too hard."

"But I'm leaving tomorrow, you know? You won't have to see me after that. Hope that makes your life easier."

"Michael, that's not what . . ."

"I'm going to Shelley's house for a few days first," I added sheepishly, trying to make Joan jealous.

"That's good. I'm going now."

"But . . ."

"Bye."

"Joan, can't I have a good-bye kiss, at least? Just two friends saying *au revoir* and all, you know? I promise I won't make more of it than that."

"Oh, Michael, stop it."

"Please."

This brief exchange had changed nothing—I still felt lost, still cared for her so much it nearly made me breathless, still knew that whatever she felt for me, she'd decided that I was a risk not worth taking. As she walked away, I cursed myself for not having listened to Mark.

On the morning of my graduation, my mother called my dorm floor telephone just after I'd returned from breakfast. She told me that she'd arrived in town late the night before along with Debby, Aunt Grace, and Pastor Cochran, the white minister of the neighborhood Lutheran church whose various community activities included administering a large summer jobs program. Although I was neither a church member nor the only kid in the neighborhood enrolled through ABC in a New England school—Ernie had dropped or been kicked out after a year, but Marty graduated the same year I did, and two other people I knew were going to schools in Connecticut—I was the first kid with any sort of church affiliation to get a diploma from one of these elite places. So Pastor Cochran, who'd driven me to the airport before the start of my junior year, who'd taken me along with a bunch of rowdy sixth- and seventh-grade boys on a field trip to Canada some years earlier, and who'd found me employment every summer I needed it, kept the promise he'd made to me when he'd learned that I'd been accepted at GDA to drive my family to my graduation.

When I told my mother that rather than come straight home, I would spend the weekend at Shelley's house, she looked at me suspiciously. She didn't express her feelings about my announcement in exactly the words she would have used had there not been a white minister present. Instead she asked me calmly about the nature of my relationship to "this Shelley." With a mischievous smile, I assured her that we were good friends, and that I simply wanted a chance to hang out with her before returning to Philly.

I put on my cap and gown and escorted them to the back lawn of the headmaster's house, where the graduation ceremony was to take place. I introduced them to some of my friends—Chip and Mark, Darryl, and others.

Once the ceremony began, prizes were bestowed to the best students in each of the academic fields, prizes that, like the service, sports, and special awards given the night before, I had no chance of winning. I paid very little attention to the speeches, anecdotes, and teary-eyed expressions of pride in the accomplishments of the Bicentennial class. I felt no such sense of pride—the mere fact that I was graduating felt like no big deal, except that it made my folks very happy—but unlike the night before, I wasn't worrying about my failures.

I sat with Mark, Steve, and Chip, glad that I'd connected with them. I searched Darryl out several times and smiled at him, proud that two-thirds of our northeastern ghetto cohort had made it through. I spotted my mother, who was listening intently to the headmaster's speech and using her graduation program like a mortician's fan in a hot, crowded black church in late summer. And I stared at Joan, who was squinting to block out the sun. I smiled tentatively at her, but she either didn't see or wouldn't acknowledge me.

After it was over, after, in our last act of bucking the system, Mark and I had walked around the hedges of the headmaster's house rather than joining our classmates in jumping over them, after my sister and Pastor Cochran took pictures of me alone and with my mother and aunt, after saying good-bye to good friends and acquaintances, I walked the Philly contingent back to the van. As they piled in, I thanked them for coming and promised my mother that I'd catch the Greyhound bus back to Philly by noon on Monday.

"You be good, Michael, okay?" my mother said as she buckled her seatbelt.

"Don't worry, Mommy. Drive carefully, Deb," I said in jest to my fifteen-year-old sister.

Just as I was about to close the passenger door, Joan appeared at my side, grinning shyly, and insisted that she wanted to meet my family.

I introduced her to everyone. I looked at Debby, who rolled her eyes and threw her head back quizzically, but she'd been too well trained by my mother to be openly rude. Aunt Grace and Pastor Cochran smiled at Joan and said, "Pleased to meet you," in a stereophonic display of civility. My mother was unable to disguise her concern. "Hi," she said coldly, looking intently first at me, then at Joan. I shot my innocent, mama's boy grin in her direction.

"I'll miss you," Joan said to me as she gave me a brief, firm hug.

"Me, too," I replied, and waved to her as she turned to walk away.

"Who's that girl, Michael?" my mother asked me when Joan was out of earshot.

"That's Joan, Mommy," I said quickly, trying to suppress a smile.

"Don't be bringing no half-white babies home and expecting me to take care of them, you hear?" she said, unable to exercise the self-discipline she'd displayed earlier in Pastor Cochran's presence.

"Oh, Tippy," Aunt Grace exclaimed, breaking her uncharacteristic silence, "leave that boy alone, now. It was nice of his little friend to come over to meet us, and here you are, making a mountain out of a molehill."

"Thanks, Aunt Grace. I gotta go, okay? Thanks, again, for coming. I love you. See you on Monday."

I watched them drive away, relieved that the stress of these meetings and ceremonies had ended. I got my athletic bag from my empty room and made my way to Shelley's dormitory.

When I returned home after my brief stay in New Hampshire, the dynamics of my mother's apartment had changed significantly. My mother's longtime partner Mr. Freddy had moved out during my senior year, having finally gotten fed up with her alcoholic antics. He'd been replaced by Mr. John, who'd learned during more than forty years of living to use his distinctive physicality—his linebacker height and girth, his jet-black skin, his huge, bald head (which he shaved religiously every morning), his deep-set, menacing, yellow eyes—to good, intimidating effect.

Having lived primarily in rural Massachusetts for three years, I'd lost any skill I'd developed for coping with urban bullies and my mother's drinking, and so I stayed as far away from her and Mr. John as possible. But since I'd lost touch with my North Philly friends from junior high and much of the attitudinal élan needed to play urban basketball, I had very few places to go. Feeling even less comfortable in my neighborhood than I had before I went off to prep school and utterly ill at ease in the apartment, I was miserable all summer.

In search of some peace one Saturday evening in late June just before Philadelphia's massive Bicentennial celebration, I decided to go to Center City. I figured that a solitary walk there was preferable to writing more mournful songs of lost love, listening to my mother's 992d argument with Mr. John, or composing another spite-filled letter like the one I regretted mailing to Joan earlier in the month. I hoped that my spirits would be lifted by a leisurely stroll; by sitting on a bench near the Fifth and Walnut Street entrance of Independence Park, watching lovers and friends return from movies, dining, and other Center City diversions; observing pigeons, squirrels, and sparrows fight for small morsels of hot dog, hoagie, and cheese steak rolls; and listening critically to blaring nationalist propaganda about the thirst for liberation of white colonists who strategically ignored the inconvenient fact of black people's underrepresented and overtaxed condition.

After an hour, the temperature had dipped noticeably, so I headed home. Instead of using Fifth Street, which would have taken me past the fences of the Presbyterian Historical Society, whose peeling and bubbling black paint I'd spent weeks scraping for my government-sponsored summer job, I turned south onto Fourth. I walked over cobblestone streets, past the Catholic church my siblings and I attended just after we'd moved to Southwark, past rows of beautiful four-story houses that dwarfed the expensive sedans and sports cars parked outside them. As I approached Fourth and Spruce, a siren began to wail loudly, and I saw blue and red lights flashing behind me. I turned around, expecting to see a white-and-red ambulance speed by, but instead a patrol car and a police van screeched to sloppy stops just inches from where I stood. Four white officers hopped out of their vehicles, guns pointed at me, and yelled for me to freeze and put my hands above my head.

They frisked me thoroughly, and one noted that the dampness of my shirt made me "a possible perp." Another of the policemen pulled my arms behind me, handcuffed me, and pushed me toward the van. I'd heard enough stories about police brutality against black men during the Frank Rizzo regimes—unlawful beatings, accidental discharging of weapons into the chests and faces of handcuffed suspects, boys hanging themselves in cells with belts the police claimed to have forgotten to remove from the suspects—to know I was in a potentially dangerous situation. I tried to deal with this danger as I always had: with humor. However, I was too troubled, too filled with bile merely to try to amuse or charm the officers. I settled for smart-ass sarcasm that amused only me.

"What am I alleged to have done? I was just enjoying the Bicentennial spirit of our historic city."

"Oh, you're a smart-mouthed nigger, huh?"

"Well, my prep school teachers would be happy to hear that some of their hard work had paid off so handsomely. My powers of articulation, recognized by Philly's finest!"

"Shut the fuck up, boy."

"Officer," I asked, remembering the guarantees emphasized in all of the cop shows I'd ever watched, "am I under arrest? Will you read me my rights? Do I get a lawyer? My phone call?"

"Shut up, nigger," one of the officers yelled, slamming his nightstick threateningly against the van.

"What crime do you suspect I committed?"

"Huh?"

"Excuse me. What do you think I may have done?"

"Nigger who fits your description just robbed a store in the area. We're taking you in for identification."

Suddenly, I felt an inexplicable sense of calm in the back of the police van. I knew I'd committed no crime, that I was innocent of whatever charges anyone could bring against me, and that the worst thing I'd done since I returned to Philly was to wish Mr. John was dead and send that mean letter to Joan. Neither of these were prosecutable offenses, even by Philly standards.

When we arrived at the police station, the officers lowered me from the van and escorted me roughly inside. A wild, white-haired man with a thick accent rushed toward us, shaking his head. "No, no, this not that punk. That nigger what robbed me! Got too much hair. Too much nose. Not dark enough. The nigger what robbed me black as night, black and greasy and ugly as horse's shit. Let that boy alone. Find the nigger what robbed me so I can spit in his black face! Hold a gun up to my woman's head, will he? Never again! Never!"

A minute later, another handcuffed suspect arrived. I recognized him as a goofy thug from the South Side who was widely known to be too stupid to plan his petty crimes well. He was much darker skinned than I, a few inches taller, with a nose and lips much thinner than mine, eyes much smaller, and a short-cropped haircut that was easily distinguishable from my five-inch Afro.

After the old man identified him—"That's the bastard, the dirty bastard! Where the gun now, you black bastard? I stick it up your dirty ass!"—one of the officers took off my handcuffs and offered to drive me home.

As soon as he started the car, I asked, "Officer, that guy looked nothing like me, did he?"

"We got only a vague description from the dispatcher."

"What did he say—he's black?"

"Yeah, something like that. Black and thin."

"Oh. I guess I better gain some weight then, huh?"

He stopped the car a mile away from Southwark. "Yo! Here's where you're getting out, pal. Let me give you some advice—you better learn to watch your smart mouth, or someone's gonna puff up them nigger lips even more."

"I have your badge number now, officer, and if I run into trouble of that sort, I'll request that you investigate the case and arrest the 'black and thin perp.' "

"Get the fuck out, nigger!"

"Yes, sir."

One Saturday afternoon, late in August, Larry and I walked to Center City, ostensibly to shop for clothes for college. He was going to a small state school in Pennsylvania, and I was headed to Brandeis. We both knew, however, that although we might actually buy something, we'd mainly come to get our last look at the honeys strutting from Wanamaker's to Strawbridge's, from The Sound of Philadelphia to I. Goldberg's. We'd gotten our signals down to a fine science—we only needed to say, "Check that out, man," or nod our head in the direction of a fine young thing to alert the other of approaching treasures—so we strolled leisurely, one or the other of us occasionally looking in clothing and shoe store windows that announced back-to-school sales.

We weaved our way around panhandlers, past blind men with signs declaring their handicaps and tin cups signaling their poverty, past urine-soaked men lying near the entrances of stores with their backs turned toward us, past cocky, wild-eyed brothers traveling in groups who got their kicks ripping off industrious young men, past sauntering couples whose heads, hands, arms, legs, and torsos would have had to be surgically separated to keep them from taking up half the crowded sidewalk, past black girls and women walking alone, in pairs, in packs, either thrilled to be noticed or offended to be having yet another encounter with the hungry eyes of strangers.

As we crossed Tenth and Market Street, we heard a familiar voice that struck more terror into us than those rare instances when one of the women we were scoping looked back at us with apparent interest. The voice was that of the most renowned hardrock in 5th Street, who was wearing a conservative suit two sizes too big, a pencil-thin bow tie, and globs of pomade in his hair. He was hawking bean pies, incense, photos of Elijah Muhammad, and copies of *Muhammad Speaks*. We tried to cross Market Street before he saw us, knowing it was better not to get too close to that crazy nigger's new hustle.

"Hey! Hey! You brothers from down the way! I know you gonna buy some bean pies, right? Come on, now. Buck fifty. Best pies in the city, brothers."

"Nah, we ain't got no money."

"Then what the fuck you doing up here, nigger? Nobody come downtown with no money. Come on, my brothers."

"No thank you."

"What? If you don't buy one of these motherfucking bean pies, I'm gonna kick your ass! I ain't talking to you, Larry—I don't want no trouble with your crazy brother—but to that burnt headed nigger. You hear me, boy?"

"I don't want a bean pie. Thanks."

As we pushed past him, he pelted me with threats and curses. We heard him shout, "I'm gonna get your ass, Bernie. I'ma get your motherfucking ass good, nigger," halfway down the block. Shaken but reasoning that he must threaten a dozen a people a day, I tried not to take his words too seriously.

A week later, I saw him standing under the high-rise in which Larry used to live with a huge baseball bat in his hands. No longer in his suit and bow tie and, apparently, given his clearly drugged state, no longer a Black Muslim, he saw me trying to duck behind one of the pillars holding up the building. "Come here, motherfucker. I told you I was gonna kick your ass. I'm gonna break both your fucking legs."

Long before this encounter, I'd learned not to run from such threats, which would necessitate my being perpetually on guard, but to try to reason with, reassure, compliment, talk my way around, or otherwise try to appease my would-be attacker. But I had no idea of how to calm this profoundly warped man. As I started to approach him, his good friend Stink stepped in front of him and put his arms around him.

"Nah, now, leave him alone. He one of them brainiacs, up there kicking ass with rich white folks. He been 'round the man so long, nigger forgot how to deal, knowwhatimean? Be cool, awright?"

"Nah, I'ma kick his black ass, Stink. I'ma send him back to them honkeys with four less teeth and a permanent motherfucking limp. Get out my way, boy."

"It's cool, Mike. Go on now. It's cool. D, you gots to chill. Cops already looking for your ass now. Go on, Mike."

The next week, police sirens unsettled the relative peace of Southwark. According to the telephone reports my younger sister received from one of her friends, my would-be attacker had roughed up a young man in a dispute about the amount and quality of reefer he'd been selling, then murdered the Housing Authority guard who tried to intervene. After blocking traffic, occupying the elevators, and searching all of the units from the first floor to the eighteenth for hours, Philly's finest found him, shivering in the empty bathtub of an abandoned apartment, his gun dangling unthreateningly from his baby finger. "Just don't shoot me here," he was reported to have said. "Just don't shoot me here."

A few days later, while I practiced my long-range shooting, someone ran toward the basketball court to report that he had been killed in a dispute with one of the prison guards. While others extolled his virtues—"He was a crazy motherfucker, wasn't he?"—I remained silent, glad that I still had all of my teeth and that I could determine how much bop I wanted to put in my step.

A couple of days before I was scheduled to begin my career as a college student at Brandeis, my mother called me to the telephone. "Someone wants to talk to you, Michael Cycle."

"Who, Mommy?" I asked, thinking it was either Aunt Grace or Aunt Peggy, wanting to say good-bye and wish me good luck.

"It's your father."

I didn't know what to say. That he was on the other end of the telephone line seemed as unbelievable to me as a dead man coming back to life or black people voting for Frank Rizzo for mayor. What was even more unbelievable than his calling our apartment was that my mother was smiling as she offered me the receiver.

I remember hearing his voice only twice: the night he banged on our door, and a few months later in Aunt Naomi's apartment, when he smiled proudly at Ricky and me, asked us repeatedly, "You boys know who I am, don't you?" and gave us money to get our hair cut. Twelve years after the latter encounter, nine months before I would be legally recognized as an adult, and three days before I was scheduled to begin college, he wanted to speak to me, and my mother—who'd told her children chilling narratives about his brutality—was eager for us to make this connection. She laughed and joked with him like they were old friends, like he hadn't broken her bones and nearly broken her spirit. She said to him, "Hold on, Junior. He's a little shy, you know, reserved."

"I ain't talking to him, Mommy."

"Come on, boy. Just say hi."

"Nah. I won't."

"Why not?"

"Why's he want to talk to me now, anyway? The hell with him."

"All right now, Michael. I won't have you talking that way in my house. You getting too big for your britches?"

"Why are you talking to him, anyway? After all the stuff you told us about? After what he did to you? Why?"

"Boy, I don't have to explain anything to you. I'm three times seven plus, and I'm your mother, not some white girl you can order around."

"Huh?"

"Say hi to your father."

"No."

I walked back to my room, slammed the door, then quietly opened it a crack so that I could listen to my mother's end of the conversation.

"Junior, he's a very sensitive boy. Don't worry about it, okay? So you saw Ricky up Ninth Street? Ain't he a good-looking boy? He takes after you."

After she got off the phone, she knocked on my door. Ignoring my silence, she entered, pushed aside the clothes I was folding to put into my trunks, and sat next to me on the bed. She'd been drinking, but she wasn't drunk. Rather, she was lucid and talkative.

"Boy, you should've talked to your father. He's proud of you, you know."

I stared at the photograph of a smiling Hal Greer that I'd taped to the back of my door eight years earlier.

"Michael, why were you so mean?"

"Mommy! What was I supposed to do? Pretend that we're old buddies? Give him my college address and ask him to send me some money or come visit? What's he to me? Nothing. If I saw him today, I wouldn't know him."

"That's where you're wrong, boy."

"Huh?"

"I want to show you something."

I followed her to her room. She reached the closet on whose shelf she kept her most cherished photographs: of her father with her nephew, Melvyn; of her mother, whose resemblance to Debby was uncanny; a professional portrait of Aunt Grace; my mother's own high school graduation picture; and a large photograph of all of her siblings taken at Uncle Ed and Aunt Josephine's wedding reception, in which my mother doesn't appear because she was lying in the hospital in a body cast the doctors said was necessary for her to wear for six months if she was to have any hope of gaining full use of

The author's biological father

the arm my father had broken. From this pile of photographs, she pulled an envelope marked "DO NOT DESTROY" in bright red letters and asked me to look inside.

"Who's this?" I asked when I pulled out a black-and-white photograph of a twenty-five-year-old man in a light, wide-lapelled, double-breasted suit whose hair was badly in need of a cut and whose head was tilted sharply to the right, so that to get a clear sense of the relation of each of his features to one another, I was forced to tilt my head at an even sharper angle in the opposite direction. While none of my features was an exact duplicate of his, except perhaps for the shape of our heads and our ears, this face—its thin mustache, its unsmiling lips, its slightly arched eyebrows, its small, watery eyes, its bruises just above the left eye and on the right cheek—was an older, rougher version of myself.

"That's Junior. That's your father."

"Nah. No. No!"

"Michael, this is the man who kicked me in the stomach when I was carrying you because he swore you were someone else's child. Now, look at you two. Couldn't look more alike. Ain't that a blip?"

"Why're you talking to him anyway, Mommy?"

"He called 'cause he's been diagnosed with cancer, and he wants to get to know you and your brother and sisters. Deathbed conversion or something, I guess. Anyway, I thought it would be good for you to talk to him."

"I can't, Mommy. I don't care about him."

I handed her the picture back. "How long have you had this picture?"

"A while now. Since Easter, maybe. Your grandmother got copies made to give to his kids. I've been holding this for you. I forgot about it until he called. You want it?"

"Yeah." I took it and packed it in my trunk.

In Paul Monette's autobiographical "manifesto" Becoming a Man, the author gropes for a broad, historically resonant image that both sufficiently conveys his antihomophobic worldview and serves to weed out all but his ideal readers. He settles on the image of a room with portraits of social actors who witnessed and responded to, in either resistant or collaborative fashion, Nazi Germany's extermination of millions of Jews during World War II. A month after his lover died of AIDS, Monette travels through parts of Europe, including Caen, "where they've built a Museum of Peace on the site of an eighty-day battle fought by three million men." Having witnessed "newsreel footage and camp uniforms, ration books, code breakers, yellow star and pink triangle," Monette describes viewing the contents of the museum—a collective "combing [of] the past" similar to his painful autobiographical musings—as equivalent to witnessing the effects of "a slow bomb."

Monette describes his reactions to the contents of a basement room filled with portraits:

> And in the belly of the place there's this extraordinary room lined with pictures on either side. On the right are the collaborators, men—all men, of

*course—who ran the puppet governments for the Nazis, . . . fawning men
with dead eyes and fat ties, grins that show the gristle between their teeth.
On the left wall, opposite, are the leaders of the Resistance—several women
here—and they're lean and defiant and alive. . . .*

*So that is what I am doing in the past, figuring out who goes on the left
wall and who on the right. For that is the choice, it seems to me: collaborate
or resist. (3–4)*

Ultimately, Monette indicates that the imagery he seeks to install as the
interpretive key to his autobiography both aids and doesn't aid his efforts to
satisfy his ideological and his aesthetic compulsions. We know, of course, as
does Monette, that however loathsome we may consider collaboration—
with slave owners who brutalized blacks, with Nazis who slaughtered
Jews, with masculinist exploiters of female labor and flesh, with homo-
phobes who discriminate against and physically harm gay men and lesbian
women—identifying the good guys and bad guys is generally never, ever
this easy, except in our "twisted," rage-filled fantasies. We know that
collaborators, who may in fact be as black, as Jewish, as gay as those who
are killed and maimed, often feel powerless before devastating machines of
mass destruction.

Monette concludes his representation of the gallery of Holocaust dissen-
ters and collaborators with an acknowledgment of the deleterious interpretive consequences of what are, for him, hard-won ideological positions: "I
don't trust my own answers anymore. I'm too twisted up with rage, too
hooked on the millennium. . . . Which is not to say I don't chastise myself
for halving the world into us and them. I know that the good guys aren't all
gay, or the bad all straight" (3). Monette's rage, resulting from his recognition that "the good guys" possessed few weapons with which to do effective
battle against forces of social oppression, limits the impact of hard-won
anti-essentialist insights. In Monette's formulations, the disempowered
figure loses the capacity to trust either the other who desires his eradication
because he is a member of a despised group or the self who feels that to
survive he must mobilize ultimately unachievable dreams of community.

For those situated in spheres characterized by vociferous or barely
audible contentiousness such as my seemingly peaceful prep school, the
struggle between knowledge and need, between truth and desire, can be
psychically devastating. While reading across the lines of difference can

serve a number of crucial functions, including satisfying the reader's need for new information about the other or for confirmation of his preconceptions, what it most ably provides is access to strategies of negotiating intra- and intercultural differences.

I suspect that it proves ultimately more difficult for "minority" intellectuals to get satisfaction by deconstructing blackness or femaleness or gayness, among other markings of difference, than it is, say, for leftist white scholars to problematize whiteness. Measured against the myriad social and institutional protections available to white (middle-class, heterosexual) people, the personal risks involved both in giving up the comforts of antihegemonic formulations of identity-as-difference and in exposing oneself to the certain sting of traditional majority responses are great indeed.

Only, I suspect, in our fantasies does recognizing a range of racialized subjectivities free intellectuals from being perceived in terms of traditional social scripts that have sought to control the meanings of blackness. Categorical blackness, an always already known set of essential(ist) characteristics, hangs like an albatross around the neck of the black scholar in postmodernism, who is expected to experience it as a troubling but powerless ghost, and the black public intellectual, who uses his own and others' awareness of its persistence to justify his existence. But even in its seemingly weakened contemporary manifestations, blackness remains both humane enough to rock you gently and, if you forget its strength for just a moment, powerful enough to squeeze the life out of you.

SECTION IV ❋ "closed in silence"

Between the end of my junior year and my graduation from Brandeis, I added fifteen pounds to my skinny body in May of 1980 through intense weight lifting. For years, I'd tried halfheartedly to transform my thin frame into some semblance of the athletic physique I'd always wanted. After months of casual experimentation with pumping iron, I started lifting seriously during the summer between my junior and senior years, which I spent in Waltham working with my best friend Dan and other Brandeis students in an enrichment program targeting elementary school–aged children. I figured that serious lifting—not just the muscle-straining and -ripping act itself but also the necessary physical, emotional, and attitudinal preparation—would help me to pass the time until the return of my girlfriend, Lisa, who'd gone home for the summer.

My increased muscularity helped me to fill out the loose jeans and athletic shirts I typically wore, inspiring me to preen, pose, and pirouette stiffly before full-length mirrors in my apartment and at the gymnasium. I especially loved admiring my torso's new hard curves as they strained against the fabric of my clothing. Even after Lisa broke up with me the day she returned to Massachusetts, I continued to experience my muscles as a victory over a genetic predisposition toward scrawniness that had always made me feel vulnerable, frail, and unmanly.

To disguise my persistent uncertainty during my senior year, I experimented with a variety of incompatible identities: the stiff-armed and -legged lifter, the bopping ghetto nigger, the carefree bon vivant, the none too suave loveman, the antisocial nerd, the chin-rubbing and skyward-gazing intellectual pondering all manner of mundane subjects. Much of my experimentation resulted from my inability to figure out how best to cope with the sense of disorientation Lisa's desertion caused me and my inability, once I believed I'd arrived at a workable solution, to stick to my script.

However heartbroken I was as a consequence of her unexplained—though not entirely unexpected—withdrawal, I never viewed it primarily as a sign of her perception of my individual

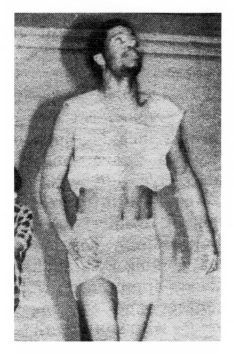

The author playing intramural
basketball, winter 1980, after
putting on fifteen pounds
through intense weight lifting

unworthiness. Rather, I saw it as a small scene in the volatile drama
of black heterosexual relations, which, as I learned as a child, were
marked by a great deal of ambivalence and contempt on both sides.
Growing up, I listened to my mother's stories about my father,
witnessed the undercurrents of hostility and moments of occasional
violence in her relationships with other men, and partially absorbed
my natal male community's characterizations of black females as
ruthless, conniving bitches. In addition, before I was eight, I'd heard
mind-boggling snippets of conversations between my mother and
her female friends, whose collective frustrations about failed and
failing marriages, long-term relationships, and more casual affairs
were articulated as general condemnation of black males.

I eagerly awaited the visits of my mother's friends, partly because

I was fascinated by the stories they told about recurring heartbreak, and also because they lavished me with gifts of candy and small change, compliments about my manners and my appearance, and predictions that I would not grow up to be like "those no-good black bastards" whom they gathered to castigate.

While I reveled in their attention, their treatment of me was also disconcerting. If they hated black men, as they insisted, why were they so demonstrative in their display of affection for me? Wasn't I a black man-in-training? In miniature? Were they as confident as they seemed that I'd be different from the men about whom they spoke with such disdain and disappointment? As I recall images of them repeatedly filling glasses with cheap Tokay wine and ashtrays with the butts of unfiltered cigarettes, I wonder whether the laughter that accompanied their tales of romantic woe was not bitter so much as filled with surprise, even wonder, that the stories they'd heard as girls about black men's flaws were actually true.

Still, they appeared to want to have men in their lives, needed them, despite or perhaps because of the pain, as confirmation of their own worth and worthlessness, their desire and undesirability, their guile and guilelessness. If so, did I represent for them uncorrupted male potential, someone they could treat with undisguised affection, could perhaps even mold because besides my youth and maleness, the only characteristic I possessed of which they were aware was vulnerability?

When I was six or seven, I overheard Miss Rose, Aunt Minnie, and my mother discussing Mr. Charley's infamous act of brutality against Miss Katie. Until I heard the story, it hadn't been clear to me what benefits there were for men in inflicting pain on women because I had no access to male analyses of such matters. Part of the thrill, I surmised, was the apparently increased self-regard that came from being able to retain women's self-sacrificing commitment in the aftermath of psychic and physical pain.

Whatever it had been before he threw lye into her eyes in a fit of jealous rage, afterward the relationship between my mother's fat, unkempt, malodorous friend and her lover-attacker must have been defined exclusively by his irrational act that robbed her of sight and him of the possibilities of seeing himself as untouched by myths of black male barbarity. By the time I finally met Miss Katie, ten years after the incident, she and Mr. Charley had moved to Southwark, and she'd given up all concern with her appearance and other superficialities. She'd transformed herself from a hot-to-trot looker, as my mother insisted she had once been, into a frumpy, perpetually inebriated soul who puzzled everyone by remaining committed to this brutal man.

When I was able to attempt to understand it at all, I read Lisa's desertion as a sign of her recognition that I hadn't really grown up to be the sweet, gentle soul my mother's friends had hoped I'd become. Driven to the brink of uncontrollable rage by her apparent emotional indifference to me and my feelings during the one visit I made to her dormitory room in the Castle to secure an explanation, I screamed at her and grabbed her by her shoulders. Having had a long, lonely month to store up pounds and pounds of despair and bitterness, I could barely suppress the urge to shake her as though she were a naughty child, smack her violently, and knock the cruel arrogance out of her.

Needing desperately to calm myself, I closed my eyes, shook my head, removed my hands from her shoulders, and tensed my muscles like a bodybuilder displaying the results of maniacal training. Standing in the middle of her tiny room with my veins, muscles, and head throbbing, I felt as though I'd turned myself into granite or ice. I refused even to breathe until I could act with the sort of soft-spoken calm my mother's friends prized and that I was typically able to achieve.

Although many of my friends and acquaintances viewed me as unnaturally mild-mannered, my self-protective displays both on basketball courts and in my previous, rancor-filled relationship that I'd ended quite insensitively in order to get involved with Lisa made me well aware that my meek facade didn't fully represent me. But despite a myriad of early difficulties, I got mad in Lisa's presence only once over the course of our brief relationship. As I sought logical explanations for her rejection of me, that display, which occurred during the second of two summer trips I took to visit her in The City, seemed the most likely cause.

We were in a midtown Manhattan restaurant, moments after

we'd thrilled to the cinematic shock of witnessing an alien jump out of the chest of an unfortunate earthling. I noticed a white man seated at the table next to us staring lustfully at Lisa. For long minutes over the course of an hour, he ogled her unselfconsciously as he chewed his food and conversed blandly with his date or wife or sister or friend.

He ignored various efforts to divert his attention from her face and the meaty curves of her breasts. Nothing—not his companion's occasional verbal intrusions, the clang of polished silverware, the periodic appearance of the distractingly gorgeous white waitress our tables shared, or the homicidal thoughts I pelted him with along with my mad nigger stare—intruded more than momentarily on his ocular assault.

I was angry and aware of my anger's inappropriateness, annoyed at my annoyance, and frustrated by my sense of powerlessness, for I'd taught myself to resist the notion that it was my masculine duty to respond actively to other males' verbal or visual indiscretions. But while he wrapped his mind around aspects of my woman's anatomy I'd been hesitant to think about for fear that unadulterated lust would sully the purity of our relationship of the head and heart, I plotted revenge.

"Can't you button it?"

"Fool, it doesn't have any buttons," Lisa said, smiling stiffly and shifting her body so as to reposition the fabric of her blouse. "Come on, MA, ignore him and talk to me."

Wasn't he aware that I was a rage-filled black man capable of bashing his head with my plate, throwing ice water in his pallid face, stabbing him with my fork, strangling him with my thick, white napkin, smothering him with my seat's cushion, cutting off the buttons of his companion's blouse with my steak knife, biting through the flimsy elastic of her bra, puncturing her pink, salty nipples with my teeth, and watching her crimson blood stain her silky white blouse, the white linen table cloth, and her companion's intrusive imagination?

We rode the subway back to Lisa's house in silence. As I stared out into the darkness at puddles of water and trash lining the subway tracks, I tried to think, first of an explanation, then of an apology that wasn't an out-and-out concession, then of what precisely I was angry about and how productively to express those feelings. During the walk back to her house from the subway stop, the only words that passed between us were, "I bought this shirt just for you, for this visit, for this evening. Why'd you have to spoil it with that macho shit?"

The closest I can come to pinpointing the precise moment when I realized I was smitten was a mid-fall late-morning vision I had during my sophomore year, just after my Shakespeare class had ended. As I began to descend the stairs connecting the humanities quadrangle to the rest of the campus, I saw her moving slowly on the walkway. Her image sharp and richly technicolored, she was the focal point of an otherwise blurry moving picture, dwarfing and stealing the light from the faceless mob of encircling students that appeared around her to admire her, hinder her progress, or obstruct my view.

She was wearing an indigo black shirt, dark blue flair-bottomed designer jeans, and a tan ankle-length sweater that both camouflaged her scrawny width and accentuated her impressive length. Her height, outfit, and carriage made her appear to be floating slightly above the mob. Though campus gossips characterized her as smug and self-satisfied, I decided at that moment that her haughtiness was a social facade erected to protect a pained soul desperately seeking self-definition: in literature, in music, in the theater, in the poses she struck in the company of her boisterous buddies. Long, lean, and lovely, she was visually striking, but she stood out for me among the freshwomen because even though I'd barely said ten words to her, I knew that she possessed a deep, dark soul, and that we were kindred spirits.

My sophomore-year obsession helped to ease the painful memory of a lonely, bored, and socially uncomfortable freshman year, full of many weekends spent getting embarrassingly drunk either at the campus bar, the Grog, or at Tufts University, where Darryl and other guys from my prep school class were enrolled. After each episode, I wondered why I'd drank so heavily, and about my drinking's potential consequences. But I had no idea how else to deal with the emptiness of being unmated and groupless, or with the feeling of looking aimlessly for ways to fill weekends that, devoid of the busyness and intellectual stimulation of classes, found me searching desperately for sensation of almost any sort. Alcohol was the surest means I knew of finding temporary respite.

I tried unsuccessfully to manufacture feelings for a black girl or two in my class, but neither they nor I was convinced by my reserved displays of interest. Dan and I warbled our got-no-woman blues constantly, moaning lustily over women who we understood would never be more than faintly cognizant of our existence. We pondered whether and how we'd flaunt our still-undetected irresistibility before members of the opposite sex.

In the midst of major emotional and psychological difficulties during the fall term of my senior year, I researched and wrote an honors thesis on the uses of existentialism and pragmatism as competing philosophies of action in John Barth's *The End of the Road*. The novel confirmed the legitimacy of my own skepticism about efforts to install any worldview or philosophy as irrefutable truth. By this point in my education, I knew that I had a rage for narrative, for stories that sought to capture and organize a series of symbolically resonant moments, stories that explored the interruption of mundane human existence by acts of social transgression, natural or seemingly otherworldly forces, or a character's brief turn off of the road of predictability.

The impracticalities of being engaged solely in a quest for immediate interpretive satisfaction—to the exclusion, even, of careerist concerns—were driven home for me during a conversation I had in my junior year with my friend Alan. On numerous occasions, Alan insisted that without a calculated series of steps that, if followed, could help me to achieve the sorts of material and psychic comforts of which my scholastic success suggested I was capable, I could very well wind up managing a fast-food restaurant in Kansas.

I told him that I couldn't imagine pursuing success with the sort of zeal manifested by many of our hall mates, who'd spent all of their upper-class lives surrounded by scores of potential role models—rich relatives, parents' friends, and neighbors with lush lawns.

"So what can you imagine yourself doing?"

"Well, I'm good at analyzing literature. I guess I could try to become a professor. Except I'm not sure I want to teach. They write stuff, too. Maybe I'll go to graduate school and become an English professor."

"Okay," Alan said skeptically, "but do you know what you have to do to become one?"

"Get a Ph.D. But I don't know what that involves."

"Then go find out, Awk! Talk to some of those professors who keep giving you those As. Do some research at Career Planning. Okay?"

"I guess so."

That year, I also had to deal with the sense of desertion my own withdrawal caused a group of boys with whom I'd entered the fringes of manhood. These were boys with whom I'd spent large parts of my first three years at college playing Ping-Pong, flag foot-ball, and intramural basketball, with whom I hung out at the Stein on Thursday and Friday nights drinking pitchers of beer, with whom I watched Sunday afternoon and Monday night football. They'd thrown two surprise birthday parties for me, invited me to Friday night movies in Usdan, to the Harvard Coop in Cambridge, and to a Chicago concert in the Boston Garden. They'd introduced me to their families and made me a part of their lives. During our senior year, they were angry with me because they believed that I'd abandoned them, that I'd changed radically because I'd chosen to live and hang out largely with three black people.

Because I'd been very close friends for three years with Marv, one of the members of this group, I felt horrible whenever I encountered the undisguised hurt etched on his face. Occasionally, I pondered how I could explain to him why I'd chosen to live and hang out primarily with Rodney, Lydia, and Valencia, none of whom had been more than acquaintances previously. However, such an explanation seemed impossible to me because I'd become far too practiced in the art of dissemblance, particularly in interracial settings. Since prep school, I had disguised my most significant vulnerabilities, afraid that my own and my family's weaknesses would be seen as pathological by whites who liked me but who'd emerged from homes and communities that I assumed were far more emotionally stable than my own. Given his secure place·in an institution peopled largely by members of his cultural group, I doubted whether Marv could consider seriously the consequences of my having had no racial community to which I belonged, no cohesive network whose commitments to unity, autonomy, and integrity comforted and inspired me. While my friendships with Marv and his ever-expanding social group made me feel appreciated, often when I was with them, I feared that I was about to lose essential aspects of myself.

His cultural history, his people's struggles, his perspectives of normalcy were sanctioned and legitimized—by the overwhelmingly Jewish student population, the names of buildings, the cafeteria menus—while my people occupied the school's fringes, searching for answers to inevitable questions: Why'd you come here? How do you like it here? Do you feel strange here? Strangeness—a condition that Brandeis, a post-Holocaust dream boldly realized, was dedicated to eliminating for Jewish American students—was simply a fact of life for those non-Jews who attended the school.

I struggled with the question of whether it was more beneficial to live with a threatened or all-consuming racial identity. As was the case at Governor Dummer, Brandeis's black community established an exclusive meeting and eating ground, two or three tables in a self-contained corner near the main entrance of Usdan's cafeteria. When I noticed it during the first week of my first year after the returning students began to show up for classes, I began to fear that others' notions of me would again revolve around how I positioned myself in terms of black public space.

Soon after I arrived at Brandeis, I heard a chilling statistic: 60 percent of the black population who'd enrolled in the school over the previous decade had failed to graduate. I knew that there were certainly mitigating factors that might have helped to explain this embarrassingly high rate of academic failure: financial burdens, scholastic unpreparedness, culture shock, and a resistance on the part of second-generation middle-class blacks to the dreams of their optimistic parents, all of whom seemed to expect their children to become doctors. Still, while I didn't understand the precise nature of the connection, I knew that there must be some correlation between the existence of that rollicking section and these embarrassing graduation rates.

Still, at times when I overheard familiar patterns of laughter as I tried to ignore the baffled expressions that confronted and challenged me, I longed for a place at the table, a point of entry that didn't also foreclose other contacts, that didn't close up behind me the second I struggled through its self-protective membrane. However, simply being among whites wasn't sufficient incentive for me to ignore the complexities and burdensome consequences of being black. The ties of race were neither unproblematic nor easily dismissed, for despite its general visibility, blackness was metaphysically as challenging a concept as Catholicism's teachings concerning a three-personed God were for me when I was seven.

Near the end of my time at Brandeis, I'd grown tired of racial disconnectedness and of being held captive by fears that in interracial settings, collectivity was forged only when all of its beneficiaries embraced a single, limited vision of cultural blackness. I wanted to be with black people, too—not instead of but in addition to my other social contacts—but my depression over my romantic troubles drained my energy and robbed me of the will to figure out how to work both sides of the racial divide. I did what was easiest—I stayed in my living quarters much of the time, got to know my housemates and their circle of friends, and felt, for the first time in years, a sense of comfort in black social immersion.

Two or three days after Lisa broke up with me, and on the day before the beginning of classes, I attended a program of music, dance, and drama sponsored by Afro-American Studies and intended to welcome the new black freshmen and women to campus. Despite my reservations, I went largely because I knew that Lisa was scheduled to perform a scene from Ntozake Shange's *for colored girls*, which she'd spent parts of the last two months of the summer rehearsing.

During my freshman year, I began to hear a great deal about this controversial play, which premiered on Broadway in September 1976. For the better part of my first two years in college, billboard

For colored girls cover

advertisements featuring Shange's attractive, sorrowful face and yellow head rag, and a multicolored, graffiti-like inscription of the play's title written on a tiled wall just above her head and her left shoulder, were plastered all over bus stops, train stations, and telephone poles up and down the northeastern corridor between Philly and Boston.

The play had been considered controversial because it highlighted the struggle for black female self-affirmation, on the one hand, and, on the other, the recognition that such affirmation demanded a serious critique of black male brutality. So I was curious about the play itself, which I'd never read or seen performed, and about Lisa's choice to interpret what she'd insisted during the summer was one of its most emotionally charged scenes.

I watched, transfixed, as she acted out the lady in red's story of "sullen," "coquett[ish]" seduction and malicious expulsion of men for whom

> she wanted to be unforgettable
> she wanted to be a memory
> a wound   to every man
> arragant enough to want her.

Describing herself as

> the wrath
> of women in windows
> fingerin shade / ol lace curtains
> camoflagin despair &
> stretch marks, (34)

she talked of lovers punished with postcoital indifference because they

> had wanted no more
> than to lay between her sparklin thighs
> & had planned on leavin before dawn
> & she had been so divine
> devastatingly bizarre the way
> her mouth fit round
> & now she stood a
> reglar colored girl
> fulla the same malice
> livid indifference as a sistah
> worn from supportin a wd be hornplayer
> or waitin by the window. (36–37)

As I watched, incensed and excited about occupying the position of overwrought spectator, I felt obligated by the requirements of that role to maintain a safe physical and analytical distance from the performer and her performance. Still, I hoped in vain that this portrait of male "arragance" and one woman's response thereto might help me to understand the actress immersed in her role.

Instead of clarity, I was left with more unanswerable questions. Watching her, I abandoned all that I'd been taught at Brandeis about the problems of assuming that texts speak the views of their artists unambiguously. Feeling defensive and interpretively stimulated, I was sure that I was gazing on an artistic rendering of sociocultural truths that contributed to our own painful drama, whose lines and rhythms Lisa controlled even more deftly than she did the words and sentiments that Shange placed in the mouth of the lady in red.

Then, as now, I wondered what the costs were of seeing one's suffering as symbolic of the pain of an entire group. Of seeking retribution for despair-"camoflagin" black women who, as a group, had been mistreated by black men. And if their despair was indeed camouflaged, how can she be certain of its presence and its manifestations?

Why does the lady in red speak in the third person? Rather than performing her own experiences, she seems to be acting out another's flawed script or artistically rendering the products of her creative, necessarily limited perception of black gender relations. What, I now wonder, are the costs—for the lady in red and any woman who speaks her words—of assuming that role or of assuming both that all black men are dogs and that all black women who stand at windows fingering shades are their victims? Can men also be victims if women are seen as blameless, as responding self-protectively to black male offenses and their threat?

I felt she was speaking of me, to me, through a character she'd embodied to articulate her own and other black women's views of me and of other black men. And though I'd seen sufficient evidence to confirm the widely disseminated view that many black men were good-for-nothing bastards, I bristled at the suggestion—clearly registered in her artistic and personal choices—that I was one of those lustful, commitment-phobic men whom vengeful, self-protective women entice sexually only to demonstrate to these men that they'd wanted nothing but sex, too. Despite my anger, I inferred from Shange's words a meaning much more significant and subtle than its presentation of male self-centeredness: in striking a putative blow for much-abandoned, much-abused "reglar colored girl[s]," women who use their bodies and souls as ammunition inflict more damage on themselves than on their easily satiated enemies.

I knew that I'd been dazzled by Lisa, enthralled by her looks, her vivaciousness, and the sorrow that lurked beneath the surface of her glittering exterior. Because I insisted on making such comparisons, if (like the character she portrayed) she "slowed to be examined," "delighted she was desired," how was I to think of the fact that I'd spent more than a year examining her, fantasizing about her, even as I professed love to a woman hundreds of miles away? And what, indeed, were the connections between the apparent indifference of the black male predator turned victim-of-sorts to his hostile expulsion and my own silent, gut-wrenching abandonment?

Enthralled despite myself, I longed to help her "gather her tinsel & / jewels from the tub," to assist rather than be banished as a consequence of her transformation back into her "reglar" self. As she walked offstage, I thought of the concept of "intentional fallacy" that I'd encountered in the preliminary research I'd done for my senior thesis. According to this theory, readers are incapable of discovering definitively the thematic intentions of artists. As I moved toward the exit against a stream of late arrivals, I felt the sort of disappointment I imagined literary scholars experienced when this theory became widely disseminated and they had to come to terms with the fact that, rather than discovering textual truth, the interpretations they offered were, at best, highfalutin guesses.

The next day, I enrolled in an Afro-American studies seminar called "The Black Woman." I did so primarily because I wanted to understand the motivations for male abuse of women, its consequences, and female intellectuals' critique of both black misogyny and women's responses to its manifestations. No course I'd ever enrolled in seemed potentially as relevant, even crucial, to my life, or as promising in terms of its ability to illuminate aspects of my personal and familial history, as this one.

Despite our twelve female classmates' apparent comfort with our presence, the professor clearly didn't trust the three male students who'd enrolled in the course, and didn't want us there. When I began to sense the teacher's hostility, I tried unsuccessfully to win her over, first with my boyish charm, then with formidable displays of industriousness and intelligence. When it became clear that she wasn't impressed with any of those qualities, I strove merely not to piss her off. Eventually I resolved to try to ignore her hostility, which I surmised was a function of her sense of all black men's deeply troubling participation in black female subjugation. Whenever I felt angry, I reminded myself that as symbolic representatives of our gender and race, the males enrolled in "The Black Woman" were being made to bear the burden of ritualized black female wrath explored in and through such works as Angela Davis's autobiography, *The Black Woman*, Michele Wallace's *Black Macho and the Myth of the Superwoman*, and *for colored girls*. Our implication was, if not biologically predetermined, then the inevitable result of our acculturation.

For my final paper, I wrote on *The Bluest Eye*, employing formulations we'd explored in class to analyze patterns of intraracial and intergender violence in the novel. And though I'd mastered the art of the college essay sufficiently to produce excellent papers in the views of all my other teachers—tenured white male professors of English primarily—my "Black Woman" teacher, who was doing doctoral work at Boston University, gave me a near-failing grade on the final paper, and a C- for the course. Ray and I were so certain that the Ds she'd given us on these final assignments were the result of an antiblack male bias that we filed a joint protest against our professor with the chair of Afro-American Studies.

Our protest proved successful. Still, when I first looked at the B on my transcript next to "The Black Woman," I wondered whether my response to her assessment of my work reflected precisely the sort of male disregard for black women's intellectual authority about which we'd spent part of the semester reading. How, precisely, do you decide between, on the one hand, individual self-interest and feelings of mistreatment and, on the other, institutional conditions from which, in countless ways, one profits as a consequence of one's privilege and by which, consequently, others are oppressed?

In addition, I wondered about the extent to which even posing the question signals one's susceptibility to the deep self-loathing that is shame—the often wrenching response to guilt, embarrassment, unworthiness, or disgrace—which may result either from one's behavior or, in the cases of *The Bluest Eye's* Pecola and oppressed people generally, from others' successful manipulations of one's views of one's relationship to the world. I was both angry at the professor and ashamed of my self-protective, potentially sexist response; was both deserving and undeserving of the department chair's intervention; was both guilty of having the potential to harm black females—and, though none of the texts we encountered in "The Black Woman" was much concerned with this reality, to be harmed by them—and not overly concerned that my charges of gendered bias might affect the professor's life or her interpretation of her own motives.

After some weeks and months of self-inquiry, I recognized that my responsibility was not to protect the professor from the potentially serious consequences of her behavior. In classroom situations, my responsibility was to do my work as skillfully as possible and make sure that I was evaluated fairly for those efforts. My guilt and shame did not keep me from rising to a level of self-righteous indignation equivalent to hers that allowed her to give me a near-failing grade in the first place. Though I was well aware that my petition could be considered the self-interested reply of an arrogant black man, and was perplexed by the host of insoluble problems posed by my cultural heritage, I couldn't passively accept this black female's apparently wrathful response.

As I was traveling home for Christmas, soon after I'd completed my thesis and after matters with "The Black Woman" had been resolved, I thought—as I had during train rides home between semesters during each of the previous three years—about my father or, more precisely, about his death. Three years earlier, a telephone call from my mother just before I left for the train station for Christmas break had alerted me to the fact that he had died. As I traveled to the station, and as the overcrowded train moved south past icy urban and suburban scenes, past dormant trees and tufts of grass in abandoned fields, I felt nothing. All my life, I knew that he and I walked the same earth, and that we were residents of the same city. I saw evidence of his rage on my mother's flesh, but he'd never seemed like a real person to me. And in the half year before his death, I could look at his picture and see that we were biologically connected. Still, he was no more than a myth to me, a symbol of the absent presence of brutal male force.

To the extent that I registered at all the news that cancer had claimed him, I was mainly concerned about the seeming inappropriateness of my response as I measured what I thought I was supposed to feel on the occasion of a father's death against my own emotional neutrality. As I witnessed my brother's tears and my mother's surprisingly somber response, a sense of guilt crept into my psyche, as it does often when I experience a profound dissonance between my own and others' reactions, and I wondered whether I was a cold, heartless monster.

My mother was the medium through which I had access to my father, the conduit of alarming tales of brutality that made me want to be different from him and to understand how she'd responded, physically and emotionally, to being thrust into the role of victim. There was no space in those stories, or in the narrative of pain written graphically on her body, for a consideration of his humanity, his motivation, his hurt. His rage simply existed, simply was.

These narratives provided me with no impetus to seek to understand or to care about him. In fact, as maternal tales of victimization, they insisted that I not consider him at all, except as a source of my mother's mark and much of her misery. She could—probably did—hate him, because she'd known him. But given that her stories failed to explore certain issues overtly, including the psychic needs that the role of victim satisfied for my mother, I felt that I was responding unsympathetically, like a (potentially) brutal male child rather than as her dutiful offspring.

Sometimes, however, I let myself become aware momentarily of these silences. At such points, I understood that these were manipulative, partial narratives that allowed her to present a picture in which, among other things, her own emotional involvement in this pattern of unjustifiable violence was hardly addressed. In her case, I was never attracted to the game of blaming the victim, but I did struggle at times with the feeling that parts of her representations of her history seemed strategically vague.

I sometimes wanted to know why she stayed with him long enough for him to have fathered four children who survived their initial journeys home from the hospital, but I was more interested in what had attracted her to him in the first place. And I occasionally wondered, even as I embraced her demonizing myths, if she could remember his first warm, inviting smile; could recall the first time his rough (smooth? cool? hot?) palms brushed against her skin, the warm (cold?) tingle of their first firm meeting of wet (moist? dry?) lips; could reconstruct the look and feel and smell of disrobed bodies, the rough tickle at the base of her neck caused by his whiskey-soaked breath and his musty, calloused feet bumping drowsily against her calves as she stared at the wall, just before she turned—moved by the spirit of morbid fascination that drew her to strangers' funerals—to inspect his tipless finger.

I'd heard a great deal about the particulars of his wild-eyed attacks—the sharp, stinging bruises his clenched fists and booted feet left on her flesh—and her sense of helplessness. She could touch her scars and recall what she had been like before him, before that deceptive smile and their first tentative, drunken act of intimacy, before she lightly caressed the site of his incompleteness and met his externalized rage.

Hating anyone, especially *him,* I'd come to believe, required knowledge and/or understanding, neither of which I possessed. Early on, I reconciled myself to certain incontrovertible facts of life: that snow is cold, rain is wet, liquid whose molecules are altered by long periods of contact with heat can scald, and my father beat the hell out of my mother.

Without a language to understand his violence as such, I approached it as history, ritual, myth, ideology, and essential truth about power relations. I knew that whatever and whoever I was, I had been formed in direct opposition to those haunting, terroristic tales of gendered and racialized acts of social control.

As I walked past his open casket, flanked by my siblings, I tried to muster up some intense emotion. I wanted to want to cry, to caress his hair with my frozen fingertips, to look at him with remorse and recognition. When these responses were not forthcoming, I wanted to want to smash his expressionless face—a face that, in death, surrounded by satiny trappings of cherubic peace, looked nothing like mine—and to spit strategically on his forehead to wash away the humanity-conferring funereal makeup to reveal the monster he really was. I wanted to want to pull out my apartment key and surgically scar his face with a simulacrum of his rage that was permanently etched into my mother's right arm.

But I felt nothing, did nothing. His dead, vulnerable body,

stretched out in this casket, visible, tangible even, in ways he'd never been to me, made him no more real than he'd ever seemed. Seated at the front of the large funeral home showroom filled with familiar-looking people whom I'd never seen before, I was moved by my grandmother's stoic silence. I was touched by my brother's sense of loss, for he had, indeed, responded enthusiastically to our father's deathbed conversion. I was surprised and, frankly, somewhat amused that Debby—for whom our father was as much a stranger as he was for me—was crying. And I wondered whether Carol's laughter was an elaborate defense against painful recollection of, if not the violence itself, then being forced into the role of six-year-old nurse after he'd broken Mommy's bones. Grateful for Carol's mocking laughter, I joined it with my own, as I'd often done when we were young parishioners devising elaborate and scandalous histories for prominent church members as we sat through another eerily familiar Catholic service.

Afterward my mother, who hadn't attended the funeral, hosted a small gathering for some female relatives of his from Delaware—a sister or two, a cousin or two, and a niece or two, if I remember correctly. Hers was a generous gesture that allowed her to mark my father's passing and demonstrate that she'd absolved him of his sins against her. But whatever his relatives' presence signaled for her, it challenged my calculated indifference, threatening to humanize him in ways that Ricky's stories about our father's generosity never had for me.

Not long after they'd made themselves comfortable, one of his relatives said, "Junior would have been all right if he'd stayed in the country. The city was what ruined him. Turned him into somebody I didn't recognize. Yeah, he was a nice boy, but this city rubbed that out of him."

Unsettled by this theory of the social and cultural sources of what were, in my mother's narratives, Carl Henry Cutler Jr.'s organic brutality, I jumped up to dispose of the near empty bag of trash that sat under the kitchen sink. On the way to the sooty hallway incinerator, I wondered what he'd been like before he migrated to the cradle of American liberty and became infected with hepcat zeal for conks, garish zoot suits, and black-and-white spats.

Before he confronted widely disseminated myths about the white man, with whom he had to learn to deal because he'd traded in the relative security and self-sufficiency of his family's Delaware farmlands for mass transportational access to the Uptown, the Royal, the Waterfront, and other seductive urban sites. Before he encountered worldly, high yellow gals with sweetly swaying hips and audible contempt for his peasant ways. Before he smiled hopefully in the bar on Ninth and Rodman Street at the thin brown woman whose averted gaze he misinterpreted as a sign of shyness, ignoring her enthrallment with the small ashtray blaze she'd built and nursed along with a shot of whiskey and a cold bottle of Schmidt's. Before he journeyed across time and space with her—past the green gates and barbed wire of Philadelphia Electric's newly installed power plant, past the convent where white women whose faith in an ancient, multiauthored book moved them to forsake earthly pleasures in favor of cramped quarters and nightly prayers for guidance on how to stimulate poor kids. Before he exchanged wringing chickens' necks in rural Delaware for breaking that brown woman's bones less than a mile from City Hall.

I couldn't listen to the mournful countermythologizing about this man whose youthful image I resembled but whose aged face, gnarled, veined hands, and whitened hair suggested that he'd become someone entirely different from the man in the picture and, perhaps, in my mother's narratives. I knew of the harm he'd caused. I learned, through my mother's act of generosity, that she was trying to forgive or had, in fact, forgiven him. What else did I need to know? He was dead and had never seemed alive to me. He was, in death as in life, if not wholly irrelevant, as forever unknowable to me as I was to him.

Soon after I arrived at the English department ceremonies, the chair began to call the graduates up to receive our diplomas. Hearing my name, I rose quickly and made my way to the stage as he announced my various honors. When he'd finished, I heard Carol's unmistakable "Go 'head, Mike" above the polite applause. In that strange building badly in need of repair, her voice echoed the structures of feeling we'd created as kids, the salve and salvation we relied on to soothe and protect us, the balm of noisy encouragement and inaudible concern we rubbed on one another despite our petty jealousies, our competitiveness, our shared sense of extremely limited material and psychic resources.

Hearing the voice that had helped to foster my intellectual curiosity, that had gathered Ricky, Debby, and me together for excursions to the Free Library to meet up with Henry and Busby and Encyclopedia Brown and other serial book characters waiting patiently for us on the shelves, I smiled, located and waved at my family, and raised the black leather diploma case high in the air in an uncharacteristic public gesture of jubilation.

Although my youngest sister was my best familial friend, and my brother my roommate, buddy, and basketball compatriot and rival, Carol—who'd taught me to read before I went to kindergarten, who'd mothered her younger siblings even when she was aware that she needed mothering herself—held a magical place in my heart and my imagination. When I was very young, I looked on her with awe because she seemed to be both a part of and apart from our plucky family drama. Hers was an involved distance that allowed her to take care of us and our mother, at that same time that our collective neediness forced us generally to ignore her psychic needs. Whenever I could, I'd followed Carol around like a lovesick, companionless dog until she shooed me away in frustration.

Seeing her at my college graduation, seated above me in the balcony next to the man she loved and who made her happy, next to our mother, who smiled with unmistakable maternal pride, next to Aunt Grace, whose kind, generous demeanor with "Tippy's kids" masked a frightening set of behavioral standards that no one could possibly meet, I was happy to have pleased them. Before that moment, I hadn't given much thought to what I'd accomplished, or to what it meant for a dirt-poor black boy from Southwark to get a diploma from such a fine university, or to the relative ease with which I'd survived my academic trials and tribulations.

I caught up with my family a few minutes after the departmental ceremonies had concluded, and I showed my mother the diploma-less case with a note that promised that the company that Brandeis had commissioned to do its printing would send the actual diploma

I'd earned once my honors had been affixed to it. Professors Fisher and Gilmore, who'd encouraged and challenged me and whose generally intimidating reserve I attributed to the intensity of their engagement with interpretive matters, smiled broadly at me, called me over, and introduced themselves to my family.

After giving my family directions to our next destination, I walked slowly over to Dan, who was waiting for me outside. We sauntered toward the outdoor amphitheater, where the general graduation ceremonies were being held. We felt happy, forced into joy, perhaps, by pomp and circumstance, by ceremonial splendor and a sense of relief. Over the preceding weeks, we'd talked about what we were convinced would be the emotionally difficult conclusion of our four years together and the beginning of our adult lives, neither of which we were anticipating unambiguously. I'd shared with Dan nearly every thought of any consequence I'd had since the first week of our freshman year, and while we knew that our bond would withstand our near permanent physical separation, we were aware also of the psychic benefits for both of us of proximity and daily contact.

Instead of dwelling on the sadness I felt over having to leave my best friend, I turned to a familiar subject.

"Dan, that's where I saw that shrink after Lisa left me," I exclaimed as we walked past the ominous gray structure that housed Psychological Services.

"The one who told you you were suffering from—what was it he called it—'maternal fixation'?"

"I don't remember."

Two months into my posttraumatic lethargy, I hadn't started writing my senior thesis, was barely able to concentrate in my classes, and had lost most of my interest in food, weight lifting, basketball, and sex. Having listened almost daily to my tales of romantic woe, Corrine, one of my close female friends, suggested that I go speak to the new black counselor whom she knew had helped some of her dorm mates to sort out some troubling academic and personal problems. I was skeptical, because I felt that by seeking such help, I would be acknowledging that I was neither strong nor smart enough to think my way past this difficulty. At the end of another week of misery, however, I scheduled an appointment.

The counselor, a black man from Philadelphia, appeared cordial and concerned, though not particularly attentive. He seemed unimpressed by, and uninterested in, my explanation of Lisa's sudden withdrawal and her subsequent refusal to speak to me, and he asked instead about my relationship with my mother. When I discussed the sense of rage and romantic emptiness I felt, he explained that children often worry that events devised to mark their success—like, for example, college graduation—are in fact frightening reminders of both their excitement about, and their fear of, independence from their mothers. When I told him that my heartbreak made it hard for me to sleep or eat or play, he asked whether my scholastic success would catapult me beyond the boundaries of family he assumed my mother had worked diligently to erect.

Realizing I was being asked to follow his line of Freudian reasoning, I said rather sheepishly, "Well, she had a problem with alcohol, and she recently stopped drinking."

"How do you feel about that?"

"Happy. Skeptical. I don't know; I haven't given it much thought. I been too concerned about Lisa dumping me and acting like she doesn't know me."

"Are you angry, too? Do you think at all about why she chose to wait until now to stop drinking? Most people would, I suspect. They'd think, perhaps, 'Why didn't she stop when I was young and needed her,' even if they were ashamed to say it."

"I don't know."

"You need to think about it, and about how you feel, including what to make of your anger. We'll talk about it, same time next week?"

"But what do I do about Lisa? How do I get through this?"

"Only you have the answer to that question, my man. Take care, okay?"

Except for a few short visits over the preceding two years, I hadn't been home to witness my mother's efforts to stop drinking. Consequently, I felt as if I were being asked to believe in a magical metamorphosis for which, as a child, I learned the futility of wishing. For years, it had been clear that her body recovered less and less well from extended binges, and since I entered prep school, the aftershocks of these binges were three or four days of bedridden agony.

I believe that notwithstanding her incapacity to continue to carry on as she had in her youth, she stopped because she'd become aware of the harm her drinking was doing and had done to our family and wanted to try to undo some of that damage. The familial nest, as it were, was empty and had been for an unusually long time. Rick, who'd moved out before he finished high school, had entered the Air Force, Debby and Carol were gone, and I hadn't lived at home for any extended period since the summer of 1978. During the agonizing process of applying to graduate school, I reluctantly included Penn, whose proximity to family chaos, I was well aware, could prove psychically and intellectually disastrous if I ended up there.

But I kept hearing reports from my siblings about my mother's resolve, about the weeks and months that had passed since she'd had a drink. During Christmas vacation of my senior year, I got firsthand evidence. She was clean and sober, subject, on occasion, to fits of irritability; but she was also more open, more forthcoming with smiles, hugs, and serious conversation than I remembered her ever being. No longer in denial, she seemed to want us to experience her as she was without booze—smart, cynical, silly, caring, put upon, amazingly giving and committed to her family and friends—and to experience us in ways that allowed her to move beyond the pat formulations, the thoughtless generalizations, into which she used to fit our behavior.

Being home with an always sober mother was both exhilarating and utterly disconcerting. I didn't know how to deal with her sobriety, with the near constancy of her physical and mental presence in the apartment. Without the counterbalance of alcoholic escapism, without the tension created by her drinking, she seemed at once too stable and too unfamiliar a person to be my mother. Although I was ecstatic about her hard-won victory, I kept expecting a return to alcoholic form, maybe even sometimes hoping for it. At some moments, I longed for the chaos of liquid addiction, which, whatever else it offered, provided the moorings of familiarity. To discover, at age twenty, a drastically changed mother, a mother defined not by her relationship to alcohol but by its absence, was, in truth, a shocking thing.

During that vacation, we spent a good deal of time talking about a range of subjects. She spoke wistfully about her inability to recapture on the old typewriter Aunt Grace had recently given her the secretary-caliber speed she'd reached as a high school student. She asked me about how welcome I felt as a black male at a predominantly Jewish school, about my career plans and my love life. Hers were penetrating questions for which I had only partial answers. I'd learned throughout my life to express my anger at my mother's alcoholism as bemused, patronizing exasperation, a strategy that at times allowed me the freedom not to have to think seriously about either her struggles or my own. Faced with her insistence on considered, heartfelt answers, I offered whiny diatribes about Lisa's behavior over the previous three months.

"Why's she acting like that, Michael? What did you do to her?"

"Nothing, Ol' Lady. Nothing I know of, anyway. I guess she just figured she didn't like me enough."

"This is the same girl you visited in the summer? The tall, skinny actress whose picture you showed me?"

"Yeah."

"Something about her I didn't like anyway. She seemed too full of herself."

"Mommy! You didn't even meet her!"

"I know. But when you talked about her, you always seemed so needy. You can't need somebody that much, like they can save you from something."

"Something like what?"

"I don't know. From what you don't have or can't figure out about yourself."

"Ain't that what love's supposed to be? One person helping to fulfill and complete the other?"

"Boy, you been reading too many books or something! Where'd you hear that?"

"In the literature I've read in classes. On soap operas and in the movies. In those *True Romance* magazines you read."

"Don't take that nonsense seriously, or you're going to spend your life chasing after something you'll never find."

"Then what am I supposed to be looking for?"

"Somebody who won't hurt you out of selfishness or fear. Ever found someone like that? That skinny actress like that?"

"Obviously not."

"Then I guess you better keep looking."

Near the end of the vacation, I scheduled a meeting with the graduate chair of Penn's English Department. Taking to heart Alan's advice that I strategically pursue my professional goals, I figured that because I was in town for the holidays, I'd signal my sincere interest in attending the university and help one member of the evaluation committee connect a face to a name on an application.

"You really gonna go there if they let you in? You're going to come back home? It's been a long time since you lived in Philly, you know."

"I think so, Ol' Lady. If they let me in and give me enough money to live on. You know, they actually pay full tuition for you to go to graduate school in English, plus they give you something like three thousand dollars a year to live on. And some schools are actually interested in having black students."

"Michael, you know I hate that word."

"Still?"

"Even more now."

"What should I call us? Negroes?"

" 'Colored' still makes the most sense to me."

"Anyway, I'm going to study black literature in graduate school. I want to write about books like *The Bluest Eye*—you remember that novel I made you read a couple years ago?"

"What are you going to say about *that*?"

"I don't know."

"You mean people actually write on those kinds of books with all that sex and violence? That woman whose Kotex fell off her? That ugly girl and her sick father?"

"Yeah. And Penn has a black professor who teaches English and has written books and stuff."

"What's his name?"

"I don't remember. I ran across a book he wrote about this poet, Countee Cullen, in the library when I was looking up stuff for my thesis. It was some city."

"Atlanta? Santa Fe? Lincoln?"

"No."

"Miami? Birmingham? Syracuse?"

"No. But it is in the South, I think."

"Michael, you're not going to give my grandchildren one of those funny names, are you? Kwami or Kofi or Muhammad or something like that?"

"Ol' Lady, I ain't even got a girlfriend. You don't have to worry about grandkids from me."

"Or name one after a city or a country like that professor? Brazil or Canada or Wilmington or Cleveland?"

"Mommy, I'm going to name the first San Francisco Awkward! Don't that sound nice? The second I'll name after you—Tippy."

"You know, I'd be really happy if you came back home. When will you know?"

"March or April, probably. We'll see how it goes."

In March, a few weeks after I'd received an acceptance letter from Penn, I went to Philadelphia with a group of black students, ostensibly to attend a party that the parents of one of my friends were throwing at her house in nearby Camden in honor of her twenty-first birthday. I tagged along in part because I wanted to experience the sense of community promised by such an exodus, and because this trip provided me a relatively inexpensive opportunity to see my mother and to see whether returning home seemed possible.

I was dropped off outside my apartment building at seven o'clock in the evening, and just a few minutes after I'd hugged my mother and set my bag on the bed of my room, the telephone rang. Insisting in mock self-importance that my fans were clearly monitoring my every move, I beat my mother to the phone and said, in the most authoritative voice I could muster, "Michael Awkward speaking."

"Hello. This is Houston Baker, calling from the English department at the University of Pennsylvania. Do you have a few minutes?"

I could barely speak. How'd he know I was here? What did he

want? I'd wanted to rest, to relax, to forget about the decision I knew I'd have to make about graduate school in the next week or two. On the other end of the line, speaking in a voice heavy with authority, self-confidence, and urgency, was the man whose name I hadn't recalled in an earlier conversation with my mother. The man whose praises my advisers had sung and whose short book on the life and career of Countee Cullen I'd read twice when I was supposed to be writing my thesis.

With the exception of a single question I asked about the numbers of black Ph.D.'s Penn had produced in the previous decade, my contribution to the ten-minute conversation consisted mostly of nodding my head in affirmation and whispering "uh-huh" like someone entranced by a rollicking, awe-inspiring sermon in an urban black church where parishioner participation was utterly essential.

My primary reaction—to his call, to the excitement in his voice when he spoke about the prospects of mentoring me, to his forceful self-certainty—was fear. This voice could dance circles around me. It was a voice that radiated not money, like Fitzgerald's Daisy Buchanan, but something I suspected was even more intimidating: hard-won power. It slipped effortlessly between King's English and hood dialect, between authoritative assertion and sizzling slang, overwhelming me on each register. Standing in front of the table in my mother's apartment where the telephone had been securely stationed for more than a decade, I felt a thrill like being on a roller-coaster ride so terrifying that not even the most uncalculated of screams could register the sensory shock of its lows and highs, its dips and turns.

I wondered whether, in addition to all of the other things I knew I'd be expected to learn to get a Ph.D., I'd have to demonstrate something close to his level of linguistic dexterity to project myself as culturally black. Prep school and college provided few sites of black cultural expression (pickup basketball games, dances, closed dormitory room doors, the Brotherhood table). In other settings— especially in classrooms—its unacceptability, signaled in all sorts of ways by all sorts of people, caused me to repress its funky rhythms, its energetic rejection of standard speech. Except when I was speaking excitedly with my siblings and trusted friends, or talking shit on the court, black speech filled me with a tremendous sense of self-consciousness.

Part of my education consisted of forcing myself to speak differently, of naturalizing tonal arrangements, syllabic structures, and sentence formations that seemed, if not altogether unfamiliar, then deracinating to a boy whose formative years had been spent trying to learn the hip talk of the cool cats and boss chicks in my neighborhood.

As his voice assumed, abandoned, and took up again a range of discursive styles, I questioned the efficacy of my having spent seven years unlearning modes of speech that virtually all the people with whom I grew up employed as a rule. The notion that one could speak both right and black, could move effortlessly from proper to street discourse, from their to our forms of verbal address, hadn't occurred to me. As I spoke with him, and for months and years afterward, I longed for the sort of dexterity he displayed.

The fear I'd felt at the beginning of the call made some room in my imagination for wonder, awe, and excitement. I was thrilled by the prospect of having a committed black male mentor, developing such verbal fluency, and gaining access to my elite hometown university's luscious greens and well-protected buildings, which had seemed both so unwelcoming and so full of promise when I was a child.

When I got off of the phone, I smiled at my mother and told her that I planned to accept Penn's offer.

"Who was that on the phone? One of your girlfriends? Seems like you didn't get a word in edgewise."

"Mommy! That was that professor I told you about who teaches at Penn. His first name is Houston."

"That's a different name. Where's his people from?"

"We certainly can't talk about 'different names,' can we? He called to tell me he really wants me to come to school there."

"That's what you want to do?"

"Uh-huh."

Dan and I sat together in the blinding sun that soaked the graduation ceremonies, barely listening to the president, barely paying attention to the various voices that conferred postgraduate and honorary degrees. Sweating profusely, I listened, respectfully at first, then with genuine interest, to the commencement speaker, Elie Wiesel, whose thinning hair blew wildly as he stood at the lectern on the sunlit stage and spoke of what he hoped would be our responses to the atrocities that people had suffered in the past. Rather than amuse and delight us with the typical sort of motivational speech I'd heard at every graduation I'd been a part of or attended, he exhorted us to consider the importance of remaining continually mindful of the motivations and likely recurrence of Nazism and its philosophical equivalents.

I listened to and watched the varied responses to Wiesel's call to the graduating class to honor the six million Jews who'd died at the hands of the Nazis and millions and millions of others who perished in clashes with a variety of ignorant armies of oppression. As I had on numerous occasions over the previous four years, I looked first at Dan, whose general thoughtfulness and secular Jewish skepticism often provided me with useful strategies for dealing with my Brandeis experience. But I had no idea what he was thinking.

I wasn't sure how material strivings, thirty years after Hitler's demise, could challenge anyone's sense of the still-terrifying effectiveness of Nazi slaughter. Nor was I clear on the practicalities of expecting from young adults of my generation active remembrance of devastation that they could experience only through newsreels, photographs, concentration camp markings, books, and survivors' increasingly hazy memories.

In a country whose increasingly guilt-free remembrance of its own acts of savagery against my people was and is nearly as shamefully self-serving as was the peculiar institution itself, perpetual mourning—anything more, in fact, than an annual, compartmentalized ritual of loss—was inconceivable to me. Americans seem to monumentalize grief and pain because we want to remember on the one day when we know we have to, and forget when remembrance would be, among other things, inconvenient.

During my years at Brandeis, America reached the peak of its participation in the disco era, marked by the 1977 release of the movie *Saturday Night Fever*, starring John Travolta. Eschewing the casual preppie Izod shirts, chinos, Levi cords, and Docksider shoes I'd grown accustomed to seeing at Governor Dummer, an infinitely more ostentatious, urban, and self-conscious crowd of cool Jews sported Sergio Valenti and Gloria Vanderbilt jeans; shiny, bright, large-collared shirts; thick, polished gold chains; wide bell-bottomed pants; and dangerous-looking platform shoes.

Like much of America at that time, my class aspired generally to be a chic, good-times crowd, leaving our cares and woes as far behind as we possibly could. Our externalized egotism shocked the sensibilities of Americans who had come of age in both the button-down fifties, when rock and roll was impetus for aural rebellion, and in the wild-haired sixties, when youth passion for freedom of all sorts transformed the nation into something that even the most astute of secular visionaries hadn't dared to prophesy. During my college years, except for sporadic anti-apartheid demonstrations, there were no sustained outbreaks of the sort of political agitation that marked Brandeis's brief history, symbolized, for me at least, by Angela Davis's revolutionary renown after her time on the Waltham campus. That lack of agitation was in part a result of the fact that we were still sorting out the social, political, and cultural consequences of the transformations that students had helped to create in the previous two decades.

Listening to Wiesel, I wondered if people are inclined generally to pick at individual and collective wounds perpetually. Was there a statute of limitations on how long we'd define ourselves and our communities exclusively in relation to executioners' theories and machines of mass destruction? How, precisely, do we measure the price of willful personal and communal forgetting against the costs of struggling to maintain or, in many cases, *produce* what passes for vivid memories of that horror? How, I wondered, does Jewish engagement with such painful group narratives relate both to my people's energetic repression and, since the civil rights period, our indignant detailing of American slavery's inhumanity and persistent effects? On that sunny, windy day, when Wiesel extolled the virtues of a life lived in self-conscious service to the past and to one's people, dead and alive, I thought he was a brave—if obviously traumatized and hopelessly naive—old fool.

Still, on my last day at Brandeis, I wondered what, precisely, was the responsibility of survivors to those whose past suffering helped to determine the course and parameters of their lives. Listening to Wiesel, I thought of lyrics from an Ashford and Simpson song about the end of a love affair: "This time / the debt is settled in my mind." I know now that there were, obviously, other times—moments before "this time"—when the song's lovers were similarly secure in their beliefs that they'd paid in full, that they were free and clear, only to discover, like Arthur Miller's tragic salesman and his afrocentric updating in the form of August Wilson's fenced-in Troy Maxson, that the psychic costs of such struggles are not easily transcended even when the mortgage is paid off and the protective domestic fence has seemingly been completed.

How, precisely, do we know when we've honored our forebears sufficiently to be cleared of our debts to them? Absent the watchful eyes of whatever gods we worship or choose not to worship, absent a clear sense of either purpose or the possibilities of success, what compels our Sisyphean struggles with rocks and hills we can move around and on but can only dream of conquering?

By the time Lisa initiated our generally friendly reconciliation two months before I graduated, I'd gotten involved with someone else and had stopped idealizing Lisa and expecting her to explain her abandonment of me in ways that could help me understand her, myself, what we'd been to each other, or the culture that produced us.

A year or so after I left Brandeis, she began making somewhat frantic telephone calls attempting to involve me in devising solutions to her problems while she manifested little or no concern for mine. I visited her three times over the course of three years in a series of small apartments in Boston suburbs when I was in town seeing Dan. These visits were marked by an inauthentic, nostalgic glee that quickly gave way for me to an overwhelming sadness. Looking at her, I knew I'd lost the capacity for the sort of idealized love I'd felt for her and that had animated my soul and my imagination for much of my life.

She continued to look, talk, and walk the same, albeit with

somewhat less affectation and unguarded optimism, but she ceased to be the beautiful, wonderfully self-satisfied character whom Dan and I jokingly called the Divine One. As it became clear that her struggles against camouflaged pain were becoming increasingly difficult, and her vulnerability became the trait that seemed most to define her, all I could imagine as a fitting expression of the residual emotions I felt was making love with her. The movement from transcendent love to primal desire, I was well aware, was my necessary, joyless, self-protective adjustment to the consequences of soul-shattering betrayal.

As we rode public transportation to the Trailways Bus Depot near the end of her tear-filled visit to Philadelphia in the summer of 1983, I knew that I needed to remove myself from this emotional entanglement. Whatever else she was, she was also a reminder of my loss of a sense of faith in deep, true, selfless love. Still struggling, as I was, with the implications of that loss, I knew I couldn't be confronted by her sorrowful presence, too.

In 1991 I received a message that she'd called my office while I was away at a conference on Afro-American studies (whose most memorable—and difficult—moment for me was the affirmative eruption of black women in response to the insistence by one prominent feminist professor that black male literary scholars were, as a group, so full of masculinist arrogance that we were not capable of recognizing our black women colleagues as intellectual equals). A few weeks later, Lisa and I had a brief, uncomfortable conversation, during which she told me that she'd seen a copy of my book on black women novelists in England, where she was touring as a spoken-word artist. She suggested to me that an important feature of her therapeutic efforts to exorcize whatever demons she'd internalized was contacting those whom she'd damaged psychologically.

As we talked, I rocked my year-old daughter on my lap, feeling none of the tug of nostalgia that allowed me to ponder endlessly the music, sports events, and cultural styles of my past. I experienced neither sorrow, nor empathetic horror, nor admiration. I certainly didn't experience the sensation of remembered joy I felt as I spoke with Joan during her two visits to Brandeis to cheer on Governor

Dummer's resurgent basketball team during its consecutive trips to the Independent School finals. At most, what I felt was uncomplicated disinterest.

Two years after this conversation, I turned to the Black Entertainment Television Network for my monthly dose of hip-hop flavor and saw Lisa fronting a smoking jazz band, the spoken-word artist's equivalent of Sade exuding a sense of comfort, charm, and practiced, stylish grace. Soon thereafter I saw her in a fashion layout in *Vibe* that celebrated eclectic styles of youthful urban dress; she looked virtually the same as I remembered her and had miraculously lost five years in age, a seemingly harmless—and certainly time-honored—play with historical truth that *Vibe*'s editors didn't bother to check. Then *Essence* and the *Voice Literary Supplement* mentioned her book of poems, emphasizing her black and primarily female artistic legacy, which included Gil Scott-Heron, Chaka Khan, and, not surprisingly, Ntozake Shange. A year or so later, a CD appeared, with production assistance from several faded hip-hop luminaries.

What struck me most about the book's engagement with Shange's choreopoem was not the book's derivative style or its curious refusal to explore similarly painful material from Lisa's own life experiences. Indeed, I was ultimately disturbed that the Broadway show, which she recognized as a significant textual event in her personal and artistic development, served as another occasion for "camoflagin" or theatrical dissembling. In order to seem fresher, newer, a down Generation X member rather than a soon-to-be played out baby boomer, closer chronologically to those hot, young, shameless thangs for whom female blaxploitation style is the latest fad instead of a well-remembered embarrassment, her book's biography plays freely with truth, claiming that she was eleven when she saw a performance of *for colored girls*. Somehow, lying about her age to a hip-hop magazine seemed less offensive than being unnecessarily deceptive in her first book. To perpetrate this age-old fraud (whose calendar-defying precursors in the black literary tradition include Zora Neale Hurston), and to represent herself as a young(er), natural wonder from the hood, Lisa's biography makes no mention of her having attended college at all.

I wondered how those professors and friends who tutored, applauded, and consoled her felt when they picked up her book and realized that they'd been erased from her strategic accounting of history. Did they question, as I did, why she'd embraced the style but not the antiracist and antipatriarchal substance of Shange's work? Was it simply to profit from the comforting flame and reflected glory of its massive cultural work without having to endure some of the troubling consequences of that legacy? Artists position themselves vis-à-vis their precursors strategically to establish the registers of their own authorial voices; Alice Walker, for example, lauded Hurston's contributions to the preservation of black culture and her presentation of black women's social obstacles while condemning Hurston's autobiographical obfuscations. That knowledge tempered the skepticism of my responses to Lisa's efforts to claim Shange as a precursor while (1) separating herself from facts of her own history that enabled her first performative engagement with *for colored girls*, and (2) participating unselfconsciously in a commodity culture wherein, rather than prodigious talent or a more easily attained quality, ideological engagement, youth—real, imagined, or proclaimed—is the key to the representational kingdom.

Recently, I came across a copy of the CD of the jazz artist in whose music video she'd appeared. In separate photographs on the back cover, he appears with three of the guest performers, including the "beautiful Lisa Manning." Encountering her unfamiliarly gleeful face, I was overcome by a sense of horror well out of proportion with my occasionally self-righteous male feminist streak. I knew, for example, that like sociopolitical 1960s male leaders such as Eldridge Cleaver, whose subsequent promotion of mainstream values shocked their serious and casual followers alike, the bleached blonde tresses sported by Black Arts movement stalwart Nikki Giovanni, and by Shange herself, signal a stylistic sea change in the possibilities of black self-representation. In a world where blonde has become a widely embraced aesthetic possibility rather than an obvious sign of black self-hatred, surely I understand the necessities of using come-hither looks, long legs, and cleavage to move some merchandise. Like everyone else I know or knew, Lisa is creating a persona by her picking and choosing among the painfully small self-promotional packages with which females are confronted in the 1990s if they wish to get a foothold in the record industry.

Of course, 1970s feminism was focused on securing equal rights, privileges, and opportunity for women, including the right of individuals to reject certain formulations in favor of others. The feminism that enabled *for colored girls,* in other words, was about choice, including the choice of what counts as one's authenticating narrative. While creating cultural space for a female Gil Scott-Heron or a Shange-influenced spoken-word artist is undoubtedly a good thing, the terms on which one assumes the right to speak are crucial, too. Otherwise the gains of this movement, like so many others, get appropriated and turned into superficial gestures with limited capacity for significant social comment or intervention. Glamour, glitter, and the projection of the self as stylized entity have largely become the point of many contemporary black cultural performances even as they link themselves to sampled, decontextualized racial glories of the past.

Somewhere at Brandeis, perhaps in our literary methods class with Professor Gilmore, we learned that what is deemed lasting, important art (and at this point in history, *for colored girls* falls into that category, though none of our English professors would have viewed it as such at the end of the 1970s) is typically the result of superior technical skill used in an effort to challenge extant forms of psychic or physical violence and other subjugating social formations. From *The Canterbury Tales* to *Jazz,* the perceived importance of literary and other art forms is determined largely by how skillfully texts depict social misery—its causes and consequences; the self-delusional states into which it throws representatives of both empowered and unempowered classes—and proffer ways of alleviating it.

To place oneself in artistic succession to such truly challenging and progressive art as *for colored girls* and Gil Scott-Heron's *Winter in America* is to invite sizable comparative burdens. However, overattentiveness to surface similarities—like those once discussed between Janet Jackson's engaging postfunk fluff *Rhythm Nation* and Marvin Gaye's brooding, melodic, and transcendent *What's Going On*—limits our capacity to scrutinize carefully what ties some artistic performances strictly to the moment of their creation and dissemination, and what qualities in other works mark them for enduring significance.

According to some contemporary thinking on the subject, artistic significance is the result of talent, thematic and historical particularity, luck, familiarity with extant traditions, an ability to represent the current flavor, and, increasingly, the capacity for shameless self-promotion. Claiming formal linkages to historical personages and racialized styles can help to establish you firmly on the artistic map. Occupying a niche, however, requires more than imitative style and youthful energies. As much as anything else, it requires either a flawless recapitulation of the status quo—witness Boyz II Men's marginally talented juggernaut and Mariah Carey's increasingly vapid output—or the ability to market oneself as a constantly evolving hot thing.

On the page, Lisa's words flow smoothly but say little that hasn't already been said much better by others. On disc, the cascading sheets of jazzy music are overwhelmed by an annoyingly theatrical voice that, quite frankly, I can't listen to for more than five minutes. I look unsuccessfully for her efforts to grapple with the world she has lived in or creates in ways that distinguish her explorations from those of a host of others, and for explanations of her erasures, of her own strategic silences.

Still, because I am aware that I, too, am driven by acknowledged and unacknowledged concerns, fears, enthusiasms, and antipathies, I know that I am also making strategic choices, even here, in a chapter concerned with the performance of social scripts like those that help to determine racial and gendered identity. I've necessarily left out a great deal, for that's what writers must do. In *Shadow and Act,* Ralph Ellison insisted that "the function, the psychology, of artistic selectivity is to eliminate from an art form those elements of experience which contain no compelling significance" (133). Of course, what is significant to one writer or artist (and in one artistic moment) may be insignificant to (and in) another, but we have to read the silences, the pregnant pauses, the unrepresented, along with what actually appears on the pages and in the grooves of recorded history.

As I wrote the bulk of this chapter, I carried Lisa's CD and book around with me from my home to my campus office, expecting to engage them as deeply as the hundreds of texts I've analyzed in a variety of professional settings. I hid them from family and friends as if they were pornography or, as someone joked, evidence of my sadomasochistic tendencies.

Her texts are compelling to me because they challenge my sense both of the power of time to heal wounds and promote forgetfulness and of the malleability of imagination, interpretation, and memory. Rather than awaken unresolved feelings, as some of my friends have intimated as they stared at her striking appearance, they threaten my sense of the importance of events, some of which I've related here. These texts fascinate me, not because I find them artistically powerful especially, but because their tangibility confirms the value of remembering the past—my versions of the past—and tests the extent to which those memories are confirmed by surviving or existing documents in the present.

In the final analysis, I'm more compelled by the existence of these works than I am frustrated with their glib surfaces and the bold liberties they take with truth. Because works such as *for colored girls* explored aspects of black women's pain as Shange perceived them in the 1970s, persuasive challenges exist to male and to white female assumption of the power to determine the meanings of blackness and womanhood respectively. Anita Hill's signal contributions to our national discourse notwithstanding, in the future, scholars may decide that unlike the 1970s, the 1990s did not constitute a decade devoted to artistic exploration of the benefits for black women of breaking silences but, rather, one devoted to investigating more carefully the consequences of strategic, partial articulation. Remaining "closed in silence" (3), to use words from Shange's choreopoem, has its advantages, too, after colored girls—and boys—abandon thoughts of self-destruction in favor of efforts to figure out, as one of my Afro-American studies professors at Brandeis so memorably put what he saw as a fundamental characteristic of black self-presentation, how to survive with style.

SECTION V ❖ The Mother's Breast

In the fall of 1993, tensions erupted at the University of Michigan in reaction to an incendiary photograph on a poster advertising the "Culture Conference" sponsored by a faculty group, Contemporary Study of Social Transformation (CSST). This group sought to problematize—and begin to break down—disciplinary boundaries that its members saw as increasingly stultifying and irrelevant to their conceptualizations of their institutional place. The photograph CSST used to signify its deconstructive concerns featured a bare-breasted black woman nursing an apparently Caucasian baby.

My own reaction to the poster was complicated, at least in part, by my multiple professional roles and responsibilities. As the recently installed director of the Center for Afroamerican and African Studies, I felt compelled to make an administrative decision about whether the poster's display within the center would be considered sufficiently offensive by students and faculty to warrant its removal. (Two female professors took the poster down, thus relieving me of the burden of deciding.) As an educator who was at the time teaching a course on the novels of Toni Morrison, I saw the poster as an effective means of stimulating classroom discussion about one of the issues that her work engages time and time again: the responsibilities entailed in the act of interpretation. Last, as a participant in debates about who could ably interrogate representations of blackness generally and black femaleness in particular, I had to decide what it meant for someone to argue that the poster's subject was, in this contested public space, taboo. Was its visual representation more objectionable than Beloved, for instance, in which Morrison discursively displays the breasts and physical and psychic scars of a character so thoroughly brutalized by slavery that she would rather kill her children than see them ensnared in its dehumanizing clutches?

The poster's offending scene displays the torso of a dark-complected black woman whose sweater is unbuttoned and frames her upper body while a strategically illuminated infant whom we might call an optic white baby, cum the Liberty Paints section of Invisible Man, suckles at her left breast. This play of light and dark serves to highlight their dichotomized roles and cultural places: black / white, nurturer / nurtured, giver / receiver.

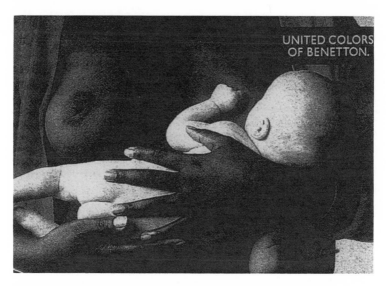

Benetton ad, used to promote "The Culture Conference" at the
University of Michigan, 1993

*Indeed, the baby's exaggerated horizontal position, when seen literally
against the backdrop of the black female torso's verticality, emphasizes—if
we view this obvious generational and racial contrast as containing a
telling spatial dimension—the geographic intersection that this black woman's (voluntary or coerced) act of nurturance permits.*

*Seen in historical terms, the black female figure assumes for many the
position of the lactating slave mother forced by white hegemony to feed
offspring not her own, but the framing of the photograph requires the
spectator to determine, or perhaps even produce, the black female subject's
reaction. Strategically de-facing its black subject, the photograph reduces
her to her dark skin, breasts, and potential service to the white baby, to a
specifically racialized biological function, without providing her the capacity to comment, even subversively, on her role or her reduction.*

*All this being said, I was not then, and still am not, able to articulate a
response to CSST's use of this photograph that reflects mere outrage at its
display in contested public space. It is not that I cannot decide, as the terms
of the campus controversy encourage, whether certain invocations of a
particularly painful historical memory are more relevant to my sense of our
contemporary institutional imperatives than the admittedly intriguing sort*

of problematizing that csst obviously intended. Rather, I am always aware that such reactions—particularly my own—are situationally delimited. I imagine that had the location of its display been, say, an urban museum of African American history and culture, and its artist assumed to be black rather than a white photographer for the United Colors of Benetton, this photo might have been seen as a powerful critique instead of an uncritical reiteration of this trope. Frankly, I am privately torn between a black feminist materialist response and an urge toward the promise of "social transformation," between the pain of black women's past and the sense that focusing solely on that pain erases the possibility of serious interpretive engagement.

Before the beginning of the conference's scheduled events, a black female from the University of Michigan's Women of Color Task Force read a prepared statement on behalf of the group in which she spoke of the hurt and feelings of violation caused by the photograph's display. Although I did not share her sense of the impropriety of csst's choices, I joined other members of the audience in giving her a rousing ovation after she completed her remarks. At that moment, I recognized—with some discomfort and as if for the first time—that regardless of our ideological commitments, gender can indeed lead Afro-American men and women to be differently invested in a politics of black female representation.

In my efforts to engage arguments about men's place(s) in feminist criticism over the previous decade, I'd objected strongly to pronouncements that men couldn't write as and like feminists because men were incapable both of a deep concern about gendered inequity and of sufficient interpretive empathy. According to such arguments, whereas we might read the poster as motivated by racialist insensitivity, black men's investment in maintaining a phallocentric status quo would necessarily limit our ability to share the Task Force member's gendered hurt, anger, and outrage at the black woman's public exposure and, by extension, black women's historical pain and humiliation.

And though when asked by friends about my views, I emphatically rejected the notion that the differences between her feelings about the poster and my own were a function of my male interpretive inadequacies, for weeks I harbored secret, debilitating doubts. Frankly, I felt uncomfortable about the fact that rather than being primarily upset by its display, I found the photograph analytically rich, and the ensuing campus controversy fascinating, including the Task Force member's acknowledgment of a possible biological connection between the white child and the black woman apparently nursing him or her. According to the Task Force member, despite the abolition of slavery and the represented woman's sporting of thoroughly (post)modern Benetton apparel, this biological connection seems plausible only if the baby were the result of the woman's having been raped by a white master.

In the following examinations of this poster and instances of maternal exposure and apparent violation that, for reasons that will become apparent, seem directly connected to the death of my mother in 1986, I attempt to produce readings that move beyond mere outrage. In other words, the following analyses of the display of black maternal breasts seek, in part, to legitimize both my support of the Task Force member's moving comments and my excitement about what I considered the controversy's interpretively provocative features. As I see it, my task as a male feminist scholar is to deal productively with such seemingly bifurcated responses, which may in fact reflect necessary tensions between masculinist and feminist compulsions and between autobiographical and scholarly imperatives.

Academic examination of people, places, and things burdened by a history of representation, as the Benetton photo doubtlessly is, must begin with a strategic placing of the scrutinized object in the context of appropriate investigative categories. Our responsibility as scholars, however, is never to be content with apparently simple assertions about complex matters, including the notion that x means y because it has always meant y. In other words, we are professionally bound to problematize others' placements, others' acts of interrogation, others' histories. In addition to contextualizing representation, our livelihood depends on our ability to ensure that meaning does not remain fixed. Hence, while I recognize the inescapability of assigning objects a specific sort of cultural situatedness and representativeness, I also understand that academic discourse, like art generally and autobiography specifically, is forward as well as backward thinking.

In their efforts to confront the implications of the display of this image in contested public space, commentators, seeking to fill in the de-faced black female subject's desires by, in effect, reading her through their own ideological agendas, ignored the desire the photograph does indeed display: that of the optic white baby. Indeed, if our interpretive glance drifts to the photo's *horizontal rather than or along with its vertical region, it is possible that our readings may shift—though, certainly, not necessarily change alto- gether. Has the proliferation of leftist interventionist modes of analysis rendered us incapable of attending to the baby and its unambiguous biolog- ical needs? What interpretive angle could make the baby visible, make it as significant a subject as the de-faced black woman?*

In attempting to speak the seemingly unspeakable, I want to look briefly at Beloved's representations of scopically white babies born to black female slaves, babies abandoned, cast overboard, and otherwise (albeit under- standably) deprived of the sort of intimacy and nurturance the poster displays.

In "trying to make up for the handsaw"—for choosing to murder her daughter rather than let her live as a slave—Sethe seeks to explain to the woman she believes is her resurrected Beloved some of the debilitating consequences of her understanding

> that anybody white could take your whole self for anything that came to mind. Not just work, kill, or maim you, but dirty you. Dirty you so bad you couldn't like yourself anymore. Dirty you so bad you forgot who you were and couldn't think it up. (308)

In effect, white people had the power not merely to wound and kill, work and rape, but to de-face the black self, to erase black will, self-consciousness, and feelings of self-worth. For Sethe, slavery reduced the black self to a state of biological availability for manipulation by any representative of white hegemony. The difference was slight, Sethe's words imply, between being a de-faced slave and a "headless, feetless torso hanging in the tree with a sign on it" (308).

Obviously, I am trying to forge explicit connections between the Benet- ton photograph of the headless black woman with white child and Morriso- nian images of headless torsos and signs that advertise an imposed black selflessness. Such connections are irresistible, but also, I think, instructive, particularly if we consider Beloved's delineation of black mothers' re- sponses to children born to them as the result of dehumanizing white male acts of sexual violation. Sethe's mother, for example, threw the products of white rape overboard slave ships but cherished the daughter who was the result of her consensual union with a black man. And Ella—who "consid-

ered love a serious disability" because her "puberty was spent in a house where she was shared by father and son, whom she called 'the lowest yet,' " "who gave her a disgust for sex and against whom she measured all atrocities" (315)—"had delivered, but would not nurse, a hairy white thing" (318). Ella's contribution to the black female wall of sound that helped drive Beloved out of 124 Bluestone Road was motivated by her fear of "that pup"—"fathered by 'the lowest yet' "—"coming back to whip her" in the ways that the murdered daughter was "whipping Sethe." Although it is difficult to tie Morrison's text down to a definitive statement about maternal infanticide and neglect under such conditions of dehumanization and de-facement, Beloved does indicate clearly that such acts have cosmic consequences that the mothers must consider and for which they may have to pay.

Especially when viewed alongside the de-faced black mother and optic white child in the CSST poster, Morrison's formulations compel us to read such scenes contextually, with a mind to their intellectual, figurative, and moral complexities. Rather than seeing the picture as an occasion, ultimately, to reproduce a narrative of black female victimization, I want, somewhat more hopefully, to emphasize its strategic invocation of the possibility of a post–civil rights, perhaps even postmodernist, social transformation.

In the transformed world that one of Beloved's central characters, Paul D, envisions, movement away from Sweet Home's defacements is, also, a potential step toward "a place where you could love anything you chose— not to need permission for desire—well now, that was freedom" (199). Can we imagine an intimate space, a site of freedom wherein this photo represents a mutuality of desire, the suckling of a loved child whose white father the de-faced woman chose and was chosen by? Could the mother be nursing the baby for reasons other than that she has been reduced to the status of will-less pawn of white hegemony or that she is compelled by a desire to stave off otherworldly haunting? In acknowledging such a possibility, am I articulating utopian dreams that are interpretively unimaginable rather than merely ideologically disquieting to some?

My mother died on the morning of Monday, November 17, 1986, of pancreatic cancer, at age fifty-seven. I don't recall the exact time of her death. But I do remember that I learned the news as I was facing away from a stiff late-autumn breeze, standing outside a photocopying center on Thirty-eighth and Walnut Street, on the campus of the University of Pennsylvania, and that I'd just copied onto twenty-bond paper the dissertation on Afro-American women novelists I'd retyped on flimsy erasable paper late that summer. I'd arranged to deliver the dissertation to the graduate secretary of Penn's English Department that day.

I knew that handing it in in approvable physical form, though more difficult in those cut-and-paste days when I didn't know the first thing about floppy disks, hard drives, and megabytes, was merely a formality. I'd traversed the last, truly difficult hurdle of getting credentialed several months earlier, just weeks before my wife, Lauren, and I were to head off to Ann Arbor, when after my nearly three years of planning, drafting, redrafting, and re-redrafting, my charming taskmaster of a dissertation director, Houston Baker, told me that my work was, finally, sufficiently professional, and that this stage of my academic initiation was complete.

Rather than walk immediately to the English department building, I stopped at a familiar pay phone near the copy center to call my mother's apartment to tell my younger sister that I'd soon be heading to the airport to catch my flight back to Michigan. Hearing the forced cheerfulness in my voice, Debby paused, I am now sure, to try to find the right words, and said, "Um, Michael, Mommy died." I didn't reply immediately. I looked at my watch, saw that it was 11:30, and tried to figure out how to respond.

Clutching the two copies of my dissertation tightly, I whispered, "I'll see you in a little while." As I walked slowly away from the phone, I thought about how badly I'd wanted my mother to see my finished dissertation. About watching with trepidation as she read the first part of my chapter on *Their Eyes Were Watching God,* her legs crossed, her right hand picking at hairs emerging from her chin, and I worried that she would think it was incredibly pretentious. About her confirmation not of the persuasiveness of my insights or even of the impenetrability of my prose, which I'd come to believe was the most telling sign of true profundity, but of the accuracy of Zora

One of Penn's unscalable gates

Neale Hurston's depiction of black gendered politics ("That's just how niggers act"). About the fact that my accomplishments never felt truly significant until I'd had their importance confirmed by her. About wanting desperately for her to see me walk across a stage somewhere at Penn to receive my Ph.D.

The University of Pennsylvania, *the* university in my city of origins, had occupied a significant space in my imagination from the time I was a child. It was on Penn's grounds that my family transferred from trolleys to the South Street bus after gatherings at Aunt Peggy's house in Darby, and at Aunt Grace and Uncle Ed's West Philly homes. When the trolley's iron wheels sparked and screeched to a stop, I'd hop off ahead of my family and race up the always-inoperative escalator stairs to escape the stench and dimly lit dangers of the underground station. As we crossed the street between the station and the Thirty-sixth and Spruce Street bus stop, stepping

on, over, and around half-read pages of newspapers and hastily dis-
carded catsup- and mustard-stained wrappers, I'd stare at the deco-
rative strip of fierce gargoyles and lions perched on the exteriors of
the university's building.

Sometimes I imagined seeking shelter from harsh Christmas
winds or Independence Day heat on the other side of the unscalable
gates and impenetrable fences of this structure. Feeling as I suspected an anxious peasant would have as he approached a lord's
castle door to request protection from rampaging bandits who had
ransacked the village at the lord's behest, I knew that these beasts
would deem me unworthy and might, in fact, be amused by my
suffering. Still, while I had no idea what sorts of activities took place
beyond those dark, impenetrable fences, I felt an inarticulate yearning that I associated with their promise of respite from the dangers
and dramatically shifting climates of urbanity.

But then I recalled my mother's labored breathing, which had
filled the stale air of the hospital room, ambulance, and hospice
room in which I'd sat uncomfortably with her for much of the two
previous days. Immediately I felt a sense of guilty relief that her
ordeal—and ours—had ended. Instead of heading directly to the bus
stop and the Southwark projects in which I grew up, I stumbled
toward Bennett Hall, where the English department is housed, to
complete my final task as a student.

My mother died near the scheduled end of my third visit to Philadelphia after I'd learned that she was seriously ill. I was in my first
semester as an assistant professor at the University of Michigan,
struggling to survive the type of teaching schedule—I taught five
mornings a week—I've subsequently learned that virtually no one,
particularly not a beginning assistant professor, is assigned at major research universities, which expect young scholars immediately
to begin producing voluminous amounts of first-rate scholarship. I
felt overwhelmed by my teaching and committee responsibilities,
which, because of my interest in black women's literature and, more
importantly, the dearth of black women on the faculty, included
serving as an institutionally naive and extremely uncomfortable
member of the Women's Studies Executive Committee. Often, it

seemed that the administrators overseeing my joint appointment had involved me without my consent in another, even more brutal, stage in the ritual of academic initiation.

Before my first postgraduate return to Philadelphia on Debby's birthday in mid-October, I'd last seen my mother in August, when I bid her a teary-eyed farewell a couple days before Lauren and I drove to Ann Arbor from Westchester County, New York, where my wife had worked for a year for an economic consulting firm and I had finished my dissertation. Seemingly well though clearly thinner than her usual pencil-thin ninety-five pounds, my mother smiled and waved good-bye to me in the parking lot of Mother Bethel Church, where she supplemented her welfare income by working as an assistant to her sister Grace, who'd become the church minister's secretary about a year after my sixth grade graduation. Soon after that October visit—during which I tried unsuccessfully to ease her severe pain by rubbing Ben Gay on her aches, watched her drift frequently in and out of sleep, and was amused by the fact that she was using Russell, the teddy bear I'd bought her a few months earlier for Mother's Day, as a pillow—her illness was diagnosed and categorized as terminal.

My sisters, brother, and I were determined that my mother would not make the ambulance trip without one of us. I volunteered to accompany her on the journey from Einstein Hospital, which was a half mile or so from the apartment she'd lived in for nearly two decades, to the hospice in North Philly where she was being sent to die less expensively. I was grateful for the opportunity and sought to cast my journey home in heroic terms—I had traveled more than five hundred miles to be present at my mother's final journey toward easeful death—rather than see it merely as an opportunity to assuage some of the guilt I felt because I couldn't stay in Philly for extended periods of time.

Also, I tried to think of something about my relationship with her that made my assumption of this duty seem particularly appropriate. I wanted the ambulance trip to have some palpable thematic significance, to explain or exemplify what I meant to my mother and what she meant to me. I needed it to be more than just repayment of a debt nearly all children owe to even the most neglectful of parents for caring for them with at least a measure of selflessness. The best explanation I could come up with was that my journeys—to Philadelphia and in the ambulance—were recompense for her having traveled to hospitals and clinics for treatment of my various childhood ailments and injuries with more frequency than she did for all of my siblings combined.

On each of the mornings before what must have been twenty afternoon visits to the eye clinic of Jefferson Hospital before and after my surgery to correct my strabismic right eye, I was truly afraid that she'd be drunk. And though she was not a barrel of laughs or a paragon of overt maternal affection during what would invariably be four- or five-hour ordeals, she recognized the importance of her sobriety on such occasions. She didn't ask me to discuss my feelings about my impending surgery, or try to explain its potential long-term benefits, or examine how her own, more pronounced afflictions had affected her, or even attempt to take my mind off of this worrisome subject. If we talked about anything, we discussed the weather, the length of time we would have or had had to wait in the clinic, or why we couldn't stop at the Horn & Hardart's bakery, whose inviting aromas we passed during each visit. (H & H sold inexpensive, day-old, sickeningly sweet cinnamon buns that my siblings and I could rarely afford and absolutely loved.)

Usually, though, she barely talked to me at all, and I assumed that she was silent because she was annoyed that she had to accompany me instead of getting plucked up. Still, these were memorable excursions for me. I was happy to have any excuse not to have to go to school, and it was wonderful to be with my mother without the intrusive presence of my siblings and the scent of alcohol. As we walked from our apartment near Ninth and Lombard Street to Jefferson Hospital, I made a game of trying to coordinate my own short, quick steps with her longer, slow strides; of avoiding all the cracks in the pavement; and of stepping on all the gutters and metal business cellar doors I could reach, in anticipation of—or despite—her protests. Or I'd walk slightly behind her and search in vain for some remnant of the childhood gait that inspired her sister Peggy, their childhood friend Sis, or some other Darby resident to dub her

"Tippy." And when one of the doctors' assistants gave me pupil-
dilating eyedrops that distorted my vision for hours, I'd feign near
sightlessness so that I could walk home holding my mother's warm,
dry hand.

My mother was being moved, I knew, because the state didn't want
to continue to pay exorbitant hospital costs for the care of a welfare
recipient whom cancer would kill in a matter of days. Indeed, her
condition had deteriorated to the point where there was nothing
even highly trained doctors (including the surgeon who'd diagnosed
her and in whose blackness my siblings reveled with the sort of
perverse group pride of which only the historically dispossessed are
capable) could do for her except numb her pain a bit with morphine.
I was uneasy about the move, however, because her departure from
the neighborhood she'd lived in for nearly two decades signaled an
ending for which I had barely begun to prepare myself.

After dropping my luggage off at my mother's apartment, where
Debby lived with her two children, I walked slowly to the hospital.
Along the way, I thought of the five or six times my mother and I
had walked to this very hospital during the summer of 1970 after my
left shoulder had been fractured. My sisters had warned me that my
mother hadn't been lucid for a week, and that she wouldn't recognize me. But when I entered the room, I still expected some sort of
response: not necessarily the hugs I'd gotten when I came to visit on
weekends during my years as a doctoral student at Penn, not the full
kiss on the lips I'd once gotten in reaction to my constant com-
plaints that she was unaffectionate, not even a pained, small smile
I'd received a month earlier, but at least a brief instant of eye contact
that demonstrated that she knew her baby boy was in the room.

But when I was young and it seemed that her greatest priority was
to create a second childhood for herself devoid of parental responsibility, there had been many times my mother failed to recognize
me. Sometimes when she was in the throes of an extensive wine
and/or whiskey binge, usually just before losing consciousness
and succumbing to a need for rest and, perhaps, rehabilitation, she
would look at and talk to her children as though she knew us but

associated us with Darby experiences we were aware of only because her storytelling impulses had been compelled and lubricated occasionally by liquid spirits. Incapable of distinguishing past from present, her children from nameless acquaintances in whom she must have entrusted aspects of her self, she would implore us, "Take me home! Take me home!" She'd slur—in fact, nearly sing—the final word so that it hung in the air, like a musical note from a badly tuned piano or guitar, and her request was accompanied by the stench of vapors so pungent that I often had to back up a step from her prostrated body and rising head in order to breathe. In her mouth, at such moments, home was an idea whose connotations of safety and security were emphasized and clearly, in her mind (and ours), unachieved.

Dripping with a sense of nostalgia I resolved never to feel, her request punctured the air, filled the room and my imagination with an almost tangible sense of my mother's disenchantment. I was aware of the depths of her sadness and regret about the course of her life, including, I was sure, being a mother of four children, and felt overpowered by the knowledge that she'd much rather be there—"home"—than living the life she'd made for herself and for us. Eventually I found myself wishing not for her to stop drinking permanently, which I understood might be impossible, but for her to drop into a long, silent sleep that would release us for a few hours from the responsibility of having to take care of an adult whom we wanted more than anything else to attend to our significant needs. After a host of disappointments, I'd learned never to wish for the improbable, to dream big dreams, and nothing seemed more improbable to me as a child than the idea of my mother giving up pluck.

These occasions confirmed beliefs I held throughout my childhood: that she viewed her children's reliance on her as an obstacle to the life of total irresponsibility she must have sometimes craved, or to her coming to terms with her deep psychic pain, or to the possibility of letting go permanently of her grip on reality in the ways that her consumption of massive quantities of alcohol temporarily enabled. On such occasions, it wasn't our comfort, security, or love, wasn't her health or clearheadedness that most concerned her, but protecting herself from the pain of the present, typically by immersing herself in a fiction of a comparatively idyllic past. She was a poor black child of the Great Depression, but her parents were alive then, her brothers and sisters a rich part of the tapestry of her existence, and the sorts of joyful experiences she spoke excitedly of during moments of drunken storytelling still possible: traveling to Philly on the rickety Number 11 trolley with her father to see Cab Calloway or Billy Eckstine or Erskine Hawkins at the Royal Theater on South Street; making herself appear shorter at the ticket counter so that she, my Aunt Peggy, and their friend Sis could all be admitted into the balcony of Darby's segregated movie house at the cheapest rates; sneaking onto neighbors' porches in the winter to steal icicles.

We'd try to convince her that she was already home, imploring her to look around the apartment and recognize its modest furnishings—and us—as hers, and to come back to us, to return to a conscious present of which we were an important part. She would continue to plead with us until, still unaware of where she was or who we were, but exhausted by her efforts and their futility, she lost consciousness and sometimes began to mumble wordlessly. It was only after she'd fallen into a near-silent, restless sleep in which she was no longer a threat to my sense of personal significance that I allowed myself to breathe deeply, and to think about how I'd feel when she eventually awoke and recognized me. If neither more alcohol nor more money with which to purchase it was available— or if in an act of will as mysterious as the Holy Trinity to me inspired her to take a break from the bubbly—that recognition would compel her to take me into consideration, to connect again with me, her other children, and her parental obligations.

I was afraid I'd fall apart if I looked closely at her dying, emaciated body, her face so gaunt that I was sure there was nothing but a thin surface of brown skin covering her protruding cheekbones, her eyes occasionally opening and staring blankly at everything but me, her lazy eye even more noticeably than usual following its own visual course, her lips sucked in to cover her dentureless gums. I knew we'd reached a moment I feared from early childhood—when my mother would not, could not, return to me. When my presence meant nothing to her. The only sign of life she exhibited before our ambulance ride to the hospice was slow, tortured breathing. Her lungs were filled with fluid her body could no longer expel, and especially during the first hour I was with her, I was certain that each breath would be her last.

She was in the same room to which she'd been taken after she'd slipped out of a coma two weeks earlier and into what seemed an incredibly vibrant dementia during which she talked—in a manner not dissimilar to drunken mutterings—to long-dead relatives. I comforted myself with the belief that she was speaking to relatives who were preparing a place for her in a celestial space by a heavenly riverside where she'd be free of all of her earthly burdens and pain. A celestial space with a comfortable reclining chair on which she could rest her always-aching feet. A space where she could see her mother and father again, her brother Jackie, about whom she spoke in reverential terms, and perhaps even her five dead children.

In that room, I'd seen her perform the most courageous, most important act of atonement and demonstration of deep affection I have ever witnessed. Despite the atmosphere of seeming antipathy that sometimes surrounded her relationship with my brother, Ricky, she worried about him constantly, perhaps because she feared he would prove himself attitudinally to be Carl's son, and perhaps because, physically and emotionally, he most resembles her. That resemblance is most clear in his long face and ample forehead, nostrils, and chin, which had been passed down to all of my mother's father's kids, but to none of hers except Ricky. Further, they shared the tendency to search for means of silencing rather than confronting fears caused by their hypersensitivity to their (utterly normal) human limitations, a sober reticence that made conversations with them often virtually impossible, and a fundamental sweetness and vulnerability they sensed they had to suppress in order to survive a world that saw these traits as weaknesses. When my mother proudly wore the kitschy gold-plated jewelry he'd sent her with a picture of him clothed in Air Force garb, their likeness was magnified, intensified, to the extent that they seemed mirror images, and he appeared to be what Zora Hurston might call the thought picture of a son she molded in her own likeness.

When my brother entered the hospital room, my mother—just out of a coma, barely strong enough to talk, for the only time I can remember uninterested in cigarettes or music, and incapable of getting out of the bed without assistance—called him over to her. As he reached her bedside, she struggled to sit up, three or four life-sustaining tubes dangling from her, and hugged him tightly, wordlessly. In her condition, I knew she should not be doing this, but she must have been thinking, if not now, then when? Her gesture was many things, is open to multiple readings, but I'm sure that her intent was to apologize and to help release him from his demons.

As the ambulance attendants moved her from her hospital bed to a stretcher, she let out a chilling howl followed by a series of long, loud whimperings. She was totally helpless, devoid of all the characteristics human socialization produces—speech, analysis, the capacity to compare what she was experiencing to what she or others had experienced, a complex recognition of family ties. She was the closest I've ever seen any adult be to the state of total dependence that characterizes the first months in the life of a newborn, except that because her life passages had also included decades of rather flamboyant alcohol abuse, aspects of this near-death state were painfully familiar to me. Again, I felt that I was nobody to her, or at least no different from the ambulance attendants or the nurses who came in to make sure her glucose and morphine drips were working and to say good-bye before her journey to the hospice.

We got to the ambulance, whose suspension, I was soon to discover, was substandard at best, and I climbed into the back with my mother. Each bump, each stop caused her to cry out and whimper like a newspaper-whipped puppy. Each manifestation of her pain increased my discomfort. I stroked her hair and hands and implored her to hold on.

When we finally arrived at our destination, the ambulance drivers, again professionally responsive to the dying and the grieving, lifted my mother's body and stretcher as though they were weightless, insubstantial, and wheeled her into the hospice. Their faces duly somber, they spoke no more of fly rides we'd sped past during

the forty-five-minute journey, no more of a seemingly endless procession of fine women whom I couldn't see through the windowless
cabin, no more of mundane Saturday evening plans—"nightclub-
bing," "skirt chasing," "gettin' high"—which, compared to my own
scheduled task, seemed divinely inspired.

The trees surrounding the entrance had lost most of their leaves,
whose crisp brown corpses crunched under our feet. As we entered
the vestibule and found the elevator, I tried to attend to everything—
the bright whiteness of the walls, the antiseptic smell, the ambulance drivers' hushed conversation—except my mother, whose
whimperings and pained expression revealed that my presence had
done nothing to ease the pain of her journey. If she could not even
recognize me, couldn't hear or understand me, why did I come
home? Why did I endure this journey that I knew, even as I was
experiencing it, would haunt me as long as I lived? To repay her for
ensuring my safety during my own perilous journey to life? Because
I couldn't just sit in Ann Arbor and wait for her to die?

As we got off the elevator and the attendants wheeled my
mother's body toward the nurses' station, one of the nurses came
over to check the condition of the patient on the stretcher. I looked
at my mother's pained expression and, turning my eyes away, saw
that one of her breasts had slipped out of her hospital gown. And
though my discomfort had been pronounced throughout the day, it
suddenly became immeasurable, unbearable. Did I have to confront
her nakedness, too, a breast with no maternal or erotic potential?
Lacking a father to complete the Freudian triad, and unable to
envision possessing my dying mother on any terms, I didn't think
myself capable of experiencing such embarrassing, childish distress,
even during moments potentially rife with postadolescent Oedipal
anxiety.

I tried to understand why the sight of my mother's breast dangling out of her hospital garb produced such anxiety in me. I told
myself that it was simply a part of her, like her braided gray hair, the
stitch marks on her right upper arm, her ashy, calloused feet, her
toothless mouth, her misaligned eye, her unplucked chin, her skele-
tal legs. Still, the sight of my mother's wrinkled breast further coin-

plicated what was an already difficult experience. Did I fear that someone else—one of the ambulance drivers?—would see it? Was I trying to protect her from the indignity of exposure? Or was I shocked because it was my mother's breast and, therefore, intrinsically compelling to me in ways that no other breast could ever be?

Keeping my eyes averted, I searched for something else to focus on while appearing to be attending to her: not her face, which illness and pain rendered nearly unrecognizable, or the attendants, who I wished would go away, or the nurses, whose presence I had a difficult time processing. I settled on the zipperlike mark on her right upper arm, and for the first time in my life, I looked at it long enough to be able to count its horizontal marks, hoping that doing so would sufficiently distract and calm me so that I could be of assistance to my mother. Staring at what had served me all my life as the most incontrovertible evidence of the consequences of male brutality, I pulled the part of her gown just under her neck toward me so that the breast would fall back into place.

Finally, members of the hospice staff got her situated in her room, and the ambulance drivers departed. Being moved from the stretcher onto the bed made her whimper and cry out again, but the pain seemed to subside rather quickly. A member of the staff suctioned out some of the fluid that had gathered in her chest during the ride, checked her IV, and, after offering me a brief, efficient look of sympathy, departed. My mother's labored breathing filled the large room, and as I watched her, the ordeal of her institutional transfer over, I wondered what I should do.

With the exception of two or three brief visits by the nurses, I was alone with her near-dead body for two long hours until Carol cautiously entered the room. After smiling faintly at me, she went to the bed, looking at our mother intently, as though to make sure no further damage had been done to her during the ambulance ride. Then she walked over to me and touched my arm gently.

"How was the ride?"

"She was in a lot of pain. The streets were full of potholes. And she cried and whimpered nearly every minute."

"You okay?"

"Yeah, I guess, except . . ."

Except what? How could I tell my sister that I was freaked out by the ride when she'd survived my mother's confession that she was scared of dying? By our mother's breathing, which she'd heard for days now? By a host of unfathomable horrors, among which was knowing that seeing Mom's breast had made me—the putatively mature intellectual who understood and should have been able to resist the Oedipal dimensions of my discomfort—Oedipally uncomfortable? Rather than experiencing an urge to tell her how sad and helpless the experience had made me feel, I was overcome with the desire to ask Carol questions I'd planned to ask our mother at some point: whether Mom had breast-fed us as children; whether the stories Mom used to tell me were true about substituting the juice of cooked cabbage for store-bought milk because we were too poor to be able to afford formula.

I didn't ask. I told her as little about the journey as I could. And I tried to forget what I'd seen, what I'd heard—the sight of my mother's uncovered breast, and the sound and fury of her dying.

Early the next afternoon, I took public transportation back to the hospice. When I got to her room, the volume of her breathing had increased, and her eyes remained closed. I wondered what was keeping her alive, and why she continued to struggle to breathe when, I wanted to believe, her way in the afterworld had been prepared, when the only sensations she now experienced were unbearable pain and the kick of morphine. It struck me that perhaps she was holding on because she didn't want to leave her children, because, as she showed when she hugged Ricky, she felt we still needed her and she knew she'd missed opportunities to mother us, comfort us, be supportive of us. Making sure her gown and bedding covered her body, I walked over to her, kissed her forehead, and told her to let herself die.

"You've done all you can for us, Ol' Lady. We're gonna be all right, I swear; you don't have to hang on for us when you're in so much pain. We'll be okay. Carol's got Kenny and Mark. And Rick'll get it together, you watch. Pat'll whip him into shape. And Deb too. She will, for Juju and Marcie Monster. And I'm doing okay. I got a good job. And Lauren and I will be okay. She's really a good woman, Mommy; I wish y'all'd gotten to know one another better—she really is. We'll all be okay, Ol' Lady. Let go. Let go. Let go."

After I'd said "let go" a third time, a tear rolled slowly out of my mother's left eye and down her cheek. I knew—I know—that this tear was simply an involuntary biological reaction, and at most a response to a sudden stab of unbearable physical pain. Certainly, it was not a sign that she'd heard me. I knew she was no longer capable of processing complicated external stimuli. But this was the closest I'd gotten to an acknowledgment of my existence, and I needed to believe this single tear was a response to my loving supplications. As I wiped it away with my right thumb and stroked one of her matted, unraveling braids, I repeated, "Let go, Ol' Lady. We'll be okay. Let go."

At that moment, my Aunt Grace walked into the room with two ministers from the First Baptist Church of Darby, which Mom had attended both as a child and after she'd stopped drinking. I felt as though I'd been busted, as though I'd sinned against God and humanity. God would take her when He wanted, which would be, to be sure, in time. He wouldn't give her more than she could bear. Her pain was a manifestation of God's power as, no doubt, would be its cessation at her death. I was sure that's how the ministers viewed matters, and that they would have counseled me to pray for her eternal soul (and for mine) rather than urging her to give it up.

Flustered, embarrassed, and more than a bit self-conscious about having my sorrow witnessed by men who had a professional understanding of how to negotiate this sort of deathbed scene, I greeted my aunt, then exited quickly. Because I was scheduled to return to Michigan early the next afternoon, I wanted to tell my mother good-bye, knowing I'd probably never see her alive again; but I knew also I couldn't endure the expressions of preacherly concern and their more practiced, better-enunciated, and potentially more effective rites of passage. I blew a kiss in my mother's direction and left the hospice.

The next time I saw her, she was lying in a blue casket in her nephew Melvyn's funeral home in Darby, a few blocks away from where she'd grown up. Her face was made up, her hair pressed and curled, her eyes closed, her tortured breathing stilled, her pain ended. Melvyn is my family's most engaging vernacular wordsmith, and one of his favorite tales centered on the fact that my mother, who found the rituals we use to accompany death fascinating, set the course for his professional life by taking him as a young child to as many funerals as there were deaths among Darby's virtuous and sinful black folk. Standing before her body, flanked by Melvyn and Carol, I recognized how wise she was to have encouraged his interest in death, for she provided herself a final send-off at wholesale prices, the type of casket and quality of mortician care and intervention that—despite Carol's equally prescient decision to take out a life insurance policy on our mother—she could never have afforded.

She had helped prepare Melvyn to render loving service to her illness-ravaged body and distorted face. I can't imagine how Melvyn managed to use his craft on the skin-and-bones body of his favorite aunt, the knowledge he'd worked diligently both in and out of school to acquire: the proper way to drain the blood, replace it with embalming fluid, dress the body, close the sightless eyes, coat the skin, set the mouth so that the look of horror and fear that accompanied its final, futile gasping for air was no longer visible, and hide as many imperfections as possible. Although I can read and talk about ghosts, murder, rape, whippings, lynchings, and mutilation (for those are the dominant subjects of canonical Afro-American literature), I could not bring myself to touch my mother's cold, bloodless hand, either at the viewing at Melvyn's funeral home or during the funeral.

I wrote her obituary, and at her funeral I read a poem I'd written years earlier that contrasted her difficult life with the look of utter contentment that came over her after she'd fallen asleep for the umpteenth consecutive time during her favorite cop show. You could say that's what she helped prepare me for: reading and writing about black women's suffering and triumph. You could say that because I could not save, dress up, or ultimately touch her flesh, my personal and professional imperatives, linked by my desire to preserve aspects of her life and spirit, are not wholly distinct from Melvyn's similarly impossible task: to represent her in a manner that resembles what she was during her life. However, unlike my cousin's profession, mine demands from me, if I am to make discursive sense of her living and dying, that I not try to hide her imperfections but, rather, lovingly interrogate them.

During the airplane ride back to Michigan, I flipped randomly through my heavily annotated copy of Richard Wright's *Black Boy*, hoping I'd run across some constellation of words that would compel me to begin to prepare to teach classes I hadn't met for more than a week. After encountering familiar scenes on which I had an interpretive handle—young Richard's suggestion to his grandmother that she kiss his ass; Wright's parenthetical remarks about the barrenness of black Jim Crow existence; his Memphis experiences with the nubile Bessie and her mother—I came across a startling paragraph on the last pages of chapter 3:

> Once, in the night, my mother called me to her bed and told me that she could not endure the pain, that she wanted to die. I held her hand and begged her to be quiet. That night I ceased to react to my mother; my feelings were frozen. (111)

After reading and rereading this passage and the paragraphs about his responses to his mother that follow it, I recognized that given the rawness of my own grief, it would be foolish to discuss it in class that week. As weeks and months and, finally, years passed, I remained compelled by this notion of frozen feelings and desperate to find a means of understanding it as being something other than a son's rejection of his mother.

I wasn't able to produce a compelling reading of young Richard's frozen feelings until I confronted the Benetton photograph and CSST poster. But having achieved a modicum of professional power and security, published essays and books through which I sought to manifest the sincerity of my commitments to feminist principles, and gained some emotional distance from my mother's life and her death, I feel confident enough after that confrontation to run the risk of reading Wright in ways that satisfy some of my deepest interpretive needs. Like, perhaps, this entire book, trying to sat-

isfy these needs exposes me to charges that I am terribly, phallo-
centrically wrong.

After indicating that young Richard's doubtlessly self-interested response to
his mother's physical paralysis is emotional distance or frozen feeling,
Wright forces his readers to grapple with what may be Black Boy's *single*
most challenging moment—his symbolic inscription of his mother:

> My mother's suffering grew into a symbol in my mind, gathering to itself all
> the poverty, the ignorance, the helplessness; the painful, baffling, hunger-
> ridden days and hours; the restless moving, the futile seeking, the uncer-
> tainty, the fear, the dread. *(111)*

Having witnessed my own mother's rapid demise during blues journeys
home to Philadelphia in my first semester at Michigan, and having recog-
nized the numbingly long-term emotional effects of surviving her incalcul-
able loss, I must read Wright's admission that his "feelings were frozen" as
potentially connoting more than a son's callousness. I believe, in fact, that
for young Richard, emotional distance from his mother's suffering is not a
treacherous act but rather a rich, analytically necessary one.

In codifying the symbolic import of his mother by emphasizing her
relationship to him, Wright employs a strategy similar to the one he uses to
deal with the threatening specter of his father. Wright offers a devastating
portrait of his father, for whom he felt "a deep biological bitterness" as a
consequence of the "pangs of hunger" *(22)*—physical, spiritual, and symbolic—that dominated his life, particularly after his father's abandonment
of his family. Indeed, Wright's manipulation of his father's image is as
essential to the writer's self-definition and developing worldview as his
reading of his mother. According to Wright, his father is incapable of
negotiating a modern, increasingly urban-centered America in which the
son thrives as one of its most influential and penetrating chroniclers.

For blacks, such negotiation requires a cleansing of the self of the
disabling residue of slavery and Jim Crow, a task that proves impossible for
his father, whose character was formed in the intersection of their devalua-
tions of blackness. Pointing out biological and tonal connections between
son and father, Wright emphasizes their essential and utter difference:
"When I tried to talk to him I realized that, though ties of blood made us

kin, though I could see a shadow of my face in his face, though there was an echo of my voice in his voice, we were forever strangers, speaking a different language, living on vastly distant planes of reality" (42). Wright distinguishes himself from his progenitor by figuring him as his antithesis, as his cultural other, a rural, toothless, uncomprehending sharecropper "fastened . . . to a crude and raw past, . . . chained . . . to the direct, animalistic impulses of his withering body" (43).

In his efforts to transcend his abusive father, Wright depicts him as psychically and emotionally stagnant, a condition that, according to the author, mirrors black southerners' relationship to white hegemony more generally. White racism, and his people's passivity in response to it, limit blacks' capacity "to catch the full spirit of Western civilization, [rendering them] in it but not of it" (45). Like other black southerners who manifest the sort of cultural fixity Wright bemoans throughout Black Boy, his father is represented as stagnant and belated, unwilling or unable to get access to the keys to the modern city.

But if the father is transcended and rendered irrelevant by Wright's confinement of him within a changeless, premodern, neoslave past, a chilling example of the double-as-other, Wright's freezing of his mother allows him actively to use her meanings in the present and preserve them—and her—for use in the future. She operates not as a sign of the past but as a timeless signifier of black American pain and as a filter through which Wright sifts all he sees, feels, knows, and believes. Whereas Wright rejects his father, figuratively killing him by confining him to a peasant land before modern time, he consumes his mother, positioning her as his ur-text, interpretive praxis, and epistemic center. His feelings for her and his interpretation of her life fixed, her suffering leads him to develop "a conception of life that no experience would ever erase, . . . a conviction that the meaning of living came only when one was struggling to wring a meaning out of meaningless suffering" (112).

Freezing his mother in time, he becomes, in effect, fixed, his interests and activities circumscribed and determined, as the "attitude toward life" he internalized from his reading of her "was to make me seek those areas of living that would keep it alive" (112). That attitude "gave me insight into the sufferings of others, made me gravitate toward those whose feelings were like my own, made me sit for hours while others told me of their lives, made me strangely tender and cruel, violent and peaceful" (112). *But if his mother is a key to understanding both Wright the famous author and a young, Jim Crow–circumscribed Richard, if that frozen image is the mother to the son's self-consciousness, it also produces what may be the most crucial determinant of this black boy's escape from the South. His attitude toward life, deriving from a strategic interpretive relationship to his mother's suffering, helped to "keep alive in me that enthralling sense of wonder and awe in the face of the drama of human feeling which is hidden by the external drama of life"* (112).

Wright's freezing of his feelings for his mother enables him to see beyond the deep surfaces of black pain in order to experience the "sense of wonder and awe" that, in his view, characterizes human existence even in the most dire of conditions. Images of hunger, pain, and death precipitated by Jim Crow's henchmen dominate Wright's autobiographical account, serving often to obscure the import of moments when the author focuses on his rendezvous with life. Even as he emphasizes the deep pessimism engendered by his maternal inheritance, Wright's own insistence on his changeless "conception," "predilection," "sense," "notion," and "conviction" regarding black life is tempered by his discussion of the "wonder" of human feeling. As emphatic in its confidence about of the liberating power of the word as Frederick Douglass's Narrative, *which holds that writing offers "the pathway from slavery to freedom"* (43), Black Boy *urges its readers to attend to both the experiences that help to shape our convictions and those awe-ful moments and texts that challenge and complicate our belief systems.*

That receptivity enables young Richard to negotiate the dangerous spaces he is allowed to inhabit in a Jim Crow system in whose near-changeless gaze he can operate only as another manifestation of black inferiority. Wright's text acknowledges the awe-ful moments hidden from the illuminations of our epistemologies, suggesting that by being both inside and outside these convictions and understanding what they enable and what they obscure, we can remain attuned to "the drama of human feeling which is hidden by the external drama of life." While our convictions, in Wright's sense of the word, help us to see aspects of the "external drama of life," to quantify, predict, and systematize human behavior as it is manifested in a variety of shapes and sizes, they are limited in their capacity to assist our efforts to respond individually and collectively to "the tantalizing melancholy," "the yearning for identification," "the speechless astonishment" whose existence humanizes and enlivens us if we are sufficiently attentive (14–15).

Black Boy exemplifies why, under conditions of unremitting oppression, objects and people susceptible to deep symbolic interrogation must be frozen, as it were. In preserving his immobile mother, Wright begins to understand her behavior and how to present his life as an exemplary effort to "wring a meaning out of meaningless suffering" that results from living Jim Crow.

The wringing of meaning necessitates our production of strategic, "frozen" analyses that, by their very nature, minimize the complexity and strategically reduce the fullness of the objects of our interpretive gazes, including, certainly, our mothers and fathers. But if we assume that such acts of strategic freezing are necessary or inevitable as we live and seek to represent, among other realities, the dramas of race, gender, and class in America, we can perhaps see Wright's gestures as emblematic of the burdens we bear as self-conscious actors in, and interpreters of, these dramas. Wright's text encourages the reader to determine what his or her "attitude toward life" is and whence it derives, and to "keep alive" "that enthralling sense of wonder and awe in the face of the drama of human feeling."

Those insights signal young Richard's own growth within his representation of his life. Early in his autobiography, Wright employs images that resonate with his discussion of his reactions to his mother's paralysis to describe his own life-threatening illness. Defying demands that he submit to familial and communal prohibitions against speech and action, a four-year-old Richard, craving sensation and stimulus, sets fire to his family's "long fluffy white curtains—which I had been forbidden to touch," destroying the home and nearly killing his family. Clearly, young Richard defies not merely his mother, who issues the edict that he be quiet, but also his scopically white grandmother, a "vivid image" whose "wrinkled . . . grim face . . . made me afraid" (9).

Wright offers young Richard's family as a microcosm of Jim Crow racial dynamics, where the circumscription of black behavior demanded by white power—represented, for him, by his grandmother—looms as more significant, more pressing, than his hunger for freedom. Here, his grandmother's power to inhibit is frightening, not merely because it mirrors that of the racial force young Richard and all blacks had to either submit to or *confront at the risk of their own and others' lives, but because of his mother's adherence to its dictates. Consequently it would not be far-fetched to view Wright's youthful act as an attempt to burn down the repressive structure that slavery built and Jim Crow maintained, whose house rules are enforced by black family members convinced that compelling him to submit is the most loving course of action they can take.*

In that context, and perhaps only in that context, Wright's reaction to being severely punished and his description of the manifestations of his resultant life-threatening illness are comprehensible. After he is pulled from underneath the burning house where he went to escape parental wrath, young Richard

> was lashed so hard and long that I lost consciousness. I was beaten out of my
> senses and later I found myself in bed, screaming, determined to run away,
> tussling with my mother and father who were trying to keep me still. I was
> lost in a fog of fear. A doctor was called—I was afterwards told—and he
> ordered that I be kept abed, that I be kept quiet, that my very life depended
> upon it. My body seemed on fire and I could not sleep. Packs of ice were put
> on my forehead to keep down the fever. Whenever I tried to sleep I would see
> huge wobbly white bags, like the full udders of cows, suspended from the ceil-
> ing above me. Later, as I grew worse, I could see the bags in the daytime with
> my eyes open and I was gripped by the fear that they were going to fall and
> drench me with some horrible liquid. Day and night I begged my mother and
> father to take the bags away, pointing to them, shaking with terror because
> no one saw them but me. Exhaustion would make me drift toward sleep and
> then I would scream until I was wide awake again; I was afraid to sleep.
> Time finally bore me away from the dangerous bags and I got well. But for a
> long time I was chastened whenever I remembered that my mother had come
> close to killing me. (13)

In his illuminating analysis of this symbolically resonant passage, Ralph Ellison argues in Shadow *and* Act *that young Richard's severe beating represents a cautionary form of corporal punishment: "One of the Southern Negro family's methods of protecting the child is the severe beating—a homeopathic dose of the violence generated by black and white relationships" (85). The beating and fear of whites positioned figuratively above him reduced young Richard to the state of silent passivity that his mother and grandmother (and Jim Crow) demanded of a black boy who*

must accept subordination as his lot. Intuitively, young Richard under-
stands that to submit is to renounce any possibility of developing a full
sense of his humanity. Iced down to cool his burning desire for full par-
ticipation, the prone, immobile black boy runs the risk of being frozen in
time, like his father, unable to catch the spirit of modernity because he has
accepted the white force's assignment of blacks to minor, silent, subservient
roles.

Unlike his subsequently infirm mother, whose paralysis leads her to
contemplate, even desire, a swift physical death, young Richard struggles to
keep from being "drench[ed with] a horrible liquid" that would precipitate
his passage into a condition that Orlando Patterson has termed "social
death." According to Patterson, social death is marked by the forced capitu-
lation to the authority of another, the result of which is that the subject has
"no social existence outside of his master" (38). The "huge wobbly white
bags, like the full udders of cows, suspended from the ceiling above" signify
both the haunting white force that looms threateningly above the heads of
potentially rebellious black boys and girls and the fact that Richard's
already socially dead mother, because she appears to have capitulated to
white hegemony's limitations of the nature of black social reality, repre-
sents a perverse, murderous maternity, a figure who is more likely to
destroy than to nurture his rebellious urge for freedom. Wright is convinced
that under such conditions, to be drenched by or to ingest mother's milk is
to sacrifice to white hegemony his right to self-determination, and to
participate in his own moral, spiritual, and ethical demise.

Ultimately, Wright is able to move beyond this vision of his mother's
figuratively whitened breasts as transmitting the milk of social death. For a
long time, young Richard believed "that my mother had come close to killing
me," strategically ignoring the fact that the fire he sets nearly killed her and
the rest of the family. But by symbolically freezing her, he invests her with
the capacity to teach him to comprehend crucial lessons about the world: not
merely the pain of living Jim Crow that made both whites and blacks able to
"accept but a fragment of his personality" but also "the best and deepest
things of heart and mind" that his dangerous rebellion seeks to protect and
allow him to nurture (284). Freezing her permits him to move beyond seeing
his mother as part of an element of black culture that retards rather than
promotes the growth of youth, as a symbolic breast whose milk would not do

a black boy's body good. Once frozen, young Richard's mother supplies him with what serves him as an astutely pragmatic epistemology.

Particularly in describing a black boy's rejection of the soul-depriving dictates of white hegemony, such a transformation is crucial if he is to get beyond simply rejecting or hating his black mother because of her roles both as what Ellison calls maternal "sanctuary" and as enforcer of Jim Crow's visions of Richard's limited place. Unlike the uncompromising disdain he feels for the other members of his family, particularly his grandmother, he embraces his mother, moving toward resolving his psychic and maturational dilemmas by figuring out how to make analytical use of her pain. Rather than reject his mother, which Ellison suggests is one of two options for the black child severely abused by servants of white hegemony, young Richard embraces (his reading of) her, internalizing aspects of her life and her behavior toward him—the beatings and poverty, her husband's desertion, her chronic, life-threatening illness, even the admission that she wants to die—so that the "undercurrent of fear and hostility" created by her beatings and reticence comes to clarify rather than obscure his understanding of the workings of the world.

Clearly, in young Richard's representation of his mother, she is not a fully realized character but a device designed to move his tale forward, a narrative that he reads selectively to confirm what we might call his emerging existential vision. But in what theories of parent-child interaction, where the focus is the child's development, are parents ever more than significant symbols, great mysteries that need to be deciphered, baffling texts to be read? Given the peculiar options open to young Richard (which, according to Ellison, are either to "embrace violence along with maternal tenderness, or else reject . . . the mother"), his choice to freeze his mother interpretively manifests his desire to honor her despite the pain she has inflicted on him. Had he not made such a choice, he would have had no alternative but to reject her as he does his father, as Hurston's Janie Crawford does her grandmother when Janie realizes the dire consequences of her forebear's imposition of her socially dead outlook on her. Whatever else the figure of Janie's pear tree represents, and despite critics' always strategic use of Hurston and Wright as figures of pure antithesis (a strategy that comments by the writers themselves encourage), Hurston's pear tree symbol resonates with Wright's view that life's meanings lie in psychic realms that intersect with, but are not wholly subsumed by, the strictly ideological.

But it is not Their Eyes Were Watching God *but rather the Philadelphia writer Andrea Lee's less well known autobiographical novel* Sarah Phillips *that provides us with the clearest comparative angle for measuring the sagacity of Wright's freezing of his mother. Lee's novel has achieved near-pariah status in some black intellectual circles because of what Sherley Anne Williams terms its "mockery of . . . the 'outworn rituals' of black community." In that regard, their temporal, gender, class, and regional differences notwithstanding, Lee's text has much in common with Wright's, according to Williams:*

> Sarah Phillips, *the memoir of privileged girlhood, oddly enough, resembles nothing in Afro-American letters so much as Richard Wright's* Black Boy, *one of the most searing accounts of deprived boyhood in the literature. In* Black Boy, *Wright literally and figuratively renounces oral culture and black traditions for personal autonomy. Andrea Lee seems bent on something of the same sort in* Sarah Phillips. *(71)*

Williams's remarks remind us of the burdens commentators have placed on Afro-American literature since at least Thomas Jefferson and others saw Phillis Wheatley's poetry as a means of assessing not her creative skills and moral clarity but her race's humanity and intellect. Further, these remarks force us to ponder other increasingly complex, dead-end, or tired questions about our age that demonstrate, at least in part, the dominance of intellectually lazy interrogations of the meanings of blackness that too frequently mesmerize black racial warriors and the general public, including: What relation can / must upper-middle-class blacks have to black vernacular culture? Can even the most assimilated of Afro-Americans escape the stings of racism? How does a black person unattached to forms of black vernacular respond to a felt or imposed need to be socially responsible to economically less fortunate members of the race? And to cite a contemporary variation on this theme, how can an Afro-American achieve—as does Sarah Phillips—a first-rate education and prepare herself for economic success without selling out?

Other comparisons between Lee's and Wright's texts are, in fact, more compelling, including their explorations of the connections between parents' worldviews and children's efforts to discover their own. Sarah is characterized by a dissociation of racial sensibility, rebelling, in what we have come to think of as a normal way, against vague hints from her parents concerning some of the social, intellectual, and ethical responsibilities to the oppressed that many have argued follow from her privileged status. For the most part, her character, like Richard's, is formed antithetically, in opposition to what her parents are and may want her to become. In Sarah's case, rebellion—which is crucial to the process of young Richard's self-discovery and production of an enabling reading of the meanings of his mother's life—obscures rather than uncovers such meanings. So when her father dies, after a life spent ministering to the souls of black folk both as a preacher in a church obviously modeled after Mother Bethel and as a participant in the civil rights movement (the type of a mass response against Jim Crow young Richard longed for, one that might have allowed him to develop a relationship to black culture that was more than primarily oppositional) Sarah adopts the role of aggrieved heroine. Still, she remains "puzzle[d] and disturbe[d]" that she is unable to codify what her father's life and work mean in her efforts to determine her own life's course. Acknowledging that "I could never decide what to think about it" (112)— what to think definitively, in fact, about much of anything—Sarah dreams of her recently deceased father in terms that conjure up young Richard's freezing of his mother.

> After his funeral I had dreamed about him. In the dream he had fallen overboard from a whaling ship—like the one in Two Years before the Mast—and had come up from the ocean still alive but encased in a piece of iceberg. Through the ice I could see his big hands gesturing in a friendly, instructive manner while he looked straight at me and said something inaudible. It was the same word or syllable I had wanted to say in answer to Stuart Penn, and I couldn't figure out what it was. (114–15)

Reverend Phillips provides a much more accomplished example of direct, overtly political struggle against racial injustice than young Richard's mother, who strives both to "teach you . . . to stand up and fight for yourself" and to make him an obedient black boy (24). But because Sarah has not been able to affix a meaning to—has no sense of how to read—her father's life, because of what, following Williams, we could term her unresolvable ambivalence engendered by the presence of a host of interpretive possibilities, she could not find the significance to her own life of his *devotion to ending spiritual misery and racial inequity, though she knew his life's work was relevant. While she is aware that his "inaudible" word and "friendly, instructive" gesture hold interpretive keys to her living in the present, in her dream at least (and, I would argue, in her life), her father hands down to her a text she does not even vaguely understand. Sarah needs to do much more work, to learn much more about the ways of the world, before she can read the meanings of his symbolic gesture, before she can make out the "inaudible" "something" he says through the ice in which she has preserved him in her dreams.*

Why, then, is Wright's freezing of his mother such a powerful and revelatory interpretive act? Because it propels him forward, clarifying for him precisely what living as a black boy means and what achieving the status of modern citizen could represent. Further, it suggests how psychically crippling it is to strive merely to survive Jim Crow and other oppressive regimes. Unlike Sarah, left figuratively wringing her hands because she cannot comprehend her father's inaudible word and confounding gesture, young Richard is prepared to seek out some of life's most resonant meanings while understanding aspects of the pain that racial hierarchization has caused. From the bleakest to the most bountiful of socioeconomic circumstances, that may be among the most significant of gifts a parent can provide for her or his child.

A few weeks after I'd returned to Ann Arbor following my mother's funeral, I dreamed that she was walking up the steep steps of my wife's and my Ann Arbor apartment, a rust-colored wig on her head and a bright red winter coat wrapped around her. In the dream, I was for a brief moment happy that she'd come to Ann Arbor to visit me, but I soon became terrified that she'd want to hold me in her dead, cold arms against her lifeless breasts, and I begged her to go away.

I didn't return home to receive my degree. With my mother's passing, the idea of participating in another graduation ceremony had lost its appeal. But at the nadir of my first interminable, sunless Ann Arbor winter, when a package arrived at our apartment from Penn's Office of Graduate Studies, I opened it with surprising excitement. Except for my name, my diploma was written in a cursive

Latin script that even Lauren, who'd studied the grand, dead language for four or five years, could barely translate.

I stuck the diploma back into the thin, brown package in which it was sent to me and placed it in one of the numerous boxes I've kept since college that are filled with irreplaceable but not necessarily invaluable mementos: my books of songs and poems; my high school, college, and graduate school essays; copies of my college transcript and commencement booklet; *Philadelphia Daily News* articles about Hal Greer's belated induction into the Basketball Hall of Fame; notes I took while studying for my Ph.D. qualifying examination; copies of articles on subjects I can't believe I was ever interested in; and a copy of the 1981 *Newsweek* that featured Toni Morrison on the cover.

Someday, when it ceases primarily to signify my mother's absence and to reawaken my own fury about a host of matters, perhaps I'll find a beautiful frame for my diploma and display it in my campus office.

Since July 1996, I've lived in a Philadelphia suburb along with my wife and two daughters and have taught at the University of Pennsylvania. It has hardly been an idyllic arrangement for me; actually, my return might best be described—to echo the title of the collection of poems Houston gave me on the day my mother died—as a blues journey home. At least once a week during my first year back home, I longed to visit my mother's grave, throw myself upon it, and beg her to let me join her rather than be forced to return to the hell my life had become. But even in the midst of often debilitating anguish, I couldn't face the pink marble tombstone, whose cold, penetrating, masonic strokes wrote her into and out of history ("1929–1986") and immortalized a childhood designation ("Tippy") that only the people directly associated with that mysterious time ever used.

After more than a decade of recruitment, a 1990 tenured job offer just four years after I received my Ph.D., and months of verbal and written assurances from administrators, I was informed on May 8, 1996, that as a consequence of a negative vote by the Personnel Committee of the School of Arts and Sciences, Penn was obliged to rescind its offer. Three years as an administrator at Michigan, during which time I was involved in efforts to recruit, promote, and retain faculty, suggested to me that this decision was, at the very least, the legally actionable result of multileveled administrative incompetence. Whatever the reasons for this surprising turn of events, I was forced into the self-protective posture of rummaging through fragments of conversations, e-mail messages, and official documents, hoping to make these fragments cohere into a narrative that, along with loving arms and other numbing comforts, could sustain me.

My family ended up in Philadelphia because after weeks of deliberations, Penn's administrative and legal teams came up with three options besides compelling the dean to ignore the recommendation of the School of Arts and Sciences' Personnel Committee. I could (1) come to Penn for two years as a visiting professor; (2) permit the university to reinstate the offer of an associate professorship it had made me six years earlier, effectively nullifying my subsequent pro-

Mother's grave

fessional achievements; or (3) stay at Michigan, as the exasperated associate dean suggested to me near the end of a particularly contentious discussion.

Penn had become a serious option only when, as part of its strategy to recruit me, its School of Social Work offered my wife—who'd made great sacrifices on my behalf throughout my career—an attractive opportunity to pursue her intellectual interests. Because I had the security of a full professor position at Michigan, I felt obliged to accept the visiting professorship. Still, Penn had placed us in financial, ethical, and parental binds from which we were unable to extricate ourselves easily. For we had, in response to administrators' written assurances, entered into legally binding agreements to sell our Ann Arbor house and to buy a house in the Philadelphia area, failed to renew our older girl's enrollment at the city's magnet elementary school, and begun officially to sever ties at Michigan. When I wasn't devising revenge plots or feeling debilitated by panic and by homicidal rage, I told myself that at worst, I'd have a horrible year, and that after my case was rejected for a second time, I'd return to good friends and welcoming institutional arms in Ann Arbor. (My wife and I agreed that with two small children, a commuter marriage would be untenable.) But that knowledge was hardly comforting.

One of the Penn gargoyles

Somehow, I endured my year as a largely unwelcomed visitor. And a year after being deemed unworthy, and after a year in which the officers of the School of Arts and Sciences faced what I imagine was a great deal of internal and external pressure, I received the unanimous support of the committee, half of whose members participated in the previous year's deliberations.

In its official response to this institutional change of heart, Penn can claim, with a somewhat straight face, that I'd been a visiting professor, and as universities have done for countless others after similar arrangements, it chose subsequently to welcome me as a member of its standing faculty. Unfortunately, I'm unable to formulate a compelling counternarrative. I take some small comfort in the fact that nearly all of the university officials who were directly involved with my 1996 difficulties saw their administrative fortunes quickly diminish and left their posts before the ends of their terms for a host of mysterious reasons. But neither their demise nor the passage of time has removed the seemingly permanent mark this experience has left on my record and my soul.

On July 1, 1997, my wife and I drove to Darby so that I could visit my mother's grave on what would have been her sixty-eighth birthday.

It was my first trip to the cemetery in the year since we'd returned to Philadelphia.

When I reached her tombstone, I tried to adopt familiar patterns of address.

"How you doin', Ol' Lady? You know they're going to take a wrecking ball to Southwark soon? Gentrification's moved further south."

Having read and viewed too many graveyard scenes, I waited for a reply. For a deep, tremulous voice or barely visible simulacrum of my mother to leap up at me. For the bright sun to hide behind the still-visible moon. For a skinless hand to reach for me from under the long-settled ground. For a piercing mist to rush through my chest and into my soul.

When it was clear that she wouldn't or couldn't reply, I moved from inane chitchat to matters of cosmic importance: "How'm I gonna do it, Ol' Lady? How'm I gonna stay?"

As I walked up the small hill back to my family's Quest minivan and to Lauren, I thought, for the first time in years, of the only lyrics I knew of the song from which my mother's nickname—Tippy—derived. Sometimes when she was joyfully inebriated and "feeling no pain," as she used to put it, she sang, in a labored, Billy Eckstine-ish voice, "I'm tippin' in." For years after she died, I searched through books and relatives' memories for the singer and title of the song.

When those efforts proved unsuccessful, I settled for committing to memory the meanings of the closest lexical approximations of her nickname that I could find.

Tip: "The end or extremity of something, especially something pointed or projecting." "To knock over or upset; topple." "Overturn." "Advance or inside information given as a guide to action."

Tipping: "To walk gingerly, quietly. To proceed with caution, even fear." (In black vernacular parlance during my childhood, "tipping" meant to propel oneself forward with an exaggeratedly soulful strut.)

Tipple: "To drink alcoholic liquor, especially habitually or to excess."

Tipsy: "Slightly drunk."

Standing above her tombstone, above the sacred ground that protected her encased remains, I felt fully cognizant, as if for the first time, of the sense of joy and wonder with which my mother filled my life along with the pain and fear. Hoping to send a message either to her or to celestial beings who could nudge her into attending briefly to my earthly antics, I walked up the final few feet of the hill on the tips of my toes.

As I entered the van, Lauren looked quizzically at me.

"Why're you smiling?"

"I don't know. I was just thinking about her."

"How was it?"

"Okay."

"You ready to go?"

"Yeah. Maybe. I don't know."

WORKS CITED OR CONSULTED ☀

Adams, Timothy Dow. *Telling Lies in Modern American Autobiography.* Chapel Hill: University of North Carolina Press, 1990.

Angelou, Maya. *I Know Why the Caged Bird Sings.* New York: Bantam, 1970.

Appiah, Kwame Anthony. *In My Father's House: Africa in the Philosophy of Culture.* New York: Oxford University Press, 1992.

Awkward, Kenneth W. "Origins of the Awkward Family in the United States of America." In *Awkward / Awkard / Offord Family Reunion Handbook.* 14 September 1991.

Awkward, Michael. *Inspiriting Influences: Tradition, Revision, and Afro-American Women's Novels.* New York: Columbia University Press, 1989.

——. *Negotiating Difference: Race, Gender, and the Politics of Positionality.* Chicago: University of Chicago Press, 1995.

Baker, Houston A., Jr. *Blues, Ideology, and Afro-American Literature.* Chicago: University of Chicago Press, 1984.

——. *Blues Journeys Home.* Detroit: Lotus, 1985.

——. *Workings of the Spirit.* Chicago: University of Chicago Press, 1991.

Barth, John. *The End of the Road.* New York: Bantam, 1958.

Berube, Michael. "Public Academy." *New Yorker,* 9 January 1995, 73–80.

Blount, Marcellus, and George P. Cunningham, eds. *Representing Black Men.* New York: Routledge, 1996.

Boynton, Robert. "The New Intellectuals." *Atlantic Monthly,* March 1995, 53–70.

Brown, Claude. *Manchild in the Promised Land.* New York: Signet, 1965.

Brown, Keith Michael. *Sacred Bond: Black Men and Their Mothers.* Boston: Little Brown, 1998.

Cade, Toni, ed. *The Black Woman.* New York: Penguin, 1970.

Caesar, Terry. *Conspiring with Forms: Life in Academic Texts.* Athens: University of Georgia Press, 1992.

Camus, Albert. *The Stranger.* New York: Vintage, 1942.

Carey, Lorene. *Black Ice.* New York: Knopf, 1991.

Carter, Stephen. *Confessions of an Affirmative Action Baby.* New York: Basic Books, 1991.

Davis, Angela. *With My Mind on Freedom: An Autobiography.* New York: Bantam, 1974.

Digby, Tom, ed. *Men Doing Feminism.* New York: Routledge, 1998.

Douglass, Frederick. *Narrative of the Life of Frederick Douglass.* 1845. Reprint, New York: Signet, 1968.

DuCille, Ann. *Skin Trade.* Cambridge: Harvard University Press, 1996.

Eakin, Paul John, ed. *American Autobiography: Retrospect and Prospect.* Madison: University of Wisconsin Press, 1991.

Ellison, Ralph. *Invisible Man.* New York: Vintage, 1952.

——. *Shadow and Act.* New York: Random House, 1972.

Farrakhan, Louis. "A Call to March." *Emerge,* October 1995, 65–66.

Fingarette, Herbert. *Heavy Drinking: The Myth of Alcoholism as a Disease.* Berkeley: University of California Press, 1988.

Fischer, Dexter, and Robert Stepto. *Afro-American Literature: The Reconstruction of Instruction.* New York: Modern Language Association, 1979.

Flack, Roberta. *Chapter 2.* Atlantic 1569–2. 1970.

Four Tops. *Ain't No Woman (Like the One I Got).* MCA 20388–4. 1987.

Gaines, Ernest. *The Autobiography of Miss Jane Pittman.* New York: Bantam, 1971.

———. *A Gathering of Old Men.* New York: Vintage, 1983.

———. *Of Love and Dust.* New York: Norton, 1968.

Gallop, Jane. *Thinking through the Body.* New York: Columbia University Press, 1988.

Gates, Henry Louis, Jr. *Colored People: A Memoir.* New York: Knopf, 1994.

———. *Figures in Black: Words, Signs, and the "Racial" Self.* New York: Oxford University Press, 1987.

Gaye, Marvin. *What's Going On.* Motown 2815 ML. 1971.

Giroux, Henry. *Disturbing Pleasures: Learning Popular Culture.* New York: Routledge, 1994.

Grealy, Lucy. *Autobiography of a Face.* Boston: Houghton Mifflin, 1994.

Gurian, Michael. *Mothers, Sons, and Lovers.* Boston: Shambhala, 1994.

Harper, Phillip Brian. *Are We Not Men? Masculine Anxiety and the Problem of African-American Identity.* New York: Oxford University Press, 1996.

Hathaway, Donny. *Extensions of a Man.* Atco 7019. 1973.

Hayes, Isaac. *The Isaac Hayes Experience.* Stax 4129. 1987.

Hemingway, Ernest. *A Farewell to Arms.* New York: Scribners, 1929.

Hughes, Langston. *Selected Poems of Langston Hughes.* New York: Vintage, 1974.

Hurston, Zora Neale. *Their Eyes Were Watching God.* 1937. Reprint, Urbana: University of Illinois Press, 1977.

Jackson, David. *Unmasking Masculinity: A Critical Autobiography.* London: Unwin Hyman, 1990.

Jackson, Janet. *Rhythm Nation.* A & M 13920-1. 1989.

Jardine, Alice, and Paul Smith, eds. *Men in Feminism.* New York: Methuen, 1986.

Jones, Gayl. *Corregidora.* 1975. Reprint, Boston: Beacon, 1986.

Karenga, Maulana, and Haki Madhubuti, eds. *Million Man March—Day of Absence: A Commemorative Anthology of Speeches, Commentary, Photography.* Chicago: Third World Press, 1996.

Kenan, Randall. *A Visitation of Spirits.* New York: Vintage, 1988.

Klein, Malcolm. *The American Street Gang.* New York: Oxford University Press, 1995.

Ladd, Jerrold. *Out of the Madness: From the Projects to a Life of Hope.* New York: Warner, 1994.

Lee, Andrea. *Sarah Phillips.* New York: Penguin, 1984.

Lee, Spike, with Ralph Wiley. *Best Seat in the House: A Basketball Memoir.* New York: Crown, 1997.

Lejeune, Phillipe. *On Autobiography.* Trans. Katherine Leary. Minneapolis: University of Minnesota Press, 1989.

Lentricchia, Frank. *The Edge of Night: A Confession*. New York: Random House, 1994.

Lesser, Wendy. *His Other Half: Men Looking at Women through Art*. Cambridge: Harvard University Press, 1991.

Marshall, Paule. *Praisesong for the Widow*. New York: Obelisk, 1983.

McCall, Nathan. *Makes Me Wanna Holler: A Young Black Man in America*. New York: Random House, 1994.

McDowell, Deborah E. *"The Changing Same": Black Women's Literature, Criticism, and Theory*. Bloomington: Indiana University Press, 1995.

Melvin, Harold. *Harold Melvin and the Blue Notes*. Philadelphia International Records KZ 31648. 1972.

Miller, Nancy K. *Bequest and Betrayal: Memoirs of a Parent's Death*. New York: Oxford University Press, 1996.

———. *Getting Personal: Feminist Occasions and Other Autobiographical Acts*. New York: Routledge, 1992.

Monette, Paul. *Becoming a Man*. New York: Harcourt Brace Jovanovich, 1992.

Morrison, Toni. *Beloved*. New York: Signet, 1987.

———. *The Bluest Eye*. New York: Washington Square Press, 1970.

———. *Jazz*. New York: Plume, 1992.

———. *Song of Solomon*. New York: Signet, 1977.

———. *Sula*. New York: Bantam, 1973.

Naylor, Gloria. *The Women of Brewster Place*. New York: Penguin, 1983.

Neisser, Ulric, and Eugene Winograd, eds. *Remembering Reconsidered: Ecological and Traditional Approaches to the Study of Memory*. New York: Cambridge University Press, 1988.

Olney, James, ed. *Autobiography: Essays Theoretical and Critical*. Baltimore: Johns Hopkins University Press, 1980.

O'Jays. *Family Reunion*. Philadelphia International Records PZ 33307. 1975.

Patterson, Orlando. *Slavery and Social Death*. Cambridge: Harvard University Press, 1982.

Pruter, Robert, ed. *The Blackwell Guide to Soul Recordings*. Oxford: Basil Blackwell, 1993.

Reed, Adolph. "The Current Crisis of the Black Intellectual." *Village Voice*, April 1995, 31–36.

Roth, Philip. *Patrimony*. New York: Touchstone, 1991.

Sadker, Myra, and David Sadker. *Failing at Fairness: How Our Schools Cheat Girls*. New York: Touchstone, 1994.

Samuels, Alison, and Jeff Giles. "Unchained Melody." *Newsweek*, 7 April 1997, 70–72.

Scott-Heron, Gil. *The Best of Gil Scott-Heron*. Arista 18306. 1984.

Shange, Ntozake. *for colored girls who have considered suicide / when the rainbow is enuf*. New York: Bantam, 1977.

Snow, Phoebe. *Second Childhood*. Columbia CK33952. 1976.

Spillers, Hortense. "Mama's Baby, Papa's Maybe: An American Grammar Book." *diacritics* (1987): 67–82.

Steinglass, Peter, with Linda Bennett, Steven Wolin, and David Reiss. *The Alcoholic Family*. New York: BasicBooks, 1987.

Suleiman, Susan Rubin. *Risking Who One Is: Encounters with Contemporary Art and Literature*. Cambridge: Harvard University Press, 1994.

Temptations. *The Best of the Temptations*. Motown 0524–2. 1995.

Veeser, H. Aram, ed. *Confessions of the Critics*. New York: Routledge, 1995.

Walker, Alice. *The Color Purple*. New York: Washington Square Press, 1982.

——. *Meridian*. New York: Washington Square Press, 1976.

——. *The Same River Twice*. New York: Scribners, 1996.

——. *In Search of Our Mothers' Gardens*. San Diego: Harcourt Brace Jovanovich, 1984.

Wallace, Michele. *Black Macho and the Myth of the Superwoman*. New York: Warner, 1979.

Williams, Sherley Anne. "Roots of Privilege: New Black Fiction." *Ms. Magazine*, June 1985, 71–75.

——. "Some Implications of Womanist Theory." In *Within the Circle: An Anthology of African American Literary Criticism*, ed. Angelyn Mitchell. Durham: Duke University Press, 1994, 515–21.

Wilson, August. *Fences*. New York: Plume, 1986.

Wimsatt, W. K. *The Verbal Icon: Studies in the Meaning of Poetry*. New York: Noonday Press, 1960.

Withers, Bill. *Still Bill*. Sussex 40177–4. 1972.

Woititz, Janet Geringer. *Adult Children of Alcoholics*. Pompano Beach, Fla.: Health Communications, 1983.

Wright, Richard. *Black Boy*. New York: Perennial, 1945.

——. *Native Son*. New York: Harper and Row, 1940.

X, Malcolm, with Alex Haley. *The Autobiography of Malcolm X*. New York: Ballantine, 1964.

Zweigenhaft, Richard L., and G. William Domhoff. *Blacks in the White Establishment? A Study of Race and Class in America*. New Haven: Yale University Press, 1991.

Amistad, 87
"Are You Man Enough?" (The
  Four Tops), 77
*Autobiography of Miss Jane Pittman,
  The* (Gaines), 82
Autocritography, 7
*Awkward / Awkard / Offord Family
  Reunion Handbook*, xvii

Baker, Houston A., Jr., 152–55, 171,
  198
Becoming a Man (Monette), 124–
  25
Beloved (Morrison), 165, 169–70
Black Boy (Wright), 1–2, 186–96
Black public intellectuals, 85–89
Bluest Eye, The (Morrison), 9–11,
  141, 152

Chicago State University's Black
  Writers Conference, 49
Color Purple, The (Walker), 51–52,
  88
Contemporary Study of Social
  Transformation (CSST), 165–67

Deep Throat, 98
Digby, Tom, 8

End of the Road, The (Barth), 9, 133

Farewell to Arms, A (Hemingway),
  9
Farrakhan, Louis, 49–52
Figures in Black (Gates), 86–87
*for colored girls who have considered
  suicide when the rainbow is enuf*
  (Shange), 52, 136–141, 160–64

Gaines, Ernest, 82
Gates, Henry Louis, Jr., 7, 85–89
Greer, Hal, 15–16, 54, 60, 122, 197

Hill, Anita, 49, 164
His Other Half (Lesser), 5–6, 8
Hurston, Zora Neale, v, 44, 160–61,
  171–72, 179, 193–94

I Know Why the Caged Bird Sings
  (Angelou), 1–2
In Search of Our Mothers' Gardens
  (Walker), 49
Intentional fallacy, 140
Invisible Man (Ellison), xviii, 1–2, 9,
  165

"Just My Imagination" (Temptations), 56–57

King, Martin Luther, Jr., 57
King, Rodney, 49

Lesser, Wendy, 5–6, 8

Madhubiti, Haki, 51
Men in Feminism (Jardine and
  Smith), 44
Meridian (Walker), xv
Miller, Arthur, 158
Million Man March, 49–52, 81–84
Morrison, Toni, xv, 9–11, 165, 169–
  70, 197
Moynihan Report, The, 51

*Narrative of the Life of Frederick
  Douglass* (Douglass), 189
Native Son (Wright), 9

Negotiating Difference (M. Awkward), 44–48

Olney, James, 7
"Origins of the Awkward Family in the United States of America" (K. Awkward), xvii–xviii

"Papa Was a Rolling Stone" (Temptations), 54
Patterson, Orlando, 192
Praisesong for the Widow (Marshall), 4, 52

Same River Twice, The (Walker), 51
Sarah Phillips (Lee), 194–97
Saturday Night Fever, 156
Scott-Heron, Gil, 160–62
Shadow and Act (Ellison), 163, 191, 193
Shaft in Africa, 76–77
Simpson, O. J., 49
Social death, 192
Song of Solomon (Morrison), xvi, 46

Spielberg, Steven, 87–89
Spillers, Hortense, 45
Sula (Morrison), xv

Their Eyes Were Watching God (Hurston), xv, 44, 171–72, 193–94
Thomas, Clarence, 49
Tyson, Mike, 49

United Colors of Benetton, 165–67

Visitation of Spirits, A (Kenan), 81–84

Walker, Alice, xv–xvi, 45, 49–52, 161
Wiesel, Eli, 156–58
Williams, Sherley Anne, 194
Wilson, August, 158
Women of Brewster Place, The (Naylor), xvi, 52
Women of Color Task Force, University of Michigan, 167–68
Wright, Richard, 1–2, 9, 186–96

Michael Awkward is Professor of English and Director of the Center for the Study of Black Literature and Culture at the University of Pennsylvania. He is author of *Negotiating Difference: Race, Difference, and the Politics of Positionality* and *Inspiriting Influences: Tradition, Revision, and Afro-American Women's Novels,* and editor of *New Essays on* THEIR EYES WERE WATCHING GOD.

Library of Congress Cataloging-in-Publication Data

Awkward, Michael.
Scenes of instruction : a memoir / Michael Awkward.
p. cm.
Includes bibliographical references (p.   ) and index.
ISBN 0-8223-2402-4 (cloth : alk. paper)
1. Awkward, Michael. 2. English teachers—United States Biography. 3. Afro-American college teachers Biography. 4. Male feminists—United States Biography. 5. Feminism and literature—United States. 6. Critics—United States Biography. 7. Feminist literary criticism. I. Title.
PE64.A88A3 1999
810.9—dc21
[B]   99-25938
            CIP